W9-CTD-667

Also by Hal Borland

An American Year
Beyond Your Doorstep
Sundial of the Seasons
The Enduring Pattern
Countryman: A Summary of Belief
Hill Country Harvest
Homeland: A Report from the Country
This Hill, This Valley
Seasons
High, Wide and Lonesome
Country Editor's Boy
The Dog Who Came to Stay
Penny
The Seventh Winter
The Amulet
When the Legends Die
King of Squaw Mountain
Rocky Mountain Tipi Tales
The Youngest Shepherd
This World of Wonder
America Is Americans
Our Natural World (EDITOR)
The Golden Circle
Borland Country
Hal Borland's Book of Days
A Place to Begin

Hal Borland's
Twelve Moons of the Year

HAL BORLAND'S TWELVE MOONS OF THE YEAR

His own selections from his nature editorials in The New York Times

Edited by Barbara Dodge Borland

G.K.HALL &CO.
Boston, Massachusetts
1985

Published by G. K. Hall & Co.
A publishing subsidiary of ITT

This G. K. Hall paperback edition is reprinted by arrangement with Knopf.

First G. K. Hall printing 1985.

Library of Congress Cataloging in Publication Data

Borland, Hal, 1900–1978.
Hal Borland's Twelve moons of the year.

Reprint. Originally published: 1st ed. New York : Knopf : Distributed by Random House, 1979.

Includes index.

1. Natural history—Addresses, essays, lectures. 2. Seasons—Addresses, essays, lectures. I. Borland, Barbara Dodge. II. Title. III. Title: Twelve moons of the year.

[QH81.B755 1985] 574.5′4′0974 84-22515

ISBN 0-8398-2867-5 (pbk.)

Foreword

Hal was completing the selection of *New York Times* editorials for this next book the day before he died. I say his "next book" because there was always a book being planned, thought about, and discussed, no matter what articles, columns, and essays were being written in his seven-day-a-week schedule.

The New York Times editorials were always a delight to him. He started writing them in 1941, as a staff man, and when he left *The Times* in 1943 to free-lance and write books or anything else, he still continued to write the editorials. And always, throughout the years, came beautiful, wonderful letters from people who shared Hal's delight in the seasons, and shared his thinking. These were a great pleasure to him, and he tried to answer every one personally.

The editorials were written under three editors of *The New York Times* editorial page: first, Charles Merz, then John Oakes, and then Max Frankel. When Charles Merz was editor, the "Borland," as it has always been called, had its regular Sunday spot. When John Oakes took over, Hal asked him if he wanted him to continue. John Oakes wrote back, "Forever." When Max Frankel became editor, Hal asked, "Shall I continue?" Max Frankel said, "Keep them coming, Hal."

There was a time when Hal used to protest the words "nature editorial." "Makes me sound like a birdy-and-bees man, which I'm not," he'd say. He wanted to call them "outdoor editorials," which always made me laugh, and I would say, "What do you think you're writing? A fish-and-game column?" He'd grin, and say tolerantly, "I guess I'm stuck with it."

Sometimes there would be a request for a special editorial to be dictated in, before *The Times* went to press. The phone call was always unexpected. I'd hear Hal say, "I'll make a try at it. If I don't dictate in within an hour you'll know it's no go." But Hal always responded to the challenge as a pro and a newspaperman.

One such phone call came on a Saturday morning from John Oakes. Could Hal write something about President Kennedy's assassination for the next day? I had engaged a piano tuner who had arrived in tears about J.F.K. A neighbor was helping me with the household chores. I asked the piano tuner to stop working and let him cry. I stopped the household machinery, and listened for Hal's typewriter. Nothing happened. Silence. More silence. And more silence. Then all of a sudden, his electric typewriter began to buzz and whirr like crazy, and I knew he had it. On Sunday, "In Memoriam" was the leading editorial.

Hal always wondered if he was turning over the bottom of the barrel, because he had written so many editorials over the years. But each one, taken separately, seemed like a newborn day. Once John Oakes called and said, "Hal, do you *have* to have a vernal equinox in this Sunday's editorial?" I heard Hal answer, deadpan, "But John, it happens every year." You will find equinoxes and solstices in these pages, because they were written over a span of some thirty-five years. In all, there are over 1,750 nature editorials, which naturally means some similarities and repetition.

Toward the end of January 1978, a month before Hal died, Muriel Stokes, Max Frankel's secretary, phoned and said, "Mrs. Borland, we have searched every nook and cranny of this whole place, and every office, and can't find Hal's 'January Thaw' to use this Sunday." Hal got on the phone and I heard him say, "But I didn't write one this year." He thought it was a great joke; New York City had an unexpected blizzard that weekend.

Hal selected nearly three quarters of the 365 columns that he had intended to include in *Twelve Moons of the Year*. Furthermore, he had earmarked many more than enough additional pieces for each month from which to select the remaining columns. *Twelve Moons of the Year* is, thus, edited by the author himself. No column has been included here that Hal did not consider suitable for this collection. I had only to select enough of Hal's earmarked columns from his scrapbooks to fill out the year, and to make sure that there was a rough chronology for each month; for example, to make sure that the vernal equinox did not fall on March 6th instead of March 21st or thereabouts. There were other minor problems—of duplication, for example. Sometimes I included columns that contained some duplication just because it would have been a shame to omit them. In a few instances, I included a column *as written* that had been slightly cut by *The Times* editors for space reasons. I did no internal editing of Hal's prose save in a very few instances where consistency of copy editing style required it.

In this collection of Hal's editorials, you may find some that are familiar to you. I hope so.

—*Barbara Dodge Borland*

Preface

In the many years I have written these brief outdoor essays for *The New York Times* editorial page I have from time to time referred to a Moon—Harvest Moon, Wolf Moon, Beaver Moon, and so on. This originally was Indian terminology. It was based on weather or natural events, and therefore varied from one region to another, even from one tribe to another in the same region. What was Snow Moon in New England was Opening Buds Moon down on the Gulf of Mexico.

Many readers have written to ask about the Moon names as I have used them. Therefore, I decided to arrange this selection of the editorials by Moons. I have been arbitrary, using a Moon as the equivalent of a calendar month which is based on solar time. A lunar month, or a Moon, is only 29 days, 12 hours, 44 minutes, 3 seconds. So the Indian calendars, the Moon years, had a correction Moon, which was added every few years to make the solstices and equinoxes come out approximately right. In this collection I have skipped the correction Moon.

The names I am using are derived from those commonly in use among several related Indian tribes when the first English settlers arrived. The translations probably were closely approximate, but there are one or two I wouldn't bet on. Anyway, here they are, with their modern, solar calendar's equivalents:

WOLF MOON—January
SNOW MOON—February

WORM MOON—March
PINK MOON—April
FLOWER MOON—May
HOT MOON—June
BUCK MOON—July
STURGEON MOON—August
HARVEST MOON—September
HUNTER'S MOON—October
BEAVER MOON—November
COLD MOON—December

I have seen June listed as Strawberry Moon, but that seems like a white man's idea. Early European explorers reported so many wild strawberries here that they could smell them several leagues offshore.

There also was a Corn Moon, sometimes inserted between Sturgeon Moon and Harvest Moon to bring the lunar year back into phase with the sun.

The Moons, as I am using them here, are nominal Moons only. Literal moons run from new moon to new moon or, in some systems, from full moon to full moon. The new moon, of course, is that hairline crescent in the western sky soon after sundown, and the full moon is that fully rounded moon which rises in the east at sundown and shines all night, setting in the west at sunrise.

The editorials, or essays, themselves deal with any number of topics, many of them rural, or at least out-of-doors. I am a countryman by temperament and by residence. I suppose the essays served in *The Times* as reminders that there is a countryside beyond the city streets. I am sure some of them reflect my disenchantment with man's belief that he owns the earth and must dominate everything and everywhere. Some, of course, are sheer celebration of life. Quite a few of them have been reprinted in anthologies, and I have adapted material from them for use in several of my books.

I wish to thank John B. Oakes, former editorial page editor, and Max Frankel, present editorial page editor, for freedom to write what I chose and as I wished. And I thank *The New York Times* for permission to use this selection of editorials this way.

H. B.

Salisbury, Connecticut
1977

Hal Borland's
Twelve Moons of the Year

January

WOLF MOON

Time of the hungry wolf pack, the howling wind, and a snug house and warm fireside.

January

January 1

January can be cold, raw, bitter, icy, edged with a wind that chills the marrow and congeals the blood. Its days are short, its nights are long, and the half-hearted sun cuts a minor arc across the ice-blue sky. January is winter, its very essence, and no doubt about it. But January also has its intervals and aspects that etch themselves unforgettably on the memory.

Sunrise after a snowfall that has smoothed and gentled all the scars and blemishes of the countryside, a dazzling sun on an untouched world of innocence. The glint and glitter of frost crystals in the air, dancing like motes of diamond dust in the sunlight. The gleaming cloud of your own breath, white and shimmering.

Midday, a gusty wind, a slow fall of snow, and a flock of snowbirds swirling like windblown leaves as they come to feed on scattered grain in a dooryard. Midafternoon and a clearing sky, a dying wind, the pines on the hillside bowed under their white frosting, free-form trees of glistening ice. Sunset, when a day of melting and a night and a day of freezing have sheathed the countryside in ice. Long light glows on the crusted meadow. Broad purple pools of shadow lie in every hollow.

Deepening dusk and the hooting of the great horned owl is twice as loud, twice as fierce, as it was in October.

Midevening and the moonlight casts ink-black shadows on the snow. The night is so full of reflected light the sky has only half its stars, a cold, bitter, ice-edged January night that engraves itself on the senses.

More Sun

January 2

Daylight lengthens. The change now becomes obvious at evening as the light begins to lengthen and there is a hint of dusk again. The sun, as we say, is moving north and cutting a slightly larger arc in each day's passage. The depth of winter is upon us, but we see in the sky the insistence of eternal change. The slow shift toward spring begins to make itself manifest.

Sunrise still lags, as even the lie-abed must be aware. Winter days are lopsided, with the sun seemingly as reluctant as the rest of us to get up. In fact, the latest sunrises of the winter persisted until only a few days ago, and even now we have only about two more minutes of morning sunlight than we had on the year's shortest day. But the sun lingers now in the sky at evening. In the past month we have gained more than twenty minutes of daylight at the tired end of the day, though the net gain is somewhat less because of the laggard dawns.

But change has come, and the change will slowly accelerate in the weeks ahead. Another month and we will have gained another hour of daylight. And after that we will be moving swiftly toward the equinox and spring, in terms of sun and daylight at least. What will be underfoot is something else again, since that will be mid-February. But change it is, and now there is no turning back. Time, not the temperature, marks off the days.

The Killer-Wind

January 3

Cold can maim, but the wind is the killer. Those who live with blizzards every winter know this and have a deep respect for the wind. Still cold, even well below zero, is tolerable because it saps the warmth of life slowly and can be endured with ordinary precautions. But when wind is added to such cold the inner fires of life are endangered because the wind sucks away the vital warmth faster than it can be renewed. From time to time, as this past week, we in the Northeast have to learn again to respect the winter wind and fear its consequences. We have to recognize it for the elemental force it is.

To a considerable degree we have tempered the direct effects of winter weather by our modern way of life in the city, the suburbs, even in the country. But the barriers we have built, dependent as they are on power and transportation, are themselves vulnerable. Combine wind and cold, add snow, and the whole intricate web begins to give way. Highways are blocked, power lines crippled, communities isolated. Then we are doubly at the mercy of the weather because we have delegated not only our comfort but our safety to the machines and those who can keep them running.

We have never really mastered the winter wind. At best, we now can hide from it a little while and hoard our inner fires. But our safety eventually lies in the weather itself, in the relaxation of the storm. Those who repair the vulnerable web ease the danger, but until the killer-wind has died we live beleaguered.

The Winter Voices *January 4*

The sounds of winter, or even the memory of them from days spent in the country, can set the cheeks to tingling. The whine of snow underfoot on a brittle-cold day, the moan of night wind in a grove of hilltop hemlocks, the groan of ice on a lake or river when the temperature has flirted with zero for a solid week.

The really shivery whine of snow is seldom heard anymore. It was at its best under the runners of a sleigh on a winter night. It could rise to the pitch of a high cello note and it had a full tone that carried half a mile if the air was right. It could make a man shiver in felt boots and a bearskin coat. The nearest we come to it nowadays is underfoot on a brittle, starlit night.

The winter wind in the hemlocks is a very different sound, and unless it rises to a blizzard howl it can be almost soothing. Particularly if one is indoors and has a healthy hearth and an ample supply of firewood.

The most ominous sound of all is the voice of the ice. It is cold thunder at times, flinty muttering occasionally. It is the creak and complaint of the ice crystals shrinking upon themselves, of water turned to steel, of stresses like those that cause earthquakes. And the ice itself is the sounding board for its own wails and complaints. It belabors the cold air that begat it in the first place. And it will continue to growl and grumble till the last floe has battered itself to pieces and the last shard has melted. For water is a restless element and full of voice, and winter gives ice its tongue.

The Unseen Tides

January 5

The great tides of the season now are lapping at the latitudes, the unseen tides of the wind. They are the restless surging of the air that curls about this earth, eternally moving, obeying some far subtler master than the moon.

We hear them now at the chimney and around the corners of the house. They swish and roar through the naked woodland, and they sigh among the pines and the hemlocks. Defying the laws that govern the watery tides of the sea, they rush up the hillsides and swirl around the summits. Sweeping down from the cold northland, they come roaring all across the continent, storming through the midlands, bellowing over the mountains, rushing far out to sea. They are the cold and stormy tides of winter.

Freight them with snow, charge them with cold, and they become blizzards. Temper them even with diluted sunlight and they are restless winds playing a chilly game with the loose litter of autumn. On a calm and frosty morning they can even whisper in the meadows in brief innocence. But on a frigid night with a late moon and glittering stars those tides can batter the hills and surge through the valleys like breakers hammering a rocky coast. They drive both man and beast to shelter.

The earth turns, and the seasons, and for all his pride and power man cannot either temper the winds or change their course. They are the unseen tides that shape our days and our years.

Winter's Moon

January 6

Midsummer's moon is the serenader's moon, sentimental as the rhymes that go with it. Autumn's moon is the golden harvest moon, big as all outdoors. But winter's moon is queen of the sky. It hurries the sun to bed, banishes all but the brightest stars, and blazons the frosty night a full fourteen hours in remote and solitary grandeur.

The January moon is no moon to dream on or to bask under. It is a distant and icy moon that glitters the hills and glints the frozen valleys. It may dance a stately pavane on the frost-flowered surface of a silent lake. It may dazzle the crystaled air over a frost-defying brook. It may etch whimsical hieroglyphics on the snow beneath the naked trees. But it is brittle as spun glass, sharp as the talon of a hungering owl.

The winter's moon makes magic of the night, but it is a sharp and frosty witchcraft. The fox knows it, and so does the hurrying hare darting from shadow to shadow. The night walker sees it in his own spangled breath, senses it in his whistling footsteps. The late homecomer observes it in the shimmer of his rooftop, smells it in the slow curl of smoke from his chimney. Even the night wind knows it.

Midwinter moonlight is no hearth-glow reflected in the sky. It is the cold beauty of a whole winter wrapped and rimed into one long January night.

Winter Green

January 7

You are most aware of them on a gray winter day with a raw wind blowing. Walking, you come to an old hillside meadow with a rocky slope beyond, and there are the hemlocks among the rocks with the white pines spilling down the slope and taking over the meadow. There are scattered hardwoods, too, on up the slope; but they stand gray and bare to the wind. It is the pines and the hemlocks that catch the eye.

Green. That is the first thought. Green in the midst of winter's browns and grays, green that is twice as green against the snow. The green that now becomes the symbol of life, in this winter world. The color that means sap, life-blood of the tree, still there in twig and needle, not withdrawn into the root. The color of that mysterious chlorophyll which makes food of water and air and sunlight even now, even when the sunlight is thin, when lakes are ice and frost seals the earth.

You stand beneath a pine and hear the whisper of its winter song, see the corded brown bark, the sturdy trunk, the five-needled grace. You go on up the slope to the hemlocks, hear their murmur, admire their feathery sweep of branch, their supple strength. And you know that one winter means little to them. Their kind knew the Ice Ages, winters ten thousand years long. They persisted, gave way when the ice advanced, crept back when the ice retreated. They were here in the earth's own springtime. They earned their winter green.

The Handsome Jay *January 8*

Maybe the blue jays don't migrate to Georgia and points south because they know how handsome they are against a snowy background. Nobody who struts the way a jay does can be unaware of such an obvious fact. In a winter landscape a jay's blue seems doubly blue, the white bands on wings and tail look white as cleanest snow, and the crest feathers are the cocked hat of a swaggering dandy. Only the cardinal can surpass the blue jay in winter plumage, and cardinals are outnumbered by jays at least a thousand to one.

True, the jay often looks like a fat, pompous alderman. That is one of his roles, and he has a whole repertoire. He can be a sneak thief or an innocent bystander, an escaped felon or an officer of the avian court. He seems to prefer a scoundrel's role, but among his own kind he can be playsome and even courtly. His voice can be a jeer, or it can be a sweet whisper. And in the summer he is a helpful mate and an attentive parent.

But in the winter the jay is a foot-loose blusterer, too handsome to be a real villain, too roguish to be a friend. Only the crows outshout him. Only the various sparrows outnumber him where there is a free meal. Few people welcome him at the bird feeders, but if he were missing from the dooryard something would be wrong. In fact, if the blue jay were a rare and sporadic migrant he would be celebrated for his beauty. Especially if he appeared only when there was snow on the ground.

Ice

January 9

Ice is ice, we sometimes say, and think that's an end to it. Then we look around and see the falling snowflake, the icicle hanging at the eave, the glare of a sleety road, the sleek or rippled surface of a frozen pond or lake or river, and we know that ice is a score of different things.

Ice is the dazzling hoarfrost on tree and bush. Ice is the delicate frost fronds on windows and the intricate frost flowers on a winter-sealed lake. Ice is the frozen motion of the wind in a snowdrift, the massive plow of a glacier. It is crystals so small, so light, that they float like mist and shimmer in a January sunrise. It can be the cruel beauty of the dazzling glaze that rips trees apart in an ice storm.

When it is a snowflake, ice is one of the most beautiful and evanescent crystals we know. As frost, it is one of nature's most powerful levers, heaving the earth and rending the rocks in the silence of long winter nights. The mountains know ice intimately, the valleys know its uncompromising presence, and even the sky has its banners of ice, its high-riding cirrus clouds that defy even the heat of July.

January

Often ice is a thing of beauty, but always it is a force, a great elemental, insensate force. And for most of us, ice is winter, and seldom is it really simple.

Dogwood

January 10

Next spring should be a magnificent season for flowering dogwood. The leafless trees now are heavily laden with flower buds, which will brave out the winter and burst into white loveliness next May. If all goes well, they should be a dazzle in the woodlands, for the buds are both big and plentiful; every twig seems to be nobbed with at least one bud.

Look closely at these buds and you get a false sense of spring just around the corner. Their stems are a faint lavender-green, a lively color. And the base of the bud itself is that soft, new green of a garden pea fresh from its pod. On top, the buds are an inconspicuous reddish-brown, but if you crouch beneath a tree and look up you see the green undersides like a dappling of young leaflets in April.

The buds even now are as much as three-eighths of an inch across and seem to be almost bursting their skins. Roughly four-sided, they show a clear seam across the middle, where they will eventually open. Peel the scales away at the seam. Two of them will come off, each like a cupped hand, and the other two scales will be seen clasping the central cluster of green pinheads which are the true dogwood flowers—or will be, come spring. The white "petals" of the dogwood bloom are more leaf than petal; they are, in fact, those four bud scales, grown big and white. And the flowers, which form the red berries harvested last fall by the birds and squirrels, are the little cluster in the center. Each cluster may contain as many as twenty-four florets.

Dogwoods tend to have alternate years of scant and abundant flowering. This year should be one of superabundance.

The Truth of Trees *January 11*

When we would know the truth of trees, particularly of the hardwoods of our Northeastern hills, we go to the woodlands in winter. In summer they are a vastness of green and an ocean of shade with islands of grassy sunlight. They are woods in which the trees are too seldom seen. Now it is the other way round. Now, reduced to fundamentals and revealed in the cold clarity of winter sunlight or snowlight, they are trees adding up to woodland.

At no other season of the year is the uniqueness of a tree so evident. Now the thick-boled indomitability of an oak is unmistakable. There is no doubt about the corded trunk of a sugar maple. The elms stand like plumes against the sky. On the hillside the birches are lithe as dancers, and in the valleys are the tall, slim javelins of ash and poplar. Now even the texture and color of the bark are unmistakable.

Trees, not a forest or a woodland. Trees rooted in earth, reaching for sun and stars, each in its own way. And each with its own symmetry, its own pattern. Trees that have known ice and storm, have been maimed, have healed, have held fast through more winters than any man will ever know. Trees waiting, as only trees can wait, for spring and summer when they will be a woodland again, a vastness of green and an ocean of shade.

The Long Night

January 12

Long nights of cold and brittle starlight, of ice and snow and sharp-fanged wind, now are ours. The snow will come and go, but the ice will persist, and the night cold. And the wildlife of this world will follow its own pattern, mostly unheard and unseen.

The coon that raided the sweet corn patch and filched from the summer garbage can will take several long naps, living on his own fat; but between naps he will raid the farmer's corncrib or hen coop, catch a few mice, uncover a squirrel's forgotten cache of nuts. The otter and the mink will be abroad almost every night, almost as busy as they were all summer, hungry and hunting for bird or beast made sluggish by the cold. Unless the snow is too deep, the deer will be wandering the woodland in search of browse, or coming down to the farmyard for hay, to the orchard for windfalls, to the dooryard for a few mouthfuls from the evergreen shrubs.

The porcupine, fat and sluggish from the summer's feasting, will be half asleep well up in a big pine where it can gnaw off strips of sweet inner bark when hunger rouses it. The fox, a shadow in the moonlight, takes rabbit and mice and partridges as they come. The skunk, its tail a high-held banner of defiance, naps and wakens and catches a few mice, and naps again. The rabbit haunts the frozen garden, gnaws the bark of sapling trees, is startled into one last shrieking cry as the stalking weasel or the pouncing fox strikes and kills.

And the great horned owl hoots gruffly, then hunts on broad, silent wings, sharp-taloned as the wind, quiet as the brittle cold.

Color and Contrast

January 13

The blue jays look more cleanly blue and white now than at any other time of the year, and the cardinals are spectacular. This isn't wholly illusion. Part of the credit goes to the winter background. The small woodpeckers are sharply black and white and the little red skullcaps the males wear are vivid scarlet. The juncos are pearly breasted and the white piping on their flight-spread tails might have been laundered last night. The gold and bronze and black and white of evening grosbeaks looks almost tropical.

The colors are there, of course, but we see them more clearly in the winter light and against the snow. In a green world with flowers blooming, only the cardinal really demands attention, and against a snowy background even the cardinal seems twice as red. The summer blue jay is just another slate-gray bird with a slight tinge of blue, blue that you can't even see if you have just seen an indigo bunting.

Perhaps we need the snow to really see the colors, just as we need snow to know how green the pines can be, and the hemlocks. The snow may not sharpen the eyes but it does sharpen the contrast and somehow cleanses the colors themselves. And it simplifies the world around us, hides the confusing clutter, the distractions. With less to see, we see more and see it clearly. Who ever admired the glistening black of a crow in July?

The Primitive Sleep

January 14

The woodchuck sleeps in mysterious hibernation, strange symbol of change and baffling proof of the quirks of evolution.

Half the year the woodchuck is a normal warm-blooded mammal. Then he retires to a hole in the ground and retreats millions of years, biologically speaking. In effect, he becomes his own remote ancestor, a cold-blooded creature whose temperature is only a few degrees above that of his surroundings and whose breathing and pulse are almost suspended. Comatose, he waits out the winter, close kin of the primitive frog and the lizard. Winter past, he spans the ages again in a matter of hours and becomes warm-blooded once more.

We know this happens, but we do not know exactly how or why. Somehow the woodchuck reverses the clock that for most creatures is irreversible. Long ago, the scientists tell us, life emerged from the marshy margins, learned to live on land; and eventually a great many creatures achieved a form of inner fire to warm the blood and maintain year-round energy. That, we say, was our long path upward from the ooze, from naked instinct to thought and comprehension.

Yet here is the hibernating woodchuck, and not even our digital computers can explain him. There, in a hole in the frozen ground, is a mystery about our own beginnings that is more mysterious than the geography of the moon.

The Waiting Trees

January 15

Autumn stripped the trees to their essentials, their trunks and spreading branches and their reaching twigs. First snow outlined the elements of their architecture, functional as the naked girders of a building. Now they stand in the winter landscape, patterned against the snowy hillsides and the icy sky, the etched grace of living line caught for a season like moss in amber.

But look up even now, in mid-January, and those lacing twigs are not bare or lifeless. They are rough with buds.

Next summer's green shade is there in embryo, and next April's inconspicuous blossom. The trees, as surely as the woodchuck, are hibernating. But the trees hibernate in the open, defying wind and winter storm. They cannot hide from the weather.

The buds are the tree's hostages to the future. The leaves are expendable, but the buds are the promise a tree makes to itself that there will be a tomorrow, another year. Even while the new leaves are unfolding in the spring, the new buds begin to appear. By midsummer those buds are nearly full grown. By November they are complete, ready for April. But winter must be endured, so they hibernate. There they are now, inert as a bead of ice yet with the germ of life, the embryo leaf and blossom, within them.

The trees stand, winter etchings against the sky, stark in their elemental beauty. But not lifeless, not even really naked. They are waiting, as only trees can wait, for another winter to pass.

The Dooryard Birds *January 16*

The winter birds come to the dooryard feeders, busier than the proverbial beavers, and even a raw and blustery January day is brightened by their presence. They bring life to a wintery world where so much lies dormant.

True, they aren't the colorful birds of midsummer, though the sight of a cardinal against a snowy landscape is spectacular. For the most part they are as gray and brown as the roadsides or the winter woodlands. The goldfinch has shed his vivid yellow coat. The orioles are gone, and the indigo buntings, the tanagers, and the redstarts. But the jays look twice as blue, and when a flock of evening grosbeaks arrives like a company of pirates their Joseph's coats are almost ostentatious.

And they aren't really singers. There is no sunrise

chorus, and even at midday they do little more than twitter or scold. They haven't time to sing, even if they had the impulse or the talent; brief daylight is barely sufficient for them to stoke their inner fires to withstand the long, cold nights.

But here they are, day after day, lively reassurance that life outlasts all winters. The twitter of a chickadee, a flurry of juncos defying the wind, the industry of a downy woodpecker at the suet won't warm the day, but they do warm the human heart.

The Day's Commitment

January 17

The slope is upward now, toward spring. No matter what the temperature or the depth of snow in the days ahead, the commitment is made. Daylight lengthens.

The sun, like the rest of us, is still slow-rising in the morning, but it sets now almost twenty minutes later than it did a month ago. Twilight lingers at the end of the day like a promise. Another month and we will have gained back another hour of daylight.

Perhaps it was for this, to know the year complete, to know the inevitability of change and the certainty of spring in the midst of winter, that man was denied the privilege of hibernation. Moody creature that he is, man needs hope and promises, the entire procession of the season, just as he needs both day and night.

True, we tell ourselves every winter that snow and ice are a trial to the flesh and the spirit, and we even migrate like the birds when we get the chance. But the slow change, the turn from deep December's nadir toward the burgeoning of May is more than a seasonal certainty. It is part of the whole, a reassuring part that gives meaning to the continuity that is life. With the days in order and the seasons wholly predictable, we can accept the haphazards as they come. We know there is daylight ahead, the lengthening daylight that leads to April and another spring.

The Open Fire

January 18

Granted, it is an anachronism, an inefficient way to provide heat, and it makes smoke. There still is something to be said for the open fire and the hearth on which it burns.

Start with the wood, which once was a tree. Its leaves gathered light and heat from the parent sun, and as it burns it yields that store of light and heat. Pine or birch, maple or oak, apple or cherry, it burns with a special flame and the fragrance of its own kind. The flame is, of all inanimate things, the most nearly alive, and the ember seems endowed with a memory of the sun, or perhaps of life itself. In a strange way that defies definition, an open fire is company.

Consider the hearth. Once it was simply the floor of a cave, but ever since man tamed fire it has been the symbol of home, of safety, of reassurance in an uncertain world. Beside his hearth a man could rest and dream of tomorrow, for it was warmth, it cooked his food, it was security from feral foe as well as from cold and darkness. Around his fire man built his home, and at his hearth he knew the comfort of family and friends.

What does it add up to? A flame, a puff of smoke, and an ember. And, strangely, a fireplace in an age that fractures atoms. And yet, the memory persists, even in the dancing flame. There is independence, there is even identity, at the hearth. There is a man, and his fire, and his home, and his own security, at least as long as the ember glows.

The Ice Booms

January 19

We think of wind as the voice of winter, the wind and the moan of the trees and the swish of sleet and snow. But the ultimate voice, the timeless voice of winter, is the boom of the ice, and it is one of the coldest voices there is.

There is the pond, or the lake, or the slow-flowing river. The cold comes and knits a film of ice, clear as glass. The cold deepens and the ice turns milky or black as it thickens. Since water expands as it turns to ice, it begins to press against its banks. More cold, and deeper ice, and more pressure; and suddenly the pressure is too great to be endured. There is a gigantic heave and a crack races across the ice; and the whole ice sheet booms like a giant drum.

Most often it happens in the night, when the cold is at its depth. The darkness seems to quiver and the very stars shiver and blink. Sometimes it happens in the daylight, and you can see the whole pond shake.

The wind comes and goes. The trees ease their moans to sighs and whispers. The sleet ends, and the snow is a drifted blanket. But the ice is restless in its bed. Ice, which split the mountains, carved the valleys, leveled the hills, must proclaim its strength. The ice rends itself in a primal convulsion. The ice booms.

The Remembering

January 20

January is a time for remembering. We remember June, so mild that we seldom appreciate it when it comes, so comforting in memory that it is perfection itself. We remember summer, with its flowers, its sun, its shade. We remember a year past, with all its four seasons.

January, and we sit before the fire and remember

warmth. We look into the flames and see beginnings beyond remembering, when fire was the primal force, before there was ice. We hold within us the vague race memory of when man tamed fire, made it his servant and his shield.

We hear the wind, the long-remembered wind of January, now come down from the Pole. The winter-laden wind that has no memory of June but only of snow and ice. The wind comes and passes, and the snow remembers the wind, tells us how it came and how it blew and how it passed.

We stand at the window and see the snow, the flakes of crystal perfection, feathering from the sky, and we remember all the winters of our lives. Snow, winter's own cold, white blossoms; and ice, the counterpart of fire. Behind us, the fire; before us, the snow. The forces that shaped our world. Fire eased and cold came, and what was molten became solid; and man, with his servant-fire, survives.

The Long, Slow Climb

January 21

We think of it as a slow and trudging journey through the valley of winter, but in reality it is a long and steady climb up the cold slope toward spring. Now we face both the best and the worst of the year's dark season, long nights, short days, brilliant starlight, a distant sun, and inevitable change.

Daylight has already begun to lengthen. The sun will be above the horizon six minutes longer today than it was two weeks ago, and a week from today it will have added another eight minutes to its stay. The gain thus far is all at the end of the day, in a later sunset; sunrise still lags, and will continue to lag for another week. But the pattern is established. By the end of January another forty minutes will have been added to the daylight. We have already passed the nadir of the night. Ursa Major, the Big Bear, no longer drags his tail on the horizon as he climbs the northern sky in the evening.

January

January is cold, and February is traditionally full of snow; what warmth remains in the rocks will ooze away and the ice fangs will bite deep, even as the daylight lengthens. But the slope is upward now. The ice will melt, in due time, and rivers will flow and brooks will leap again. Buds, already patterned on the twig, will open. Birds will sing. These things we know, for they are as inevitable as the lengthening daylight. The long, cold slope still lies ahead, but we have already begun the slow climb toward spring and April.

Winter Dusk

January 22

Winter twilight is as special, in its own way, as the long midsummer dusk. Though half an hour shorter now than it was in June, it seems to linger longer over the snowclad world, and even the early starlight is somewhat muted in its glow. The long night is slow coming, as though the glistening hills were reluctant to submit to the cold depth of darkness.

It comes swiftly, once the sun has set far off to the south. The long shadows vanish. The chill deepens. The sky in the west still glows, and all across the horizon lies an almost luminous band of ice-green color, clear and cold. Then, as the sun sinks deeper, a luminous afterglow seems to fill the sky as though every frost crystal in the air were glittering. And the earth, every drifted valley and every white hummock and hilltop, catches the light. The day's dazzle and glitter are gone with the sun, but the twilight is almost radiant. It is like moonlight reflected from a clear-iced lake, like fireglow seen through a frosted window.

But it is cold light, colder than moonlight. The air sparkles with one's frosted breath. The snow whistles underfoot. The frozen lake and river grumble and echo, and bare branches rattle in the breeze that touches the treetops.

An owl hoots and a fox barks, but no other living sound disturbs the dusk. The glow fades, starlight brightens and the cold deepens. Twilight dissolves into the brittle darkness of another winter night.

Owls in the Night *January 23*

Of all the night sounds of winter, one of the most lonely and forlorn to the human ear is the hooting of the owls. In darkness it can be an unearthly sound that seems to come from some ghostly presence. In moonlight it can throb the frosty air and almost make the shadows quiver. It can question, it can threaten, it can cajole; it can be as cold as ice and as impersonal as the wind. No wonder the owls were long considered prophets of dire happenings.

But the owls now hooting are speaking, in their own language, not of doom but of domesticity. The great horned owl nests early, often in February, and the barred owl only a little later. If a shivery chorus is heard tonight on rural hillsides lit by the full moon, it may be because moonlight inspires serenades even among owls.

The owl is, in man's terms, a useful but not a lovable bird, as the chickadee or the robin. Even the other birds fear its fierce beak and talons, its silent wings and nocturnal habits—though most of its diet is of mice and smaller animals. It has its place in the intricate system of life, and it guards that place with stubborn tenacity. It is a bird of the cold winter night, and if its voice makes the moonshadows quiver, that too is a part of winter.

The Unremitting Change

January 24

Daylight lengthens. Sunset now comes half an hour later than it did a month ago and there is even a slight gain at the beginning of the day, though sunrise always lags until March. You see a change in the way the shadows fall, especially at midday, for the sun, as we say, is steadily working its way back from the southern depths of the sky. It will be a month tomorrow since the winter solstice occurred.

Change, though inevitable, can seem painfully deliberate at this time of the year even in the country where the signs are all around you. Even when a flow of balmy air from the south brings a January thaw, it is too soon overwhelmed by another Arctic blast. Spring will come, but not yet. It is still January, and the year has to work its way all through winter to get to spring. There are no short-cuts.

To the countryman, who has lived close to the weather for generations, these barn-chore days give a man time to ponder his shortcomings and be grateful for survival. But they don't give him time to grow cynical. He knows that beyond the daily chores of January and February lies the summons of the fields in March and April, the new green, the new life of a burgeoning world. The turn of the seasons, the unremitting but deliberate change, the inevitability of spring, all are written in those midday shadows and the later sunset. Knowing, he does his chores, tends his fire, and waits.

Wolf Moon

January 25

What we speak of as January's full moon occurs tomorrow night. The Indians knew it, and the lunar month it marks, as the Wolf Moon. It was a time when the fangs of winter bit deep and the fangs of the pack were eager, when hunger drove the wolves. Unfortunately, few wolves remain, most of them in the Far North, but the fangs of winter do persist. January is cold, and no mistake about that. January's full moon marks a time of bitter temperature and biting wind. The ice now lies deep, the drifts are piled high in the woods.

Ours happens to be a land where the mountain barriers lie the wrong way to temper the winter winds. Our storms move from west to east across the country, and the winds generally come down from the north and northwest. Our mountain chains make great valleys that actually funnel those winds down across the flatlands. They come howling, like the vanished wolf packs, and blow till they have blown themselves out. Even our trees are mostly deciduous on those mountains, with little resistance to check the racing winds.

So winter sweeps across the land, and when the moon rides full, the cold deepens. The wind seems to come from far Arcturus. You can almost feel the rocky ledges being pried apart by ice. You can almost hear the ice swelling in its lakes; on a full-moon night you can hear the echoing boom as it heaves and cracks, too big for its bed.

January full moon or Wolf Moon—the naming doesn't matter. It is probably the coldest moon of the whole year.

That January Thaw

January 26

It doesn't always come, but about three years out of four we get a January thaw. Nobody seems to know just why it occurs, and there are no official dates for it, though some of the more liberal weather folk now grant it informal recognition. Country folk have recognized it for generations, and dogmatic ones among them will tell you that it usually comes between the twentieth and the twenty-seventh of this month. Earlier than that it doesn't count; later, it's just a warm spell easing us into February.

It usually follows severe cold and often it comes in the wake of a snowstorm. Sometimes it creeps in overnight, settles down for a few days and makes one think of late March. Whether it lasts a day or a week, as it does on occasion, it warms both heart and hands and lifts the spirits. Drifts melt, gutters and roadsides overflow, brooks waken and chatter again, meadows feel soggy underfoot. It is an illusion, of course, but red osier stems seem to quicken. And maple-sugar men, though they know sap won't run for at least another month, think of spiles and sap buckets.

Then, mysteriously as it came, the thaw departs. The wind turns cold, the sun is dull and remote, brooks are iced in once more. But for a few days winter lost its grip. It was as though a cold door had opened and there was spring in the next room. But that door always closes. After all, it is still January and, thaw or not, January isn't spring.

Squirrels in the Treetops *January 27*

If the gray squirrels have been more active and even seem more numerous now than they were a few weeks ago, it isn't wholly because cold and hunger are catching up with them. Another urgency drives them. This is their mating season. For a few weeks after mid-January they are as much interested in each other as they are in acorns and only the most stormy weather interrupts their vigorous courtship and reckless treetop chases. The young will be born in March and April, though we won't see them out of the nests until two months later.

The squirrels have been making out very well this winter, thanks to a better than usual nut crop last fall. High-tension bundles of energy that they are, they are in trouble when the nut crop is short because few other rations supply the concentrated heat and energy available in an acorn or a hickory nut. The speed and grace of a squirrel, the flaunt of that eloquent tail, the breath-taking leap from high limb to limb, are as much a product of the oak woods as the leaves of the trees. Young squirrels, in a sense, are nurtured in acorn cups.

But just now the squirrels are proving that biology is never remote from the sun and the seasons. January is still winter, on the human calendar, but to a squirrel it is urgent with the impulses of spring. The eternal rhythms are established in them, even as in the oak tree, and they respond, as the oak will in its own time. A squirrel can sense April now in the naked treetops.

January Wind

January 28

The January wind has a hundred voices. It can scream, it can bellow, it can whisper, and it can sing a lullaby. It can roar through the leafless oaks and shout down the hillside, and it can murmur in the white pines rooted among the granite ledges where lichen makes strange hieroglyphics. It can whistle down a chimney and set the hearth-flames to dancing. On a sunny day it can pause in a sheltered spot and breathe a promise of spring and violets. In the cold of a lonely night it can rattle the sash and stay there muttering of ice and snowbanks and deep-frozen ponds.

Sometimes the January wind seems to come from the farthest star in the outer darkness, so remote and so impersonal is its voice. That is the wind of a January dawn, in the half-light that trembles between day and night. It is a wind that merely quivers the trees, its force sensed but not seen, a force that might almost hold back the day if it were so directed. Then the east brightens, and the wind relaxes—the stars, its source, grown dim.

And sometimes the January wind is so intimate that you know it came only from the next hill, a little wind that plays with leaves and puffs at chimney smoke and whistles like a little boy with puckered lips. It makes the little cedar trees quiver, as with delight. It shadow-boxes with the weather-vane. It tweaks an ear, and whispers laughing words about crocuses and daffodils, and nips the nose and dances off.

But you never know, until you hear its voice, which wind is here today. Or, more important, which will be here tomorrow.

Simplicity

January 29

There is a simplicity about the resting world of winter that is neither stark nor colorless, once the eye has accustomed itself to the season. It is elemental and direct, and thus has its own clean beauty, which is enhanced by winter itself, by the long shadows and the tempered highlights. But it is so different from the full color of autumn and from the burgeoning greens of spring that it is our habit to dismiss it as a time of dull grays and lusterless browns.

What it comes down to is elemental form. A tree in winter is so obviously a tree, skeletonized to its very branch and twig. You can see every inch of it, every ridge of its bark and every bud-knob. Yet there it stands, firmly rooted, strong in its upthrusting trunk, purposefully branched to withstand the storm and at the same time to spread its leaves to the sun in a proper season.

The same is true of the hills themselves. There they stand, their skeleton of rock substantial against the weather. The mark of centuries is upon them, the gouge of ice and the knifing of swift water; but they rise above the valleys in clean ridges that direct the winds and breast the storms. And the streams which flow at their feet are brooks and rivers, the flow of winter waters, unshaded, unshoaled except by the ice of winter itself, their sole purpose to drain the land before the floods of spring.

Even the snow on such a landscape has this same simplicity, carved and shaped though it is by the wind. Is there anything more beautiful, in the purely esthetic sense, than a snowdrift curled in the shape of the storm's breath? In its cold, clean way it seems to sum up the direct, unembellished beauty of our icy months.

Midpoint

January 30

There is an old back-country rhyme, seldom heard anymore, that says:

When January nears its end
    On this advice you can depend:
Have half your wood and half your hay
    And you'll come safely through to May.

The assumption that winter was half over by January's end was not always borne out, of course; but it was based on practicalities. A farmer's livestock had to be barn-fed from early November till the first new grass greened the meadow, and house-fires had to be fed an almost equal time. Hay and wood were calculable indexes to the season's passage and winter was not bounded by a solstice and an equinox, no matter what the almanac said. Winter was winter, to be prepared for and lived with.

Times change. There aren't many woodpiles left to be measured when January nears its end, though most farmers can still count their bales of hay. Now we watch the degree-day totals and the oil bills when we look for signs. But the seasons persist and winter is still weather. And January's end still marks a midpoint, halfway between November and April.

The old rhyme still is fundamentally true. Once January is weathered, the chances are that we will come safely through. To May. And that is the most heartwarming part of the prediction. The old-timers who first set it to rhyme weren't aiming at March as their goal. They were yearning for violets and apple blossoms, not melt and mud.

January Evening

January 31

Sunset leaves a glow like a faint blush on the hilltops. It slowly flows down across the valley, a pinkly luminous shadow. The wind, which all day has been re-drifting the snow, filling paths and smothering footprints, eases away. The countryman, booted, mufflered and storm-coated, goes out to do the evening chores.

Slowly the pink glow fades, leaving a shadowless, lusterless world of white. The sky is icy-green at the horizon, thin blue above, skim-milk blue, and near the zenith is a half-moon that looks shrunken with the cold, pale as a snowdrift. The barns stand stark, their weathered boards dark as bitter chocolate; and their roofs are like thick white frosting on a chocolate cake. The woodshed door creaks on its chilled hinges. Across the way, the river is a winding white road; the country road itself, though plowed open, is snow-packed as though awaiting pungs and cutters.

Darkness comes, but a deceptive dark. Stars shimmer. The young moon glows. Drifted meadows and fields seem to have caught the vanished light from the sky. Naked maples cast black shadows. A man's breath puffs white and twinkling against the stars. Sounds echo in the cold, heavy air, a barking dog, a slamming storm door, a barred owl calling from the dark grove of hemlocks on the far hillside.

The countryman rubs his nose with a mittened hand, warms it for a moment. It is a cold January night. Zero and falling. He knows without looking at the thermometer, for he hears the whistling whine of his footsteps in the snow.

February

SNOW MOON

**The drifts mark the wind's
fandangos, the deepest
snowdrifts of the winter.**

Groundhog Day *February 1*

This week brings that secular occasion known as Groundhog Day, when an almost incredible combination of guesswork, speculation, superstition, and error is taken for divination. The groundhog, or woodchuck, is supposed to rouse from hibernation, emerge from its den, and decide about the weather for the next six weeks. If the sun shines and the woodchuck sees its shadow it will return to its bed and winter will continue another six weeks. If it is cloudy and the woodchuck sees no shadow it will end its sleep and winter will be at an end.

That is the old belief, which reaches back to primitive times. Early tribesmen credited various animals with the ability to forecast weather. The Egyptians relied on bears. Early Europeans turned to wolves for prophecies. In England they put their faith in otters and badgers. Early English colonists in America, never skilled in identification, mistook woodchucks for badgers, which often were called groundhogs in England. The badger was the Candlemas forecaster in England, so the American marmot inherited the prophet's mantle. And, just to round out the tangle of identities, the name "woodchuck" came from the Algonquin *wejac*, which meant fisher, a cousin of the weasel.

And that is the way the old Candlemas legend was credited to a misnamed creature that usually sleeps right through the event. Not even countrymen put much stock in the old belief, anyway. But in upper New England there is a wry twist to it. Folks up there hope for sunshine so the groundhog can see its shadow. That, they say, means there will be *only* six more weeks of winter.

This is one year when we can echo their hope. May the sun shine bright on Groundhog Day!

Groundhog Day *February 2*

If one wanted to be pontifical it might be said that Groundhog Day is a perverse symbol of man's indomitable hope. If it is bright and shimmery the groundhog will see his shadow and, being a timid soul, expect the worst and retreat to his den for another six weeks of winter. If it is dour and glowering the groundhog will not see his shadow and winter's worst will be over.

Though it is a nonsense legend it reaches back to pagan logic. On Candlemas Day the ancient Romans burned candles to Februa, mother of Mars, seeking her intercession. Mars was a god not only of war but of growing things, of field crops, and Februa could urge him to grant an early spring. Over the centuries, Februa was forgotten except in the month's name; and by a series of errors, including the mistaken identity of the American woodchuck, the groundhog became a principal in the ritual. But fundamentally it was, and still is, rooted in the insistent human hope that if we get the worst over with now, something better must follow.

So we scan the skies on Candlemas Day and hope for the groundhog's intercession, no longer believing in the old gods. But the woodchuck sleeps oblivious, having no influence with either Februa or Mars but only a dull and comatose attitude toward the whole matter, certainly unaware of any gift of prophecy. He sleeps, and we hope his sleep continues undisturbed through Candlemas Day. Let it glower, let it gloom. Let the candles burn. We don't believe a word of it, but we do believe in spring. And the sooner the better.

Half Past Winter

February 3

Now, to paraphrase the Song of Solomon, the winter is half past, and in another six weeks the flowers will begin to appear on the earth, the time of the singing of birds will have come. Not many birds in mid-March, but some. And they certainly will include "the voice of the turtle," for the turtle dove is one of our year-round birds. Song sparrows and white-throats will be singing by then, of course, and there may be red-wing blackbirds. There may be robins back from the South.

Just speaking their names and remembering their voices makes the first week of February seem akin to April. There is a similar magic in the names of the early wildflowers. But why prolong it? After all, this is February, and March itself is not April, not in our area. It now is midwinter, by the almanac, and even Solomon would have had difficulty forecasting the weather.

A few guesses, however, may not be out of order. In the next six weeks the greenish horns of skunk cabbage will be in sight down in the boglands. Those horns will open into hoods and reveal small flowers that have the odor of rancid meat, the earliest of spring blossoms. Grass along the banks of pasture brooks will begin to show green again. Sometime in March there will be pussy willows. And after pussy willows, almost anything can happen that has the look or smell or taste of spring.

Whimsical February

February 4

February probably will be capricious—it usually is; but there is excuse for that. February is the last full month of winter, by the almanac at least, and the traditional battleground of warring weather systems. It begins with the absurdity of Groundhog Day, celebrates romance in mid-month, and includes an extra day every four years. February is the only month that still approximates the lunar month—one of man's earliest units of time—yet on occasion it passes without a full moon.

According to the ancient chronicles, February was first put in the calendar by Numa Pompilius, legendary second king of Rome. It was named for Februarius, the feast of purification, and on the old calendars it was the year's final month. It ended with the feast of Terminalia, a kind of New Year's celebration that lasted several days. Then came March, the vernal equinox, and the new year.

So we inherited February, a whimsical month that can smother us in snow or set the sap to flowing, paralyze us with sleet or brim the brooks. Its days are as long as October's, but its nights can be colder than December's. Februarius and Terminalia have vanished from our calendars, but February still purifies us, in a rugged way, and when it goes we usually bid it a glad goodbye.

The Flutterers

February 5

The sparrows make late winter a pleasanter time, especially for country folk. Not English or house sparrows, those raucous little city gamins, but native American sparrows—the song sparrow, the tree sparrow, the white-throat, the pine siskin, the field sparrow, the occasional chipping sparrow. Finches, all of them, in the big classification of the ornithologists, but simply sparrows to most of us. They come to the feeding stations, they are busy as bees on the hillside where weeds still stand with a few seeds, and they chatter eagerly in the most untoward weather. On warm days they sing a little, foretaste of the lively songs they will sing after March has made its turn.

In its old meaning, the word "sparrow" meant to flutter. They are flutterers, all of them, adept on the wing. See a flock of them sweep up the hillside, wheel into the wind against a gray sky, and it lifts your heart. In such a flock there will be speckled breasts, solid gray breasts, breasts that seem striped, for the sparrows are congenial. You even see flashes of yellow among them, that bright little patch at the base of the pine siskin's tail.

They are seed-eaters, all of them. They flock to the feeders, where they eat millet, shucking off the outer shell with a quick, tongue-rolling, beak-chomping motion. Those papery shells cling around their beaks, like a small child's oatmeal around its mouth. They eat, and at no sign they all take frenzied wing, fly away chattering.

The Maples

February 6

The old-time New Englander liked to have a few sugar maples near his house, not only for sap and shade but for reassurance. It was well enough to say that if a man had half his wood and half his hay still unused by the first week in February he could come safely through the winter. But it comforted a man to see and sense that the big maples also expected spring to come. It still does.

Maybe you can't say that a tree "expects" anything, but it surely can bolster your own expectation. Outwardly, a sugar maple is as dormant as an oak or an elm. The buds on its twigs are sealed and waiting, no bigger now than they were in December. Those buds actually will be slow in opening; a dozen other trees come earlier to leaf and blossom. But maybe because it is so deliberate, the sugar maple starts preparations early. It begins to stir in February.

So when you come to those dark February days of doubt, you go out and listen to the maples, feel them, let their slow, impalpable pulse of soil and sun flow into you. You don't look at the buds or cut a twig to see if it oozes. You remember the way the stars stood on the last clear night, the way the shadows fell in the last bright noontime. And you know that things are waking up down at the root of this tree. Sap is getting ready to work its way upward. You know, just as sure as you know what day it is. And knowing, you can go on with the chores, sure as April, and May, and summer.

The Promise *February 7*

A mild day in January is a break and a momentary relief, a chance for a man to catch his breath; but when February relaxes for a day or two it is a promise. It warms a man's heart as well as his hands and makes him think of March and April. Two or three mild February days in a row, with frosty nights between, and the countryman thinks of sap. By Washington's birthday sap should be running.

The fact is that hope is as insistent as the seasonal daylight. Once the sunset holds off till a quarter after five we begin looking for signs. Hopeful signs. The countryman talks about maple sap, but he watches for partridges in his apple trees. Any day now they will be down from the thickets for an early spring salad of apple buds. When he has an errand down by the bog he keeps an eye out for skunk cabbage tips, which can melt their way right through the ice. He appraises the stems of the red osier dogwood, wondering if it's the light or sap actually quickening that seems to warm their blood-red color.

He looks at the willows against the sky. Are the buds bigger than they were two weeks ago? Maybe, just a fraction. He pauses beside a rock where the sun has melted a little patch of ground clean and looks at the rosette of gray-green leaves of a giant mullein. Then he hears a twitter, a tree sparrow singing instead of chirping, and that really lifts his heart. It's just February easing off, but it is a promise. It may be cold again tomorrow, maybe more snow, but it can't last forever. Now he knows.

The Secret

February 8

February is still winter, beyond argument; but change is in the air. Literally in the air, if you watch and listen to the blue jays.

Jays are not ingratiating birds, even among their own kind. They squabble with each other as well as with the neighbors. If there is no one else around they will scream for an audience to come and listen to their complaints and accusations.

Like others of dubious reputation, jays scream bloody murder at visitors of the best intentions. Approach a jay with a handful of corn or a crust of bread and he will scream, "Stop thief!" three times even as he flies away—flight only to a nearby treetop where he can wait till you leave your offering and go away. Then he will come down, quiet as a sneak-thief, and stuff himself.

At the feeder the jay will eat four times as much as any other bird and kick out even more than he eats. He insists on eating alone, threatening sparrow, chickadee, and titmouse with baleful eye and rapier beak. Most of his winter excitement comes from occasional attacks on smaller owls, a noisy diversion usually marked more by uproar than by blood-letting.

But when February comes and daylight begins to linger, the jays begin to feel, perhaps down in their hollow bones, that life is good and soon will be even better. They whisper this, at first, to themselves. Then they say it aloud, but softly. It is a wholly new note, actually a two-note salute to the season. It is almost musical. It really is the blue jay's prelude to a love song, a sentimental secret the secretive jay can no longer keep to himself.

Reynard *February 9*

You hear the yelping in the night and you know the foxes are out. Then you hear the fine-spun yapping answer and you know they are looking for mates. They wouldn't pass up a grouse or a rabbit if it happened to be in their path; but grouse and rabbits are year-round, and the fox's mating season is brief. So the dog fox yelps and the vixen yelps her answer, and soon after mid-March the pups are born.

The red fox—Reynard is legend and folk tale—is one of the most successful of all wildlings that live in populated areas. He can survive in the suburbs, even in odd corners of public parks. But he thrives in the settled countryside, in woodland and brushy places. Those are his best hunting grounds.

For some reason, he likes to live near a farmer's house. When every farm kept a pen of chickens that was understandable, since Reynard is a notorious chicken-thief. But now it almost seems he simply wants a human audience for his outrageous tricks—the way he toys with a field mouse, the way he walks on a stone wall, the way he taunts a farm dog into a hopeless chase.

He is a handsome creature, with that magnificent red fur coat, that white-tipped fluff of a tail, those ever-alert ears and eyes, and he fairly struts when he isn't running like a streak. If you are lucky, you see him in full daylight, for he is abroad day or night. But just now you hear him yelping in the midwinter darkness.

The Green Wishes

February 10

From now on, every sunny day is more than a break in the clouds that come swooping across the continent on winter schedule. Every day, of course, is another day toward spring; but when the sun shines it prompts greener thoughts than were possible a month ago. For one thing, it is a higher and warmer sun, but mostly it is the response of the human heart.

February zero is just as cold as zero in January, and February snow often is deeper than January snow. But the sight of the sun all through a steadily lengthening February day gives that day a dimension beyond mathematical calculation. You don't pay so much attention to the calendar or even the clock. You know the inner feeling of change, the sense of the seasons passing.

You stand at the foot of a hill and are not surprised when you hear the trickle of melt underneath the snow. You aren't so much pleased as expectant when two chickadees come to twitter at you and stay to sing a fragment of song, as though sharing a remarkable discovery. You watch two gray squirrels frisking through the big maples and know that winter games of tag have changed to mating chases.

Inevitably, there are green wishes, too. The wish for April and May, without the necessity of March. For new grass beside the brook, rustling leaves on the maples, the woodsy smell of violets. And it's still February, no matter how bright the sun may be. But you know the feeling now; you know that the change is a certainty.

Snowstorm

February 11

There is ironic paradox in the fact that man, who boasts of his mastery of his environment, still is at the mercy of a snowstorm, particularly in his cities. A foot of snow in the country creates only a brief interruption before the patterns of life are resumed. Roads are plowed, driveways are opened, and essential traffic and service are soon back in order. But in the cities the very complexity of life becomes a trap.

The countryman can fall back on older simplicities. The plows push the clogging snow off his roads and leave it at the roadside. He shovels what paths he needs. His way of life includes stocks of food and fuel for such times of necessity, so he goes neither cold nor hungry. His schedule is flexible. He is, to a degree, self-sufficient. Knowing winter and its demands, he has prepared for them. He lives with the weather, has no notion of ever mastering it. He can even see beauty in a snowdrift.

But cities are highly organized, dependent on the intricate network of transport and service. Snow is a nuisance when it isn't a disaster. There is no place to put it. It clogs streets, chokes traffic, blocks bus and truck and ambulance. And no city is self-sufficient. A snowbound city is soon in distress.

We can split atoms, send rockets to the moon, fly faster than sound, but we still can't subdue a blizzard. Our cities remain at the mercy of the bitter wind and the driven snowflake.

The Difference

February 12

There is a clear-cut difference between a major snowstorm in January and one in February, one that can't be measured in inches of snow or the degree of trouble it may cause for busy, beleaguered people.

A January storm too often comes with a kind of cold silence that is only emphasized by the shrilling of the wind. And it usually fades away into a sullen, short-day bleakness that hardly warms up at all.

But a February storm, even of the same dimension, looks, feels, and sounds altogether different. It may come with whooping gales, unload two feet of snow, tie up traffic, and paralyze life's routines for a few days. But once he has dug himself out, a man can see daylight, more daylight than he has seen since October. He can feel the sunlight, and though there may be five-foot drifts he knows that the sun is going to melt them, in due time, not merely bounce off.

And out where there are winter birds there is bird-song when the storm has ended. There is something about the passing of the storm, the brilliance of the sun in a clear sky, and the subtlety of the season that acts like a pre-spring tonic to chickadee and blue jay, tree sparrow and nuthatch, downy woodpecker and junco. They haunt the trees, the exposed weed patches, and the dooryard feeders, and they sing. Not like robins or orioles in May, to be sure, but minor songs that make a man remember April. Even in two feet of February snow.

Mr. Redbird

February 13

The cardinal, traditional Mr. Redbird of the Deep South, is no longer a rarity up here in Yankeeland. For some years this bird of the spectacular plumage and the bold, proud voice has been an occasional year-round resident here in the city and up the Hudson Valley. But this year cardinals have been seen frequently in southern New England, even well up into the Berkshires. This is not altogether new, since Massachusetts has known the cardinal at least since

1930; but Mr. Redbird certainly is more commonly seen this winter than ever before.

It is impossible to mistake Mr. Redbird for any other bird. His color, a vivid cardinal red, is unmatched. He has a jaunty crest. And his whistle is like nothing else in birddom. Unlike many other birds, he sings every month in the year. Seen in a Northern winter landscape, he demands attention. Heard on a raw February day, he thrills one with amazement and delight. There's not another winter bird that can rival him, either in looks or voice.

Why cardinals should range farther north than usual this winter is as much a mystery as why red-breasted nuthatches should range farther south. Weather can't be the answer to both puzzles, probably not to either. But there they are, cardinals and red-breasted nuthatches, overlapping generously in the snowy hill country where neither of them might be expected in any number. The nuthatches are quiet little fellows with no song to speak of. But the cardinals are neither modest nor inconspicuous. The cardinal is Mr. Redbird, and don't forget the Mr. He knows it, and you know it the minute you see him, or even when you hear him whistling somewhere down the lane.

Valentine

February 14

We come to mid-February with a variety of signs that reflect the reason. In the zodiac, Aquarius is about to give way to Pisces, water boy to fish, Uranus to Neptune. In the almanac, winter is in its last month, come snow, sleet, or whatever the weather may bring. And on the calendar stands Saint Valentine's Day, festival of hearts and flowers, occasion of love tokens and romance.

In a way, Valentine's Day doesn't make sense in mid-February. Yet we treasure it in part for its contradictions. It was named for a saint, though nobody knows for sure which of seven, possibly eight, saints and martyrs gave it his name. It probably dates back to a forgotten Roman holiday, possibly linked with flowers though the only flowers in sight in the Northern Hemisphere are in greenhouses. One legend says it marks the time when birds begin to mate, though the only birds we know who mate now are the gruff-voiced owls.

But here it is, a hope and a promise, and a good deal more reassuring than zodiacal fishes or almanac forecasts. It deals with spring, with gentling April and bee-loud May. Its sentiments are warm and flowery. It has the smell of violets and the song of bluebirds. It is—well, it is February's love song to a winter-weary world.

Subtle Signs of Spring

February 15

In one sense it is much too early to look for signs of spring. But that is the dulled sense dictated by slavery to the calendar.

The calendar lags, and if one were a stickler one could even say that spring began to assert itself when the angle of sunlight shifted ever so slowly after the winter solstice. The assertion was so subtle, and attended by such obvious sights and sounds of winter, however, that most of us missed it. You can't hear, and you can scarcely see, the alteration of a shadow, which was all that really happened.

But now there are things to be heard if one is at all attentive. At noontime on a sunny day the dooryard sparrows begin to test a few phrases of remembered song. The chickadees, which will lisp a greeting any winter day, now extend their songs, simple though they are. The nuthatches still say nothing but *yank*, but they say it more often and with a new intonation. From the woodland the male cardinal whistles as though he really means it. And the blue jays flit from leafless tree to tree, actually singing, in a kind of hoarse whisper, vestiges of what some call the melodies their ancestors sang.

True, these are slight matters, particularly on a day when the wind has a wire edge and the threat of more snow. But spring is the sum of many things, and weather is only one of them. Shadows are important, too, and those impulsive bursts of melodic notes. Spring is not yet at hand, but there is change, and there are subtle stirrings here and there, if we forget the calendar and listen.

The Courting Owls *February 16*

Mid-February, and back in the hills the great horned owls, biggest and most truculent of the nocturnal tribe, are starting to nest. The courtship preliminaries are both loud and eerie, so the nights echo wherever great horned owls are resident.

Both our big owls, the barred and the great horned, are sometimes called hoot owls, but their calls are quite different. The barred owl, only slightly smaller than its great horned cousin, usually utters a nine-note series of hoots that has been aptly put into the words, "Who cooks for you? Who cooks for you-all?" The great horned owl, with a gruff bass voice, usually uses a five-note call, "Woof-hoo, hoo, hoo-hooo." But now, in its mating season, it uses a variety of calls, challenge, question, summons, even soft cooing notes quite out of keeping with its ordinary gruffness. It can sound like a baying dog or like a group of laughing women. It can simply hoot in half a dozen tones. It can ask, "Wau-hoo? Who? Ho, hoo, hoo?"

The barred owls, which won't be mating for another month, still occasionally ask, in the deep of night, who is doing the cooking at your house. But from now till the end of February, the great horned owls will be the lords of the night, loud and gruff and full of summons and challenge.

Eggs will be laid and hovered, even in snowstorms. Owlets will hatch and demand food. Then the big owls will be too busy to sit and hoot at their own echoes in the darkness.

Those Attic Wasps

February 17

Wasps begin to appear in country houses about now, and even in some suburban houses. One sees them dart uncertainly about, hears them buzz and bang on window panes, and one wonders where they came from. They probably came from the attic, where they spent the early part of the winter hibernating. Now, with longer hours of daylight, the wasps begin to rouse and start exploring.

The sound of a flying wasp is different from that of a fly. It is a matter of vibration, of the speed of the wing strokes. Those strokes set up sound waves. Some ingenious researcher once measured those strokes with a tuning fork. Tuning forks are carefully calibrated and, by matching the sound of a flying insect with that of a tuning fork, it is possible to say how fast that insect moves its wings.

Thus it was shown that a common housefly makes its familiar buzz by beating its wings nearly 20,000 strokes a minute. The wasp beats its wings a little less than one-third that fast, 6,000 strokes a minute. The normal human ear can hear sounds with as few as 1,800 beats per minute, the beat of a dragonfly's wings.

So it is easy enough to hear a wasp. Especially now. But it isn't the sound of spring in the dooryard. It is the sound of a female wasp still half asleep. It is mid-February with a stinger in her tail.

Purification *February 18*

February gets its name from an ancient ceremony of purification, which occurred about the middle of the month. The countryman has known for generations that it is a good time to cut fence posts, prune trees and grape vines, clear out brush, and wean calves. Even when the weather isn't cutting up capers, there isn't much more that a farmer can do except take care of the daily chores and wait out the balance of the month. The signs of the zodiac, which change from Aquarius to Pisces on the 19th, aren't much help, for both are rather watery. By March a man is pretty well purified.

By February a man has begun to look ahead to March and April, and he sometimes gets impatient. He keeps telling himself that every day of sunshine is another day nearer spring, and every dark day or stormy one is another day of winter survived. But he also keeps watching the slow stretch of daylight, which is the true index of the season. There's a clear gain of more than an hour now and by the end of the month that gain will be almost doubled.

So he cuts his posts and prunes his vines and trims the brush along the pasture margin. He works his way through the days as they come. Purification isn't very painful. It's mostly a matter of learning patience again, as a man must learn every February.

Jaunty Mr. Chick *February 19*

The chickadee has a scientific name twice as big as he is, *Parus atricapillus*, but there isn't another bird in the woodland or dooryard that rates as much respect and affection, especially at this time of year.

Actually, the chickadee is one of the smallest of our familiar winter birds, weighing only a little more than a first-class letter. And a good half of that weight is feathers; he can fluff himself, on a cold day, to the size of a fat sparrow. Yet he is one of the most adept of all birds on the wing. His wings can beat thirty times a second and, though he can't fly backward, he can hover and he can fly straight up.

All birds live at high speed, physiologically, but Mr. Chick is a sprinter even among his own kind. His tiny heart beats 500 times a minute when he is asleep and doubles that rate when he is awake and active. His normal temperature, 108 degrees, would be a fatal fever for any human being. His metabolism is terrific—he needs a winter diet of about his own weight in food each day. That is one reason he is so eternally busy, so incredibly hungry.

There he is, Mr. Chick, a mere fleck of feathered life, gay, jaunty, gregarious, chipper even in a snowstorm, singing even in zero weather. He rates a salute, and hereby gets one.

Sunrise

February 20

The sun now rises well before seven o'clock, its earliest since November; and, no matter what the temperature, it begins to have the feeling of change. It no longer is the belated awakening of a deep winter day. It is still winter-quiet, with the silence of a leafless landscape. No birds sing. But the day begins fresh and rested, renewed by the night.

The most insistent thing about any dawn is the leisurely coming of light. There is no haste about it, no scurry or rush. The stars dim slowly, the darkness thins away, the sense of light is there before the light itself. Then there is gleam where there was glow, and the sun has risen. But even the first hour of sunlight is almost deliberate, with time to twinkle and strike sparks from frosty twigs and icy ponds, time to pencil long shadows on every tree-lined meadow. It is a new day, a young day, another beginning. And in mid-February we are eager for beginnings, weary of cold leftovers.

Any dawn is beautiful, even one filled with falling snow, simply because it is new, it is daylight again and a fresh span of time to be lived. And in February it is another day toward spring, which is in a way the year's own dawn. The night passes, and the winter, and each day we know the miracle of sunrise, which is the apotheosis of change itself. By noon we may have wearied, and by dusk we may have forgotten; but tomorrow there will be another dawn, another sunrise, the reminder of another day.

Sap-Rise

February 21

By tradition, this is the week when life begins to stir down at the root of things. Old-timers in the lower tier of the maple sugar country will tell you that, three years out of four, Washington's birthday brings the first sap-flow. So unless a howling storm has iced things in completely, there will be spiles in sugar maples on south slopes before Tuesday's dawn, and there will be pails of first-run sap by sundown.

How does a man know when to set his spiles? Well, he hears the jays call with a new note in their voices, and he hears the woodpeckers drumming with a new urgency. He sees the winter robins venturing out more often into his pastureland. He sees the first faint amber glow in the willow tips, and he sees a subtle livening in the red osier stems. He has seen the grouse come down to his apple trees for a taste of apple buds, and though he can't see the change he knows those buds must have begun to swell. He sees the sun rise soon after six-thirty and stay in the sky almost eleven hours.

He knows what time it is, not by the clock or the calendar but by the season itself. Everywhere he turns, he sees that the seasons are still in order. So he sets his first few spiles, and a few mild days and frosty nights start the sap dripping. When the sap rises you can begin to count the days till spring. Winter isn't over, but its days now are numbered.

The Signs

February 22

By the last week in February there are signs. The osiers have begun to blush with a lively red on stems that have been dull reddish-brown since last October. The willow twigs have an amber look and their catkins are fattening in their buds; by the season's turn a month from now their silver fur will be in sight.

In the boggy places, skunk cabbage thrusts its greenish hoods up through the rotting ice and opens its fetid blossoms to the early carrion flies. Alder bushes nearby cautiously open their male catkins and spill just enough pollen to attract a few early bees. There are signs of life in the crocus bed. And maple sap begins to rise.

The squirrels and chickadees seem to know as much about sap-rise as most countrymen do. At the right time, no earlier, the squirrels nip buds off the maple trees and lick the sap that oozes. Maybe it is a squirrel's spring tonic. When the squirrels have left on other business, the chickadees arrive and drink at the taps the squirrels have opened. Perhaps that first-flow sap is their spring tonic, too; after a few sips they sing more lively songs. And that afternoon the sugar-makers set their spiles and prepare to fire up their evaporators. By tradition, sap-run starts on Washington's traditional birthday, which is today.

It may snow tonight. The temperature may deep-dive again. But daylight now lasts almost eleven hours. That is the best sign of all.

Twilight

February 23

We call it twilight, and we cherish it now especially because it helps the days in their slow reach toward spring. It shortens the nights, which are so reluctant to relax their cold grip. It makes the sunset seem later than it is and somewhat eases the dimensions of our late winter lives.

We cherish twilight, too, because it not only has the glow of the departing day but a special beauty of its own. It is neither sunlight nor star-shine nor moonlight, though it borrows somewhat from all of them. It can be hauntingly memorable over a snow-covered meadow or in the leafless woodland. Its shadows are soft-edged, velvety. It spreads blue-black pools in all the hollows. It touches the horizon line of the sky with the green of lake ice freshly cut. The air of twilight may be brittle, but the light itself has the soft, elusive texture of mist.

Even the sounds of late winter dusk have that special quality of twilight. The jays and crows are silent, their day ended, but the great horned owl's mournful warning from the dark pine woods is less ominous than it will be at midnight. The voice of the red fox challenging the farm dogs hasn't quite the sharp, staccato note of darkness in it. The countryman's footsteps on his way to the woodshed make winter music in the crisp snow, but it is a whistle, not a frigid whine. February twilight is glow without glitter, a song that is never shrill.

In the Sun

February 24

The sun, moving steadily toward the equinoctial meridian, now has enough warmth to bring a midday touch of softness and relaxation to the south side of the old stone wall. It isn't yet the taste of spring, but it is an easing of the bite and bitterness of winter. Walk there any bright noontime and you can believe again in the benevolence of the earth.

The stones gather and radiate the solar warmth, and the snow melts around them. Their gray-green lichen maps of strange, undiscovered Utopias have a warm, moist, livened look. The moss on the oozy surface of the deep-frozen earth is green of an impatient tip that will be a six-foot stalk by July.

An alder bush rooted above the wall reaches over it to dangle reddish-brown catkins at the twig-tips. Winter catkins, still tightly closed, but pollen-laden catkins ready to open when April nears. Just beyond stands the broad bole of a big red oak, its sunward side warm as the stones. A nuthatch comes down the tree headfirst, exploring every crevice for sun-lured spiders and insect eggs. A chickadee, ever curious, comes fluttering and twittering, then perches on the alder and sings its familiar notes with a special lilt.

Not spring. Not even March. But the sun is in our sky three minutes longer today than it was yesterday.

The Deliberate Buds *February 25*

The buds on the lilacs, like those on the dogwoods, always look impatient by late February, no matter what the weather. But they are sealed with caution and are as deliberate as spring itself. Unlike forsythia and pussy willow buds, they refuse to be fooled or hastened by being brought into a warm room and cosied in a vase of warm water.

But life is there, and leaf and twig and blossom, in those remarkable buds. And that astonishing little package that is any bud didn't come into being overnight. It began to take shape last summer, well before the season's leaves fell. The buds on all the trees and bushes formed then and grew inside the bud scales until hard frost clamped down.

Then they hibernated, much as the woodchuck hibernates. They will awaken when the sap starts to stir again in response to the vernal sun and warmth.

When the buds do waken, everything in them will grow like magic. The bud scales, no longer needed, will fall in a shower unnoticed but in numbers even greater than the autumn's fall of leaves. The new leaves, delicate as a baby's skin, will stretch and expand and be filled with chlorophyll as their "baby color," often pink or lilac, fades. Blossoms will open, often from the same bud. The miracle will happen.

But that is for later. Right now the buds are waiting, a promise of April. The impatience is in us, watching them, hoping, wishing, while the clock they obey continues its slow, deliberate ticking down at the root of things.

Hunger Moon

February 26

To see the full moon as it rose in the brittle eastern sky last night was to know both awe and shivering wonder. It was round as a medallion, bright as burnished brass, and its light had no more warmth than the frost cloud of a man's breath. It was a false and lifeless sun that made false daylight of the night. It killed the lesser stars and reduced the constellations to fundamentals. It burned the darkness with neither heat nor smoke, strewing the snow with charred skeletons of the naked trees. No wonder the Indians knew the February full moon as the Hunger Moon.

Yet, as it mounted the icy sky the moon set stark patterns of beauty. Footsteps in the snow became laced traceries of purple shadows. Starless ponds of night sky lay in the meadows' hollows. Roads became black velvet ribbons with winking frost sequins. Pines became whispering flocks of huge, dark birds on the hilltop and pasture cedars were black candle flames. Warm-windowed houses and frost-roofed barns were all twins, each with its counterpart beside it on the snow. And no man walked alone as he hurried toward warmth and shelter.

It was the perfect winter moon. Tonight its edges will be frostbitten and it will rise an hour later. Tomorrow it will be still another hour laggard and within the week its rim will begin to crumble. Night by night more stars will creep back to claim the darkness, and day by day the sun will move a fraction of a degree toward March and the equinox. The Hunger Moon will soon pass its prime.

Winter Is Still Winter *February 27*

Every winter inspires one of two questions: "This is a real old-fashioned winter, isn't it?" or "Whatever happened to the old-fashioned winter?" The same answer can be given to both: Over the years, winter hasn't changed very much. We have an occasional mild winter, and we have an occasional severe winter; but when the weather records are averaged, decade by decade, they show little variation. One of the longest continuous records, that for New Haven, Connecticut, shows only about three degrees difference between the coldest and warmest decades since 1780.

We make more demands of winter, however, than they did in the olden days. Now we have traffic problems that are vastly complicated by snow and cold. Our complex network of utilities is often at the mercy of snow, ice, and wind. We resent cold weather, indoors and out, and demand warmer temperatures in our homes and offices than were available in the past. Our urban and suburban ways of life are geared to a different tempo, and even our rural life no longer waits out the weather as it once did. Winter hasn't greatly changed, but there has been a revolution in our winter habits and demands.

Winter is still winter. It has been, apparently, for a long time. Some years it is mild, and some years it isn't.

Even Thomas Jefferson asked, more than 150 years ago, "What happened to our old-fashioned winters?"

Prophets of Tomorrow

February 28

This is the time of year when prophecy proliferates. Between the garden seed catalogues and the almanacs we can look months ahead and know not only what will happen right here on earth, but in the heavens. Hope and promise are in these pages, and all tomorrow's triumphs.

What will June be like? Turn to the Old Farmer's Almanac. For the ten days beginning with St. Barnabas: "For this cool weather be grateful, the storm in its wake may be fateful." Turn to the catalogue. A gardenful of roses, succulent peas, savory chives and scallions, crisp lettuce. And June? Sweet corn, long, fat, yellow ears, luscious, not even sullied by an earworm, petunias, snapdragons, zinnias, morning glories. August? Asters big as saucers, dahlias, marigolds, gaillardia, giant hybrid delphinium in second bloom. "Weather you'll find often changes its mind." But tomatoes ripen, tomatoes big as soup plates, tomatoes by the bushel.

These things we know, now in February. Yes, we know, too, that March and mud, April and icy rain, May and an aching back, June and insects, July and weeds, all lie ahead. We know, but memory dims. Particularly in the face of glowing descriptions and full-color pictures on coated paper. All these wonders will happen. It says so here! All honor to the prophets, in February, at least.

March

WORM MOON
Melt and mud, and the frost comes out of the ground, the angle worms with it.

March

March 1

March comes, a kind of interregnum, winter's sovereignty relaxing, spring not yet in control. But the pattern is now established.

The incredible but annually commonplace change that is life eternally renewed has begun to stir. Out of the cold and dormant earth will come the leaf, the blossom, and the twig. Out of the pupa, the egg, and the womb will come the palpitant swarming of gauzy wing, chitinclad body, feathers, and fur. The pulse of plasma with its green chlorophyll or red hemoglobin begins its slow vernal throb. Sap stirs. Blood livens. The protoplasm of life begins to quicken.

It is a deliberate process with its own rhythms and responses that are unchanged over the eons. Only man, keying his life to his clocks and calendars, is impatient. The bud and the egg can wait, for a safe temperature or a precise span of daylight. Man measures; they respond. And for all man's vast store of facts, he still cannot alter that response. To grow a blade of grass he must start with a seed or a root, then wait. To hatch a bird he must start with an egg, which contains its own inflexible schedule.

March comes and the sap quickens down at the root of life. Buds, set on the twig last summer, begin to swell toward April. In the woodland's litter and debris there is a slight stir. Ice melts on warm afternoons. Water begins to flow. Chill darkness checks the slow awakening, but another day starts the deliberate throb again, the slight breath of change, the incredible, inevitable renascence of life.

Weather and Prophets

March 2

We don't hear much from the old-time weather prophets anymore, the goose-bone seers and the fur-and-feathers oracles. Meteorology did them in. But most countrymen have a weather sense, even though they supplement it with the morning's forecast. They know the Weather Bureau doesn't invent the weather, and they see their own signs and sense their own portents every time they go out to the barn or the hen house or out to the woodlot. They grew up knowing that almost everything, including weather, is a matter of cause and effect.

Except in hope or as a joke, the countryman knows better than to guess the weather two weeks ahead. But he does know the set of the wind and the lay of the land in his own valley. And no matter what the report said, when he sees snow clouds moving in he makes sure the snow shovel is handy. He lives with the moon's phases and knows that weather often changes with the moon. He is suspicious of a gaudy sunrise and a flaming red sunset. He takes warning when sun or moon wears a halo. He watches the birds, which sense weather even better than he does and feed heavily before a storm. He knows the likely meaning of sun dogs and mares' tails and clear dawns.

He doesn't think of himself as a prophet, but he has lived with the weather every day of his life. It's in his bones, and when his joints ache he suspects something more than rheumatism. His weather sense is built in, like his stubborn love for the land. But prophet? No! He's just a cautious countryman who doesn't like to be taken by surprise.

March

March 3

March has a dubious reputation at best. There is the hint of madness in the very mention of the March hare. There is the threat of dark deeds in the ides of March. There is the lamb-and-lion belief. There is March mud, there are March floods, there are the winds of March, and there is the folklore of the March Blizzard of '88.

That isn't the whole story of March, of course. To tell that story you must remember the vernal equinox, the daylight at last exceeding darkness again, the red-wings clamoring in the pondside treetops once more, the pussy willows in silvery catkin. And you must surely remember those rare March days, unpredictable and splendidly surprising, when the air is warm, the breeze is gentle, and the sun is as friendly as late April. March is these things, too. March can be hylas wakened and calling in the warm afternoon. March can be hepaticas in bloom, if you can find them.

Maybe we give March its bad name because we are so impatient. With February out of the way, we want it to be May, or April. And it isn't either of them. It is temperamental March, a time of change. We have to wade through the mud of March to get from February to April. We need the floods of March, in moderation, to wash away the snow and ice of January and February. But March is neither sinister nor mad; it is old endings and new beginnings, a jumble of them that won't get sorted out till April.

Song Again

March 4

By early March you can begin to hear April, even on dour and lowery days. The winter birds now find time for a few songs when they have stocked their inner fires and pause for a few minutes in the lengthening daylight. Despite snow or ice or sleety rain, the unseen forces of spring are beginning to work in the very fiber of life, and the birds respond.

Dooryard chickadees that have twittered companionably for weeks now indulge in full phrases, five and even seven notes, and there is the lilt of song, not mere greeting, in those notes. Tree sparrows, which can sing even in a snowstorm, now make even the dark days somewhat brighter. And song sparrows come out of the thickets and achieve the melodies that inspired their name, songs as lively and bubbling as an April brook.

Crows have no song, but their calls are less raucous and less defiant now as they watch the weather in the naked treetops. And blue jays, those jeering dandies who can make the most harmless prank look criminal, whistle haunting two-note calls that echo like the exuberant mating call of the cardinal.

Winter slowly frays out. March melt and mud still lie ahead, and probably March snowstorms. April is still a hope and a promise, but its faint, far-off song begins to tremble on the distant hilltops. The birds hear it and now testify to its truth.

The Signs

March 5

The temptation is strong, on a bright day in early March, to go looking for signs, green signs. The air has a chill, but the sun rises almost east and the shadows of the naked trees point a new, hopeful direction. Brooks begin to burble, at least by midday. Surely there must be some quickening of green life. One goes to look, beside the brook and the road and in meadow and woodland.

There are signs, but only a few. Spring is cautious. Our March is not a green month. In a sheltered cove beside a flowing brook there are a few blades of new grass in the withered clumps. In a boggy place are the primitive purplish-green hoods of skunk cabbage, which has no respect for ice and little respect for time. Beside a sun-warmed rock in the edge of the woods are small, young leaves of the hardy wood-nettle. But no violets, no anemones, no bloodroot. Dig in the woodland litter and you may find their budding roots, but it is promise that you find, not green, only green to come.

The quickening is there. But it is a response we feel and sense rather than see. The earth, the soil itself, has begun to lose its cold and gather warmth. The slow pulse has begun imperceptibly to quicken. There is a restlessness down at the roots, a stirring of slow sap. And that is where the green begins. The green itself is a precious thing, not to be trusted to March.

There are signs, yes; but few green ones. The going and the looking is a sign itself, a sign of vernal hope. The green will come, inevitable now. We feel the quickening, which is why we go.

Winter Robins

March 6

Occasional mild, sunny days now will bring out the robins and there will be the annual reports that robins are "back" and spring must be coming early. In virtually every instance, the robins seen and reported will not be migrants at all, but birds that are spending the winter here and have come out of the thickets to look for food on suburban lawns and rural meadows. All it means is that the birds, even as the people who see them, appreciate a fine day.

Every year a few robins spend the winter this far north. Nobody knows exactly why. Even up in the Berkshires winter robins are so persistent that they are sometimes spoken of as year-round residents. And this is no new phenomenon; it has been reported for many years. Sometimes the winter robins are seen in flocks of a dozen or more, usually in brushy areas where they find both food and shelter. Occasionally, but not often, they patronize a dooryard bird-feeder.

The truly migrant robins seldom get this far north before late March. When they come, they come in flocks, not a few at a time. And they have an uncanny temperature sense, almost never appearing before the average twenty-four-hour temperature is at least thirty-five degrees. Meanwhile, it is reassuring to see a few robins on the lawn on a sunny afternoon. But it doesn't mean that spring is just around the corner of the house. Not yet, it doesn't.

Partridge in the Apple Tree *March 7*

Maybe partridges perch in pear trees at Christmas in some places, as the old song says, but in our part of the world they mark the latter part of winter by perching in apple trees. When the countryman is startled by the loud whir of wings beating from his dooryard apple tree toward the woodlot, he knows it is early March. The partridges have been down to his house for an apple bud salad.

The ruffled grouse, our common partridge, has an uncanny sense of the season. All winter long it varies its diet of seeds and berries with the tiny dormant buds of birch and poplar back in the woodland. Then the strengthening sun beckons to maple sap and the dooryard apple tree begins to waken. The casual observer can't see much change, but the partridge knows better. It knows, almost to the day, when those buds quicken and start to push against the brown protective scales. Then a new substance and succulence, undoubtedly rich in vitamins, is at work in them. So here come the partridges, to perch in the apple trees and eat as eagerly as the countryman will eat when the first spring greens appear on his own table.

Some of those eaten buds would make apples, of course. But the countryman seldom begrudges them. Before the buds become blossoms in May the partridges will be stuffing themselves with bugs and beetles by the thousand. They pay for what they take, in their own coin. And right now, when a man sometimes wonders if the ice will ever break up, a partridge in the dooryard apple tree is worth its weight in hope and reassurance. The bird and the bud both know that spring is now inevitable.

March Winds

March 8

The winds of March are as inevitable as the vernal equinox, and they can be as variable as the moods of the season. They can be as cold as February, as warm as May. They can bring snow, and they can bring flocks of birds from the Southland. But fundamentally, March wind is the dying breath of winter, the first triumphant gasp of spring. It is clearing of the air. It may howl or whisper, soothe or punish, but it is the wind of change, the voice of seasons in transition.

March winds act as they do because they come down from the still frigid Arctic and up from the steadily warming tropics. Vast weather systems are marching across the land and when they meet, as they do here in the Northeast in March, strange things happen. March weather is the counterpart of the storms that so often accompany the autumn equinox. But in autumn it is the surge of on-coming winter beating back the rearguard of summer. Now it is the other way around. Winter is on the defensive and will be routed in the end.

So we take the buffeting and the comforting as they come, as we take mud and ice, cold rain and melting snow, knowing they are a part of March. We often wish they weren't. But before we can have spring, winter must be torn to tatters. And that is what happens by the time March has blown itself out. March is no picnic, or even a time for one, but it isn't blowing December our way. It is blowing us right into April, and May, and summer.

Promises *March 9*

The signs are subtle, but down at the root of things the processes that will add up to spring are busily at work. The leaf and the flower so compactly waiting in the buds on lilac bush and maple tree will not burst into being over-night. They had their beginning last summer, and in some mysterious way they are almost ready now for April. Most of the flowering bulbs needed the winter rest to rouse their summer vitality, and many of the wildflower seeds would not sprout without having felt winter's icy bite.

There are only a few visible signs. But on a warm day in the woods you can sense the subtle fragrance of the resin that coats the buds of poplar trees and cottonwoods. It is being softened by the strengthening sun, so the bud scales can loosen, at a proper time, and release the new leaves. You can see a more lively color on the bark of young birch and aspen twigs. It is too early for the blush to mark red osier dogwood stems, but the withes of willows have begun to quicken. Pussy willow catkins are not far behind that liven-ing turn.

There are even a few hidden blossoms. Some alders and

hazels and other bushes that have male catkins tightly sealed all winter now begin to open them, tentatively, on sunny afternoons. They gild the air about them with pollen, and the very earliest bees begin to gather at the feast. If you look in the sheltered corners of the vegetable garden you may even find a few insistent chickweed flowers.

The signs are subtle and often hidden, but they are there, promises of change not far ahead.

Shade-Tail

March 10

A good deal of the talk overheard in the woods these days is the talk of the red squirrels, which can scold like a catbird, chatter like a flicker, shriek like a jay. They have been out and around all winter, unafraid of weather; but now they are courting and mating and full of the season.

The young won't be born until late April, and they won't open their eyes until late May. It will be July before they are weaned and out on their own, but from there on they will be like pranksome small boys, all action and noise. And since there are usually four and sometimes six in a brood, they will be all over the woods until the owls and the hawks take their toll.

The squirrels get their common name from their scientific one. *Sciurus.* And *Sciurus* literally means shade-tail, which makes one think of the big gray squirrel with a tail like a plume. But the red squirrel's tail needs no apology. It is shorter and less fulsome than that of his big gray cousin, but it is twice as emphatic. He uses it to emphasize and punctuate his cries, and always he uses it as an exclamation point. When he screams in anger or warning, he screams from nose to tail-tip.

The red squirrel might be called the swallow of the

squirrel tribe. He darts, he scurries, he plunges headlong, and he is superbly graceful every instant. Two of them chasing each other in the treetops strain the eye to follow. Two of them fighting are a fury of fur and recrimination. One alone is as cute as a chipmunk.

A red squirrel can be a nuisance, particularly if he quarters himself in an attic, and a family of red squirrels can be a plague. But in the woods where they belong they make March as busy as June.

The Home-Coming

March 11

You can't predict the day, but you know that by mid-March the morning is not far away when the back pasture or the side lawn will be lively with robins. Not the few hungry, winter-worn robins that emerge from the thickets between February storms, but sleek migrants that arrive by the dozen, by the score. You know them by their numbers, by their chatter, and by the deep southern tan on their breasts. They look well-fed and self-assured, and they go about their breakfasting like excited travelers come home, more talkative than hungry.

There are no songs, at first. Now and then one will pause and sing a few notes but seldom a whole phrase, more an exclamation of delight and satisfaction than a salute to life. And the restlessness of travel is still upon them. They run about, fly a little way, come back again, as though going from room to room to make sure all is as they left it. They can't quite settle down.

They will be restless for a week or two, coming and going. Then one bright morning a few of them will salute the sunrise. That bold, full-throated song will echo again from the leafless treetops. After all, they are thrushes, and thrushes must sing. Hearing that song you will know that buds will open, violets will bloom, bees will hum again. The robins proclaim the certainty.

But first must be the home-coming, the morning those chattering, sun-tanned flocks return. The certainty now is that they are well on their way.

The Big Melt

March 12

The ice melts and you know the fundamental turn has come, no matter what happens now. We may have more snow and we certainly will have more frosty nights; but now the earth is unlocked and there will be no more long imprisonment until another winter. Upland brooks and rivers flow again, some of them in spate. Lowlands ooze. Frost in the ground slowly retreats, making quagmires of open fields, sodden sponges of pastureland. Snow that has lain in upland woodlots since December trickles away in a hundred rills.

It is a soggy time. Water is everywhere. But this is the very juice and sap of spring, this water. It is the fluid of life. Without water the land is barren, the seed lies dormant, the bud withers unopened. Life began in the primordial waters, as nearly as we can trace beginnings, and it still needs water for its annual renewal. Only in water can the vital salts be dissolved and fed to the fundamental protoplasm. Water is the basic broth of both blood and sap.

So the water drenches the land, suffuses it, as the cold, insistent rains of March beach the ice. Melt begets more melt. Channels open. Boglands overflow. The earth is an ancient, watery planet again whose land is slowly rising to warm itself in the strengthening sun and clothe itself in green. We have had the big melt. We are ready for spring.

Washing Winter Away

March 13

Despite March's windy reputation, winter isn't really blown away; it is washed away. It flows down all the hills, goes swirling down the valleys and spills out to sea. Like so many of this earth's elements, winter itself is soluble in water.

And water now begins to flow. You hear it on a warm afternoon, trickling down the southfacing slopes as the drifts begin to melt in earnest. The hollows in the meadow turn slushy, then overflow, and you hear the soft gurgle as myriad little spillways create temporary brooks. Rocky ledges drip, pattery as eaves in April rain. The brooks themselves waken and begin to chatter, leaching the white ice from their stony banks, spating toward the rivers. In the river, shards of ice loosen and crunch and mutter as the rising current nudges them downstream.

It is a wet world, winter's harsh grip beginning to relax. The open field lies oozy, watery proof that the soil's frost moves upward. An outcropping ledge on the hillside sheds its beard of icicles and becomes a seep spring that drips into a shallow pool that feeds a growing runlet. There is a twinkle of water at the country roadside. February's cold plowing now becomes the guttered drainage of a macadam furrow.

The wind helps, but mostly it is the flowing water. After all, Neptune is the season's planet, and Pisces, the fishes, are its zodiacal sign.

The Response

March 14

There is something in a mild March day that can touch a man to the very quick of his being. Just what it is cannot readily be stated, but it must be compounded of sunlight and air and warmth and an immeasurable mystery that is partly summed up by the word "promise." There are other things, too, but they are inside, responsive, part of a man's being.

You go outdoors, on such a day, and you feel that mysterious promise. You look up and see the slim terminal twigs of an elm fatbeaded with buds. You see the damp, dark ooze of sap on a maple branch where a woodpecker two weeks ago dug out an insect tidbit. You hear a chickadee singing; not twittering, but singing a dozen consecutive notes. You feel a breath of mild air on your cheek. Two months hence such a breeze will feel chilly, but today it is warm because it lacks the bite of February's wind.

You feel the sun on your face, another kind of warmth, hospitable, inviting. A month from now you will want to sit and bask in that sun, but now it makes you want to walk, go, look. Look for what? For something up the road, across the hill, something green and new. It isn't there, of course, Not yet. But you feel the promise, the inevitability of green newness to come. You can't say more than that, but there it is, in the air and the sun and the whole being of the day. And in you. Something in your blood, in the very depth of your being, responds.

Beyond the Promise

March 15

Now we begin to hear birdsong again, not the full-throated ecstasy of robins and orioles in a mid-May dawn, but considerably more than the January twitter of juncos and chickadees. Some of it now is the sweet chatter of tree sparrows, but more insistent and melodious are the voices of song sparrows. And in the background are the surprisingly soft, haunting notes of the blue jay's mellow Spring-song.

What we are hearing, beyond the promise of April, is the exuberance of life itself. The notion that birds sing only to impress mates and warn off rivals makes no sense at all in early March. Birds obviously sometimes sing merely because they feel like singing. The idea that song must have a meaning and beauty a purpose doesn't wear well out in the open, especially in spring.

Before long there will be violets and spring beauties and bluets and all the other early flowers that delight the human eye. It was long believed that their color attracted pollinating insects; but now we know that many of those insects are color-blind. Bright butterflies will be a-wing in the weeks to come, but every one of them could fly just as well on drab, brown wings. Sunrise and rainbow will glorify the skies, but to what practical purpose?

The fact is that nature abounds and overflows with what we know as beauty, whether it is song or color or rhythm or form. It doesn't have to be useful any more than the sheer delight we sense in the voice of the song sparrow now.

Sap

March 16

The watery tides rise, not only in the springs and brooks and along the surging rivers but in all the growing things that are rooted in the soil and soon will spread leaves to trap the energy of sunlight. Sap begins to move again. Red osier stems along the waterways flush as though suffused with blood. Limber willow withes look as though their mysterious veins were pulsing with amber honey. Sugar maples yield their sweet flow to the sugar makers. The vital juices begin to quicken root and stem and fattening bud.

Life, we say, came out of the ancient seas, and it can survive only as long as it maintains a minor sea within itself. Hence the sap, the pulsing, watery fluid that is the life-blood of grass blade and twining vine and towering oak. Sweet in the maple and the birch, acrid in the oak, resinous in the pine, it is the vitalizing current that flows from the farthest root to the topmost twig. Girdle a tree, cut the channels of sap flow, and that tree dies. Prune a grape vine when the sap is rising and it will "bleed" for days.

Sap, akin to sapient and savory because man has long recognized its vital purpose. Thin as water, yet rich with earthy minerals and salts, pregnant with the stuff of chlorophyll to be fed to the leaves, once the buds have opened. Sap, rising with incredible pressure, the pressure of spring tides themselves. Unseen, unheard, and yet the very flow and surge of all the green life that soon will clothe the earth.

The March Buds

March 17

Buds fatten on the elms, beading their twigs against the sky, and in the lowlands the red maples begin to shrug off the scales that have protected their crimson florets from the winter's cold. In the dooryard the lilacs are in such big bud they make you wonder how much longer they can contain their swollen packet of leaves and stem and blossoms, all purple tinged for May delivery and celebration.

Out along the pasture fence the cedars are in full bloom and strewing pollen from blossoms you have to look thrice to see. Beside the brook the alder catkins have been at the pollen stage for some time. A few early bees know it, but the alders don't have to wait for the bees. Alder and cedar and most other trees and bushes of older lineage are not dependent on the insects. The wind has been their pollinator since they outgrew spores. That is why their blossoms have no petals, only stamens and a pistil. The wind needs no signal flags or landing platforms.

Go to a grove of poplars now, on a sunny afternoon, and the fragrance of poplar gum will be there, faint but tanged of spring. The gum that seals the catkins in their fat buds is melting, loosening the scales. Pause beneath the willows and you will see bud scales falling, may even mistake them for motes in the sunlight, though no mote ever sheltered a willow's silver-furred male blossom.

The winds still belong to March, gusty and often edged with ice. But the trees trust their buds and early blossoms to those winds, as they trust their roots to the soil.

Coltsfoot *March 18*

At a quick glance it looks like a dandelion blossom, perhaps flattened a bit or skimped by the chill of early March. But it isn't a dandelion and it hasn't been shrunken by the weather. It is coltsfoot, one of the earliest of all our wildflowers, and it is in bloom now on sheltered banks that catch full sunlight.

Only those bright yellow blossoms are in sight. No leaves will appear until the flowers fade into fluffy heads of floss-borne seeds. Then the leaves will come, broadly heart-shaped or, if you prefer, the shape of a colt's hoof. The flower stalks are solid, not hollow like dandelion stems, and are covered with red scales and reddish-green bristles, almost fur-coated.

Like many of our wildflowers, coltsfoot is an alien. It was brought here by early colonists for use in herbal medicine. A decoction of the leaves and roots was believed to be good for coughs and those late winter colds that could turn into pneumonia. John Gerard, in his *Herbal*, recommended it another way: "The fume of the dried leaves taken through a funnell, burned upon coles, effectually helpeth those that are troubled with shortness of breath and fetch their winde thicke and often."

In England, it was also known as foal-foot and horse-hoof. Its botanical name, *Tussilago farfara,* is a combination of Latin *Tussis* for cough and *farfarus* for the hoof of a colt, with nothing at all about winter's end or brightness on a dark March day.

The Quickening Willows

March 19

It is no longer a trick of the light or a matter of contrast. The willows are quickening. Sap is rising in them and their withes have the lively glow that means it is mid-March and April coming.

You see it in the weeping willows that stand like great honey-colored fountains. Against a clear, blue sky it now is the warmest color anywhere around. You see it in the riverbank willows, those dark-stemmed old trees that wear a bristly crown of golden hair as their twigs are revitalized. You see it in a ruddier shade of the pondside shrubs called hoary willows, an especially live color that reminds you of the warm blood beneath your own skin. You see it in the pussy willows along the margins of the lowland bogs, not in the livening color of their dark twigs but in the silvery plush of catkins already thrusting aside the brown protective bud-scales.

There is a midday trickle from the deep drifts back in the woodlands. Brooks gurgle and flow again beneath their rotting ice. The icy locks are giving way, slowly and deliberately. But down underneath, even before the frost in the ground has shown any sign of relaxing, the roots have received the message. The vital fluid that suffuses life, both red and green, has quickened and renewed the mysterious pulse that will throb through leaf and blossom, fruit and seed, as the days lengthen into spring and summer. You see it now, in these late days of another winter passing, the first beat of that pulse in the willows against the sky of mid-March.

Still in Order *March 20*

The vernal equinox is a marker on the great wheel of time, a reassurance of order in a world where confusion and disorder too often seem to have the upper hand. It is a promise of predictable change, certain as sunrise, from the rigors of winter to the benevolence of spring. It is variety in a time of doubt and uncertainty.

No equinox ever burst a bud or sprouted a seed. Dawn will not be marked by a chorus of vernal birdsong, nor will dusk be loud with the call of newly wakened hylas. Those are consequences, not causes, of change. But once the sun has passed its equinoctial marker such consequences are assured. Violets will bloom again. Maples will come to leaf. Grass will clothe the hills.

Man is prone to boasts of omniscience and omnipotence, but all he can do about the rhythmic seasons is chart them and, if he would live in comfort, cooperate with their conditions. Neither the power of his armies nor the efficiency of his machines can hurry or delay a solstice or an equinox. The wheel turns, time flows, and the earth responds. Spring comes, and man responds, too, knowing deep in his being that the universe is still in order and that he is privileged to be a part of that universe.

Ready for Spring

March 21

Watch the willows and you need no almanac to know when the season turns. They respond to the tides of daylight as few other trees, gauging the sun's progress northward as certainly as a sundial. By the time of the vernal equinox, which occurs today, they are ready for spring. Their catkins, kitten-soft and fresh as the dawn, have begun to burst buds, and once they appear the green leaves are not far behind.

But even before the catkins, the willows have signaled the season. By early March a few warm days bring them to life. Their sap begins to rise and their lesser stems quicken with color. You can almost see the slow throb of sap-pulse just beneath their thin translucent bark. Weeping willows become great amber fountains. White willows and yellow willows and even the big black willows of the riverbank achieve a honey-blond look that catches the winter-weary eye.

Once the sap begins to rise the buds respond. Frosty days may hold them back, but the strengthening sun is urgent. Ice melts. Bogs begin to ooze and one warm day the bud-scales of the first silvery catkins appear, first of all on the pussy willows. You see them, fat and furry, opalescent in the shifting light, and you know what time it is. Spring is at hand; not yet here, perhaps, but not far away. Once the willows bloom, the tides of spring have begun to rise.

The Primitive Peepers

March 22

Some years the spring peepers start calling in mid-March, some years not until the first week in April, depending on weather and place. But whenever it happens, the peeper chorus is the voice of eternal spring. There is nothing else quite like it. Robins sing and maple sap rises, but the peepers in full voice are the ancient and triumphant cry of life enduring. The message is as unmistakable as sunrise.

It is one of the pleasant puzzles of nature why this small tree frog, *Hyla crucifer,* this mite of amphibian life which still hibernates as its progenitors did 100 million years ago, should so unmistakably personify the surge of spring. Perhaps it is because spring itself is ancient beyond reckoning, or perhaps it is because all the life we know had such minute beginnings and because, so far as we know, it too originated in the warm waters of ancient time. But why this voice, this shrill proclamation from such a tiny remnant of the distant past? A dozen peepers make less than a human handful, but their voices can fill a whole evening.

You can hear the peeper chorus half a mile away, but you can scarcely see a peeper three feet in front of you unless you see him inflating his bubble-throat. *Hyla crucifers* are only about an inch long and blend so well with the background, be it white bark or brown, that the tiny frogs are all but invisible. But you don't have to see them. You hear them, and you try to find some simile for their voices—chime of silver bells, sweet whistled notes, chirps. But none of them quite suffice.

Astronomically, yesterday was the first day of spring. The peepers know nothing about vernal equinoxes, but they do know what time it is. They can be frosted into silence or briefly driven back into the mud, but not for long. They are the very epitome of insistent life, making minor compromises with things as they are but never surrendering. Their trill is an announcement that winter is on its way out. It is only one note in the vast vernal chorus now beginning. It is primitive and ancient, just as spring is very old and very simple.

March Doth Make Liars

March 23

Shakespeare never used it in his plays, but he must have several times been tempted to say, at least as an aside, "March doth make liars of us all." For March in London was as perfidious as it was in Stratford. And Stratford March is not too different from March in Manhattan, or in Queens or Bergen County or in nearby areas of Connecticut. March means maybe, but don't bet on it.

By next week, we say, crocuses should be in bloom, now that snowdrops are out all over the place. Then we turn around and crocuses are in full and even fading blossom everywhere. So we amend the forecast. Daffodils will be up and budding soon, we say. And there are daffodils, in fat bud, ready to open tomorrow. We start to say something hopeful about pussy willows, but before the words are said the fat, silvery catkins are open to the sky.

The red-wing blackbirds, of course, should be arriving soon, in another week or two. And the loud "Ok-a-lee!" in the nearest streamside tree proclaims us wrong again. The red-wings are back, dozens of them, treefuls. And if we so much as mention migrant robins or spring peepers being due in early April, they will also "make liars of us all" and be here and in business whether March lions out or lambs out.

There are no rules for March. March is spring, sort of, usually. But whisper it when you say it. Otherwise there's no telling what will happen.

Waiting

March 24

Late March is a time of waiting, and by now the fabric of human patience has worn a little thin. That is why this is a difficult time, a time when we wish the weather systems would settle down and be through with whimsicality. We even tell ourselves we would welcome cold rain and slithery mud if mild air and sunshine were sure to follow. Rain that has the smell of spring, not sleety rain or rain that could turn to snow any minute.

We want the world to get on with the basic business of spring, without having to keep looking over its shoulder ready to face another interruption from the bedraggled forces of winter. We want to hear robins and orioles singing, not jays and crows jeering. We want to see violets, not snowdrops.

So we wait, impatient, and the seasons take their own time. This is a kind of interregnum, with neither winter nor spring in full control; and such transitions usually are difficult, uncertainty their signet. We know that May will come, with lilacs and apple blossoms, but we don't know what the day after tomorrow will be like. That's the gist of it. We want to hear spring peepers and see the green haze spreading through the treetops, and we are weary of waiting. And if we seem to be captiously impatient, that is a hopeful sign. Such peevishness is an early but dependable symptom of spring fever.

Red-Wings *March 25*

As usual, the red-wing blackbirds have timed their return by the season rather than the weather. At least a few of them regularly arrive here in the Northeast by the end of February. The big flocks will be along any time now, surely before April. These early red-wings are males. The females travel separately and about two weeks later than the males. They also are differently garbed; they look like big sparrows, striped and mottled in brown and whitish gray.

Those early red-wings put up with the weather, calling

loudly and almost defiantly even in a snowstorm. They forage for early insects and fill the gaps in their diet with weed seeds. High on their list of preferences is ragweed, which makes them friends of hay fever sufferers.

By mid-April they will begin to scatter and mate. Then every damp swale and wooded brookside will echo with their calls and flash with those red-epauletted black wings. There will be nesting among the reeds, and pale blue eggs spotted and splashed with black and purple. And chicks that are feathered much like their mothers, like strange sparrows.

But now those early travelers are calling from the leafless trees and flocking from icy pond to icy bog. Singing, whether we call it song or not: "Kuk-karee, karee." Waiting for April and mates.

Dawn

March 26

Dawn comes early, almost an hour earlier than it did when March began. It is a crisp dawn, icy around the edges, and every roadside pool of yesterday's melt is filmed with a brittle, glassy pane. The pasture brook that chattered all afternoon and into the frosty evening is reduced to a whisper, the flow from the hillside's persistent drifts awaiting another midday's warmth. Turf that was soggy underfoot yesterday now is crusty to the tread. Dawn and dusk, day and night, abide by the season's deliberate rhythm of change.

A robin scolds in the young daylight, then sings a tentative song. Another robin answers. A blue jay flies to a leafless maple, gray against the sky, and twitters a Spring-song that hasn't one jeering note. Two red-wing blackbirds, fluffed fat against the chill, talk hoarsely to each other in a willow whose cautious catkins are still half sheathed. A cardinal whistles, waits, then whistles imperiously as though summoning the sun. Winter's silence has ended, but spring's jubilation is still to come.

The sun rises just a trace north of east. A man's breath twinkles, a faint cloud in the frosty air, and a trail of thin mist rises along the whispering brook. Four black ducks skim the naked treetops, wings swiftly beating, necks outstretched, silent as shadows. A man faces the sun, feels its glow, and knows that March, like the snow on the wooded hillside, is fraying away, flowing down the brooks, making way for April.

Three Gardens *March 27*

Every garden is grown three times over. The first time is when the seed catalogues arrive and fill January days with dreams and perfection, all achieved without one callus or one drop of sweat. Then comes late March. The second garden appears, in the village hardware store.

You walk down the street, no matter what the weather, and there are the spades, the hoes, the rakes, sprouted in neat and shining array. They appear overnight—brand new, sharp, and shiny. You stop and heft a spade, test its balance, appraise its spotless blade. You run your thumb over the working edge of a hoe. You test a trowel's shape in your soft palm, and you admire both the paint and the motor on the tiller.

Then you go home. You put away the car and go out and look at the garden patch. It's still muddy with March and frosty down beneath the mud. But you can see scallions, crisp lettuce, succulent peas, sweet-kerneled corn, luscious tomatoes. Then you remember that pile of work gloves at the store, off to one side like an afterthought, with the dusters and sprayers and the insecticides and weed killers hidden behind them. And you look at the garden again and see cutworms, flea beetles, bean beetles, tomato worms. You see purslane, chickweed, quack grass, German weed.

You see that third garden, and you know who is growing it, and where, and how—come May, come June and July. And you wish they had kept those work gloves out of sight just a few more weeks.

The Spring Furrow

March 28

Some years the spring plowing doesn't get under way until late April, or even May; but this year has been different. The robins came north several weeks ago—those that hadn't spent the winter here—in great flocks. They salute the sunrise, they scatter over the pasture lands, and they follow the chuffing tractors and the plows, certain that spring plowing is done specially for them. Go out into the open country and you can see the black furrows open to the sky. You can also smell the fragrance of fresh-turned loam, which is like no other smell in the world—earthy, rooty, elemental. It is the smell of spring, of growth. Few farmers will admit it openly, but one reason for spring plowing is to open up the fields and free that fragrance. It is better than any store-bought tonic for a man who lives with the land.

Plowing is hard work, but not nearly as hard with modern machinery as it was with a team of horses and a walking plow. But even in the old days there was a sense of accomplishment in following the furrow, in seeing the smooth turn of fresh soil from the polished moldboard. The ability to turn a smooth, straight furrow was and still is, a gauge of the farmer's skill. The expression "He plows a straight furrow" was long in the language and is still heard occasionally. But only farmers and gardeners know the vernal smell of a fresh furrow. It does something to them.

Anyway, April is not quite here and the plows are busy on many a hillside and many a flat forty. That doesn't mean there won't be frost, hard frost, still to come. It does mean that deep frost is out of the ground and that the smell of spring is there waiting, the smell of the spring furrow newly turned.

March Dusk

March 29

The March full moon, which occurs tonight, has emphasized the lengthening daylight most of the past week; but it is the day-end glow, not the moonlight, that now tells the true time of year. Dusk has begun to linger and the long nights are slowly retreating. We have a softening light at sunset, no longer the cold winter light that winked out abruptly and left the world to brittle stars. Winter dusk has a sharp and icy edge, but the dusk of March begins to soften the rim of darkness.

No season ends overnight. Change comes slowly. Winter must be melted and blown and washed away, just as spring must be leafed and blossomed and gradually grown into summer. But the hard blue shadows and the ice-green sky of January and February have now relaxed into an aftergrow that gentles the hilltops and eases the valleys with tones of pink and rose. Even the blustery winds of March tend to fall away at sunset. The winter night's dark fang is somewhat dulled.

The earth's long sleep is not yet ended, but the slow awakening has begun. The sun's warming fingers have begun to reach down to the very roots of life with their subtle summons. There is yet no urgency, no demand for haste. That comes later. But there is an insistence, which we feel at dusk, and see and sense. And one of these lengthening dusks the peepers will hear the summons and waken and give the evening its vernal voice. This we know even now, as we watch the deliberate change in the slowly gentling dusk, the long light of March's strengthening days.

Hepaticas

March 30

Some call them hepaticas, some call them liverworts, but all know them as the first flowers in the woodland. The blossoms, no more than an inch across, vary from lavender-tinged white to pale purple and they burst bud on hairy stems that rise from winter-worn leaves before the first new leaves appear. They grow on rocky hillsides where rich pockets of leaf mold catch the ooze and trickle of late March and early April. On a sunny day they are like flecks of cloudless sky on the littered floor of the leafless woodland.

We cherish them not because of their special beauty but because they bloom so early. They are, in a sense, the trimuph of spring, the first triumph of the vital root and the urgent bud. Snowbanks may still be melting on the slope above them. Nights may still be fanged with frost. But the hepaticas dare to send up a stem and fatten a bud, and the petals open with what we can only call confidence that the earliest bees will come to their pollen. They bloom when April is still deliberating the reality of spring.

In another few weeks they will be lost in the spreading shadow of new leaves and even the bees will ignore them. Anemones will be sparkling the woodland, trout lilies will be in bloom, and violets. Bloodroot will spread its waxen white petal. Columbine will demand the eye with its flash of gold and crimson. The pollen-rich rush will have begun. But first come the hepaticas, early April's convenant with spring.

The Wings of Spring *March 31*

The morning is mild, the sun warm, the air calm. You look up at the elms, hopefully, but there isn't yet a trace of green in the lacy pattern of their twigs against the sky. Then you see a butterfly, wheeling, circling, soaring like a hawk on glistening dark wings. It seems incredible, but there it is. It drifts down, settles at the roadside, and you see the satiny purple-brown wings edged with pale yellow, dotted with blue. Then it is off again, a mourning cloak, flitting across the tawny meadow, soaring through the leafless woods.

The mourning cloak is the earliest butterfly, appearing with the crocuses. In England it is the rare Camberwell Beauty, but here it haunts streamside willows, poplar groves, and elm-lined streets. Here its distinction comes from its early wakening from hibernation. It is out to greet the first spring flowers and by the time the violets bloom it will have laid its eggs on the willows and elms where its larvae will feed on young leaves.

But first this big brown butterfly must explore the leafless world, glorying in the sunlight. It seems to have neither haste nor hunger, only that need to ride the air, absorb the sun, be fully alive again. Its long winter is over. And seeing it, following its flight, you sense the awakening. On those fragile wings the whole urgency of spring begins to move across the meadow and through the woodland, not yet soaring but warmed by the sun, eager to take flight into April and May and June.

April

PINK MOON

Hepatica first, pink and white
and lavender, then early azalea,
rhodora, spring beauties.

First Smell of Spring *April 1*

The smell of change comes even before the trees open bud, before the eye can verify what is happening. The precise date is unpredictable, but one warm afternoon the change is in the air, winter turning to spring, and it is more than sunlight, more than warmth. It is a kind of presence smelled and felt most keenly in the open country but also in a suburban street and even in a city park.

It is a compound of many subtle scents. It is the earthy smell of soil stirred by little, seemingly inconsequential movements—the thrust of grass stems from wakening roots, the spring house-cleaning in a colony of ants, the thrust of earthworms and their fine-grained casts. It is the fertile smell of leaf mold and rotting twigs in a woodland, a rich, damp, vegetative odor. It is the clean, silty smell of flowing water at a brookside, the misty smell of wet stones, the damp, almost green smell of moss.

The only place it has even a tinge of rankness is in the bogs, where decay is swift and water stagnant. Even there it is the smell of life, not death, life teeming in the soggy rootbed, preparing to emerge green and urgent. And on those wet margins the bog smells are already livening with the resiny odors of poplar and willow buds straining at their seams. Soon the faint polleny smell of willow catkins will be there.

It is the odor of quickening life, the first fragrance of spring, thinner than mist, warm as sunlight. Change is in the air.

Easter

April 2

It is written in the bud. Life begins at the root, hidden and mysterious in so many ways, and its urgency mounts with the sap; but the bud is its manifestation, the truth revealed.

A bud begins in summer, in the midst of growth and fruiting. It is a mere fleck, an insignificant beginning unseen among the leaves. It grows, takes inner form even as the tree completes its cycle. Autumn comes, leaves fall, and there upon the branch the bud persists. Cold comes and the tree withdraws its sustenance to trunk and root, stands naked to the winter storm. But on the branch, the farthest twig, the bud persists, its purpose still intact, the unseen promise.

Winter wears away. Sunlight shifts and strenghens. Spring creeps in day by lengthening day. Roots quicken, sap rises, and the bud responds. The leaf, the blossom, the tender shoot, take form, incredibly compressed within those thin brown scales. Life, the miracle of life itself, begins to strain at the dark walls of confinement reaching for the light, the glory of renascence. And at last the bud bursts, the miracle is fulfilled. Where there was darkness there is light; where there was only hope there is achievement; where there was restraint there is freedom.

We call it spring, and we celebrate it as Easter and as Passover. It is renewal, rebirth, release from the winter of the soul. It is faith and belief triumphant. And it is written in so simple a place as a bursting bud.

The Buds

April 3

The bud is a marvelous thing, almost as marvelous as a seed. Within the bud's slight scope a tree somehow packs an incredible store of leaf and blossom, the perfect device to trap sunlight and manufacture food, the whole complex means of creating a fertile seed and fostering another tree. There it is, this astonishing summary of the process of life, compacted inside a few scales that now are little more than dark beads along the branches. There is every tree's hostage to time, its bid for eternity.

By April you begin to see the buds against the sky. They are still so small that even the pattern they make is elusive to the casual eye, but they subtly change the dark lace of branches that marked the winter landscape. The poplars and cottonwoods now look nobby and faintly green with pointed oval buds. The beeches are full of slim lacy points along their slender stems. The elms look as though their twigs are dotted with brown raindrops, and the willows quicken, withe and stem-hugging bud, day after sunny day. Swamp maples blush with buds as crimson as the coming blossoms.

There on the branch in the April afternoon is next July's cooling shade, still tightly furled. There in the woodland is next October's color, ready to fill spring days with pastel tones. There are the complexities of catkin and raceme, of pollen and petal, of stem and spreading leaf, all packed within the waiting bud that is smaller than a baby's fingertip.

Wild Goose *April 4*

The geese are on the wing, moving north with April. You hear them in the night, like small dogs yelping in the far distance. You see them in midmorning, a penciled *V* against the sky, high overhead and pointing northward. You pass a country pond and see them in late afternoon, resting and feeding, gray bodies and long black necks with white chin straps sharply outlined against the luminous water. You hear them gabbling in the dusk.

Robins return and sing paeans to domesticity. Peepers emerge from muddy hibernation and shrill the boglands with celebration of life's resurgence. But the wild goose comes north with the voice of freedom and adventure. He is more than a big, far-ranging bird; he is the epitome of wanderlust, limitless horizons, and distant travel. He is the yearning and the dream, the search and the wonder, the unfettered foot and the wind's-will wing.

True, the goose is no songster, by any stretch of the imagination. He is neither brilliant in color nor really spectacular in flight. He is neither romantic thief nor colorful villain, neither wastrel nor philanderer. We call a fruitless errand a wild-goose chase and we use his name as a synonym for stupidity. Yet the cry of the wild goose and the sight of a migrant flock can send our hearts and imaginations winging. It may have been by chance that the goose feathered the winging arrow and quilled the poet's soaring pen; but we doubt it every spring when the wild geese come gabbling north again.

The Pressures

April 5

It is only natural that we impatiently gauge the progress of the season by the height of the mercury in the thermometer. But there are other measurements. The height of the sun, for one. The height of the sap, for another. And both are more reliable than the temperature, which can change overnight.

The sun is high, past the equinox, and as its angle changes the sap responds. You can see it in any woodland, along any pond or watercourse. The red osiers are vivid now, as lively a color as though blood, not colorless sap, were just beneath their bark. They have come alive after winter dormancy. And the willows glow. Weeping willows are huge honey-colored fountains, their withes full of amber vitality, and even the dour black willows have a greenish-amber look to their slim twigs and young branches.

Even more pronounced is the look of the poplars. There is a temptation to say the pressure of their rising sap has begun to force their buds, for you can see them against the chill April sky, fat and almost bursting their seams. Swamp maples show it too, their buds already slightly flushed. And the birches are like paint brushes whose tips have been dipped in rouge.

The pressures of sun and sap are strengthening day by day and the green surge of spring waits only for a week of seasonable warmth. When it comes, as it will, the miracle will seem to happen overnight. But it is all there now, ready to burst from uncounted millions of taut and waiting buds.

When the Robins Arrive *April 6*

It is a moot question in some quarters whether the robins bring spring or spring brings robins, but it won't be long now until the first robin reports come in. Some of them will mean nothing more than that a few of the hardy, or foolhardy, robins that always winter here have come out of the thickets and onto the lawns where spring-hungry people can see them. But when a whole flock of robins appears, particularly if a flock of red-wing blackbirds is seen too, then change is definitely in the wind.

Actually, spring and robins travel north together. We still don't know all the reasons for migration, but we do know that food and weather largely dictate the birds' spring schedule. They have enough sense not to outrun the food supply, and they know what freezing rain and biting cold can do to them. Migrant robins, red-wings, and geese follow rather closely the thirty-five-degree isotherm. When the average twenty-four-hour temperature hits thirty-five degrees and holds there, robins can be expected.

Even the birds aren't infallible, of course. On occasion the robins have guessed wrong, been caught in a blinding snowstorm, and had to back-track. They can easily fly 250 miles south in a day, find more hospitable weather and wait out the storm. One of these days the robins will arrive, along with that thirty-five-degree isotherm. There won't be either flags or ticker tape to greet them, but celebration certainly will be in order.

The Silence Ends *April 7*

April is still in its first week, but the silence is ended until November's frost again bites deep. The lesser sounds of new life, life resurrected, have begun, and in their sum they will soon outspeak the wind.

They began with the trickling of water, the melt on the hillside, the splash of the brook, the renewed current in the river. But those were inanimate sounds. The animate ones began with the bees. The early bees came out to course the brown span of March and found the bright cups of the crocuses. There was excited buzzing, the bee-hum of discovery, and there was swift, pollen-laden flight. In their eagerness the bees climbed over each other, buzzing their welcome, summery sound there in the crocus blooms. Then there was another buzzing in barnyard and pasture, fly-buzz as larvae hatched in one afternoon of warm sun.

Then the birds. They hadn't been altogether silent, but they had little conversation and few songs. Then the first robins came, and the blackbirds, and even the chickadees, the tree sparrows, the jays, and the crows remembered last summer's songs. There still is no chorus, but there is a tuning up, a beginning, a celebration of life and new beginnings. It will increase, day by day, as will the insect chorus. Dawn will be loud and noon will be sibilant.

Life, as always, is being reborn and revived, and with it is sound, much of it of a joyful nature, all of it an expression of living. For that is a fact of spring and of every year. The silence ends. Life is renewed, and life sings its own songs.

The Newness

April 8

Few things in this world are newer, and look newer, than the tiny leaves as they start unfolding from the buds. They have been there all winter, to be sure, but not until April do they appear. They have to be brought to the precise degree of readiness by the sun and the sap, by all the urgencies of April before they burst the bud. Then, at that moment, the birches on the hillside and the willows in the hollows are hazed with green, with leaves too new to add up to more than a kind of pastel shimmer.

Actually, the look of green in the treetops is tentative to begin with. The leaves are so new they have a kind of baby look, pink and rosy, that persists until the sap has suffused them with chlorophyll and set them to work. But first, like butterflies just out of the cocoon, they must unfold and stretch and open their veins and be warmed and strengthened by the sun. Before there can be the cool texture of summer shade there is the gleamy shimmer of spring lace.

And all the while there is the added newness of the little flowers, the pale green catkins of the poplars, the crimson florets of swamp maples, the tiny yellow tassels of the oaks, the pale tufts on the elms. And the subtle changes that shift the emphasis from day to day, that add new stanzas to the poems written on the hillside, in the meadow, and along the riverbank, poems old as time but issued in a new, revised edition every April.

The Green *April 9*

The green is doubly welcome after a long winter. Our eyes need the comfort of grass and leaves, with another wavelength than that which glances off a snowbank. So every year we watch the coming of the green with as much eagerness and satisfaction as we get from the gradual warming of the air. The "feel" of spring is always welcome, but the "look" of spring lifts the heart.

The grass comes first, as though it were specially driven by that urgency which makes spring of winter and drives on to summer. You see a brookside bank turn green while snow still melts in the meadow. You see the meadow lose its winter grizzle and warm with a greenness underneath while the drifts in the woodland shrink and rill away. You are surprised to see how quickly the city park can turn green again once it's April; at how insistently the green reaches for sunlight through cracked pavement and vacant-lot rubbish.

Then there is the haze of first leaf, of maples opening flower bud, of willows and poplars in catkin. You see the green against the sky, thin as gauze, a hint of green outlining twig and branchlet.

First green in the trees is tentative, not so much uncertain as deliberate. It comes quickly in the bushes, the underbrush, perhaps because brush is closer to the forthright grass. But it comes, the green of grass and leaf, and the eye feasts, the heart celebrates.

The Songs *April 10*

The winter birds have begun to sing again, and before long the migrants, which include the real virtuosos, will be here and making the mornings loud with music. Spring will arrive full of melody and even the casual listener will be aware of it.

There was a period when it was considered sentimental and unrealistic to call birdsongs music. Birds uttered calls that might seem musical but actually lacked that essential of song, which is emotion. There were mating calls, territorial calls, warning calls, alarm calls, rallying calls. But no songs, as such. Fortunately, that period of disenchantment seems to be passing. It never did seem valid to those who really studied birdsongs—or birdcalls.

Who can listen to a robin, which may sing as many as fifty different songs, and deny the bird emotion? All thrushes have a variety of songs, and few songbirds have as few as half a dozen different melodies. They sing in courtship, sometimes both sexes. The males sing during nesting and after nesting. Many birds obviously sing merely for the pleasure of singing. Who can deny that the brown thrasher enjoys the thrill of his songs, or that the house wren is full of ecstasy? The mockingbird knows he was born to sing. And the catbird even has a sense of humor.

To deny the birds a sense of song is to deny man his own sense of music. Who taught man to sing, anyway? Not the fishes or the frogs, certainly, and not the apes. In any case, dawns will soon be full of song, and the birds will be the ones who are singing.

Spring-Hungry *April 11*

It isn't quite time to celebrate spring, but one needn't be dour about the season either. Song sparrows are singing, no longer cautiously tentative. Migrant robins are strutting the lawns and pastures and managing a bit of jubilation of their own. New violet leaves are in sight along the margins of chattering brooks. Crocuses begin to fade and daffodils are in bud. Lawns are green. So are dandelions.

Aries rules the zodiac and the governing sign is the lamb. Mars, who was god of fields and growing things before he was a god of war, is a morning star. Venus rides high as an evening star. The celestial omens have a hopeful cast. Daylight now surpasses thirteen hours, a longer span than we have had since late last August. Shadbush will soon be in bloom.

Garden seeds are on display in the hardware store, and hoes and rakes and spades; but work gloves are still out of sight under the counter. Sap flies haven't yet hatched. It's too late to prune the grapes, too early to mow the lawn, and the only digging that should be done in the garden is for angleworms.

Streams are still in spate, back in the hills, and elms there are still in bud. Frosty nights have persisted, but the icy fang is dulled and worn short. Winter has lost its grip. March is gone and May is coming. That's sufficient for now, spring-hungry though we are.

The Bee and the Crocus *April 12*

The first bees out, these April afternoons that have been so much like March, have been the big golden bumblebees, and they have looked twice as big as the bumblebees we shall be seeing a month from now. They have been specially busy at the crocuses, which are generous with their pollen, carrying off load after load of the golden grains.

They are big bees. They are the pregnant females that wintered over, often in a field mouse nest. Now each of those big bees has lined such an underground nest with dead grass and is gathering pollen to moisten with honey and spread on the grass. That done, she will make a small waxen pot, fill it with honey of her own making for food on rainy days, then lay a clutch of eggs on the bed of grass and pollen.

If all goes well, her work now is nearly done. She will incubate the eggs, which will hatch in ten days or so. The larvae will eat the pollen and a special food the mother-queen will make from pollen and honey. They will spin paper-thin cocoons from which they will emerge ten days later as small but full-fledged workers. They will go to work. The queen will lay more eggs, then live in state the rest of the summer.

In one of those remarkable twists of fortune, the timing is perfect. This first brood of new bumblebees hatches just in time for the first apple blossoms. The trees will be loud with bee-hum, and the next hatch of bumblebees will be fed on apple pollen. Apple blossoms will be fertilized. Apples will grow and ripen. Cider and apple jelly will be ours because a bumblebee found a crocus in bloom in April.

The Songless Songster *April 13*

Even people who like all kinds of birds seem to merely tolerate grackles after they have seen the first dozen or so in early spring. Just looking at a grackle, this seems rather strange, for a grackle is a large, graceful black bird with a beautiful iridescent sheen on its feathers. It has a graceful tail, it is well proportioned, it flies well. It struts when it walks, and it walks instead of hopping, as a robin does. It comes north early in the spring.

Having said that, you have about exhausted all possibility of praise for a grackle. And just about then the grackle, which is technically classified as a songbird, opens its mouth and makes a noise. As an individual bird, a grackle can croak, squawk, make clattery noises, but it can't sing a note. A flock of grackles is an offense to the ear. Some have likened their noise to that of a fleet of squeaky wheelbarrows. Others think of rusty gate hinges, thousands of rusty gate hinges.

Give the grackle credit, though. He doesn't sail under false colors. The very name "grackle" goes back in origin to European words meaning "croak" and "garrulous." He has been grackling a long time, and everybody has known about it. Even his Latin name has a kind of grackle sound: *Quiscalus quiscula quiscula,* harsh and repetitious. He undoubtedly got his common name from the farmers who knew him best, who watched him in the springtime, when insects were plentiful and grain was scarce, and in summer, when grain was plentiful and insects had no lure.

Anyway, the grackles are here, clattering away. And pretty soon there will be some songbirds that can really sing.

Crimson Maples

April 14

Most of April's blossoms get little notice because they are so small and hang so high. They are the flowers of the common trees of the woodland, and because they are so often green or greenish yellow they are lost in the first vernal haze in the treetops. But the red maples refuse to be anonymous. In the damp lowlands they come to early bloom like bursts of dark flame. Every twig is outlined with crimson, every tree a huge, glowing bouquet, and streamside thickets are red as a stormy sunset.

All maple flowers are tiny, their petals not much bigger than a gnat's wing, but those of the red maple are garnet-red and bloom in clusters. The twigs themselves are red, and when the leaves first appear they are so near the color of the blossoms that one must look closely to tell which is which. Even as the leaves grow and turn green, the red persists in vein and stem.

Spring is not a red season. Its early flowers of pasture and meadow run to whites and yellows, with purple violets for accents. We think of reds as summer colors. But the wetland maples abide by no such rules. They are a fiery tribe, accenting April as they will dominate October. They command the eye, not by spectacular blossom but by the vivid spectacle of uncountable florets, by an overwhelming display. Who can ignore a crimson cloud in the April woodland?

April Rain

April 15

A good deal of nonsense has been written about April showers, most of it by indoor poets and those who write rhymes for sentimental songs. April rain is warmer than sleety March rain, but it isn't really green rain and it isn't full of violets. Daffodils bloom in the sun, not in the rain, and wood anemones and bloodroot don't wait for a rainy day to open their buds.

Rain in April tends to be showery because the weather is changeable. The earth is still damp from the melt of March and a few warm days fill the air with evaporated moisture. A cold wind comes along, condenses the moisture, and it rains, often locally. The wind passes, the shower ends, and the sun shines again.

Grass thrives. Trees begin to open bud. Early flowers bloom. And the showers make all these changes seem a special benevolence. One can walk with April rain, satisfied with the rightness of the world. The rain doesn't slash or sting. It burbles in the gutters and chatters in the brooks with a friendly sound. One can live content with April rain, knowing it is a vital part of spring, and spring is a stimulating season that grows better day by day. But it is still rain, not floral confetti, April rain that nourishes the root and sprouts the seed and advises the ready blossom to wait for a sunny day.

The Migrants Return *April 16*

With the migrant birds returning, an old, old question presents itself again. Why do they come back?

Migration has baffled man for a long time. We now know far more about it than ever before, but most of our knowledge is about the how rather than the why, the way birds migrate rather than their reasons. We speculate about food supply, and nesting habits, and living space, and even about the ways dispersion benefits the species and the effect of climate on fertility and growth. We know a great deal about flyways and migration routes, and we can chart schedules by the weather maps. But all such knowledge still leaves the basic question unanswered.

Why should hummingbirds return all the way from Central America? Certainly not because they are crowded there, nor because they are hungry for the nectar from bee balm and jewelweed. Why do the swallows return? Northern mosquitoes surely are no more tasty or nourishing than those that breed in Southern swamps. Why should Orioles come back? Merely to hang their nests in Northern elms?

The migrants filter in and begin to sing. And as the chorus grows, all through April, the puzzle becomes more baffling. The birds sound almost exuberant. They sing like exiles returning to a beloved homeland. And none of the explanations really explain. They flew away last fall, and now they are coming back, as they have done for eons. We still don't know why, but we welcome them.

Morning Fog

April 17

Fog, which technically is nothing but a cloud in contact with the earth, can be a nuisance and a hazard to travelers. But if one can stay where he is for a few hours, a morning fog—especially in early spring—creates a degree of magic that makes one forget hazards as well as technicalities.

It comes in the night and it lingers through the dawn, soft, chill, faintly luminous. You step out into the dooryard just before sunrise and you are on a familiar island in a strange, new world. The trees that were just down the road yesterday, the hill that was across the way, even the horizon itself, have vanished. On every side and even overhead hangs that soft white veil, unsubstantial as smoke but impenetrable to the eye. Even a tall tree only fifty yards away has no top; it is a damp-dark pole stark against the fog. Somewhere above that pole a robin sings, and far off in the white distance another robin answers; but there isn't a bird in sight.

Then the sun comes up. It isn't the familiar sun; it is a shimmer, a warmth of silver light that seems to come from everywhere. A wisp of breeze swirls the fog and the tall tree has a top again. For an instant there is an incredibly blue patch of sky. Then it is gone. The shimmer becomes a dazzle and the little island-dooryard begins to widen. The hill is there again. Slowly the sun warms the air and the magic vanishes. The fog rises and the familiar world reappears. But for a little while the fog made a world all its own, a fantastic, mysterious world, evanescent as the fog itself.

Spring Plowing *April 18*

The reason for spring plowing, the countryman will tell you, and look you in the eye when he says it, is to turn the soil and prepare a seedbed. He will go on, perhaps, and say that you plow as soon as the frost is out of the ground and it's dry enough to "get in" so you will be ready to plant oats early, or corn, or grass. He believes that.

Then he gets on his tractor and starts plowing, and if you watch him closely you will know that he told only half the truth. Spring plowing is to prepare the soil, yes, but it is also to prepare the man. He, too, has to get winter out of his bones. He has to get the sun into him again, and the wind. He has to know April if he is to know May and July and September.

So he plows his land. He turns the clean, straight furrows and something of the soil is plowed into him, the smell of it, the look, the feel. It isn't quite the same as it was when he walked the furrow behind a team of horses and felt the earth beneath his feet. But he still feels it, as he feels the morning, as he hears the blackbirds, as he smells the fresh-turned earth.

He plows, and the mild sun beats down, the robins strut, the brook just across the way prattles and shimmers. He is working with the soil again, the soil and the season. But—and this is the other half of the truth—the soil and the season are also working with him. The earth belongs to him again, but he also belongs to the earth.

Breathing Space *April 19*

Grass begins to green our corner of the earth again, the new young blades of the least pretentious of this world's everyday plants and the most important to mankind.

Grass is simplicity itself. Not the simplicity of unicellular life in stagnant water, but specialized simplicity unmatched in the fields. All the grasses, even the corn and wheat and barley and oats, have achieved a kind of perfection by eliminating nonessentials. Their stems are seldom branched. Their flowers have dispensed with petals, scent, and honey, since they need neither bee nor butterfly to pollinate them. The wind does that job. Even the roots of grass are uncomplicated.

The trees and the grass not only cool and help clarify the air we breathe but constantly restore oxygen to that air. Chlorophyll's power of regeneration is far greater than anything man has ever devised. The city's parks and the suburban open spaces are not only pleasant green oases; they are literally breathing space. And the meadows, the pastures, the cornfields, and the wide grasslands of the country provide oxygen for every breath we take.

So there it is, the simple, priceless grass, perfect for its purpose and found almost everywhere that plants can grow. It grows tall, as bamboo. It grows generous, as corn and other grains. It grows lush and cool, as bluegrass. It is a weed, sometimes, but it is a green hillside, a lawn in the village, a hayfield, a thousand-acre field of wheat. And now it is greening the earth again.

Green Again

April 20

The grass is green again, and that makes all the difference. Now all the flowers of spring can come to bloom, and all the trees can burst their buds and come into leaf. This won't happen overnight, but it is possible now. Until there was green grass in the meadows there couldn't be fresh green leaves on all the trees. That is one of the rules nature has made for itself.

Of all the green-growing forms of life, grass is one of the most humble and at the same time one of the most insistent and assured. There are about 5,000 species of grass. Some grow in the hottest tropical areas, some well up inside the Arctic Circle. Grass finds a roothold where nothing else but lichens can survive. It asks for only a minimum of rootage; it makes the most of a tiny crack in a granite ledge. Some species can survive a long drought. Some can endure long, deep cold. It is typical of grass that it reclaims land after fire, after flood, after storm, neglect, and even after man's abuse.

Few things are more beautiful than a New England meadow green with the freshness of April. Few things are more amazing than the vast plains of the West when April greens grass that stretches mile after mile, grass that was there before the first man came. All over this continent the grasses grow, wild or tame, bluestem and wheat, grama and oats, bamboo and corn, the marsh grasses, the sorghums. The ubiquitous grasses, green again with spring, with life itself.

The Ferns

April 21

Fiddleheads uncurl and the bright new fronds of the ferns begin to spread themselves at the foot of the banks where violets and Dutchman's-breeches are full of bloom. If there is something venerable and touched with mystery in the uncurling of a fern, there is reason, for the ferns are literally as old as most of the hills. Their beginnings go back millions of years, and fern fossils found in the ancient rocks show little difference from those now opening in the warm May sun. Counterparts of lady ferns and maidenhair, woodferns and cinnamon ferns grew here in the days when our mountains were still mud flats washed by the young, restless oceans.

For generations men were baffled by the ferns, which bore no flowers and had no seeds, yet throve and multiplied. Ferns were magic plants, and those who dealt in magic believed that if they could only find the seed of a fern they would have the ultimate in mysterious power. They never found a fern "seed," of course, for ferns multiply by a complex of spores and intermediate growth in the form of prothallium. It is a process that requires seven years from spore to mature fern, and it goes on so secretly that few are aware of it.

Yet ferns are everywhere. In some size or form they grow in almost every region of the world. And every spring they come nosing from the leaf mold along our roadsides and in our woodlands, common as violets, yet still overlaid with their ancient air of mystery. Like the very old and very wise of our own race, they seem to have outgrown haste and impatience and the need for sharing secrets.

The Dipper *April 22*

Regardless of the weather, the stars point the season. Go out now and look up and to the north in midevening. The moonless sky is filled with stars that still glitter with winter's brilliance, but the Big Dipper hangs high overhead, higher than at any other time of the year, well above Polaris and with its bowl inverted, no longer a winter Dipper.

Astronomers have called this constellation Ursa Major, the Big Bear, for thousands of years, but in Homer's time it was also known as Maxama, the Wagon. A little later the Romans called it Septentriones, the Seven Plowing Oxen. Both these names went to England with the Roman occupation, and for a long time the constellation was called the Wagon of Charlemagne, or Charles's Wain. Then it became The Plow.

Ancient Arabs saw the constellation as a coffin followed by a funeral procession. But Arab names left little imprint on popular astronomy in the West. Among American Indian legends was one that made the constellation a bear followed by three hunters, one so sure of success that he carried a cooking pot on his shoulder. Sharp eyes can see the pot, a small star close by the middle star in the Dipper's handle.

But we still prefer it as The Dipper, an old-fashioned dipper filled with new flowers and new leaves and exuberant birdsong, and now spilling this springtime generosity over the whole Northern Hemisphere.

The Beautiful Dandelion *April 23*

There aren't many flowers prettier than a dandelion, if you can look at a dandelion as a blossom, not a weed. Its color is magnificent, one of the most rich-toned yellows anywhere around. Its shape is the economical sphere, beautiful from every angle. It blooms early, and it keeps blooming until the first daisies appear.

Dandelions grow almost anywhere, and that is their undoing. You have to work to be rid of them rather than to grow them. They will take root and come to bloom in a crack in the city pavement. They will thrive on an ash heap. They love the soil of a suburban flower bed. They happily put down root beside the onions and cabbage in a rural garden. They find a pampered lawn, anywhere, an ideal background for their golden extravagances.

In the country, out where grass is for cows and corn is for the silo, the dandelion has become Number One on the Least-Wanted list. It will take over a farmer's whole meadow or pasture if given one season's start. It will even overwhelm the stout-rooted alfalfa. And every bright blossom that ripens sends a double-handful of fluff-borne seeds to take over more acres.

The dandelion's old virtues are almost forgotten, nowadays. Its self-blanched inner leaves made an excellent spring green, fresh or cooked. Its roots were used for potherbs. Wine was made from those bright blossoms. The dried roots were ground and substituted for coffee. But that was before the dandelion became a dooryard weed.

Partner of the Elements

April 24

This is going to be a garden year, as every seed seller can tell you. More people than ever before are going to grow vegetables, hoping to beat inflation or at least to hold it somewhat at bay in the kitchen. That plot of ground to be planted and harvested has other yields besides cabbages and carrots, however. One of the most important is contact with the soil and growing things.

As has been said many times, man does not live by bread alone, not by lettuce and carrots and beets and peas and broccoli and tomatoes. Man happens to be a sentient as well as a hungry animal. And the real gardener, whether he has ever grown an onion or a carrot, has a deep instinctive need to make contact with the soil. Planting seeds is a good excuse today, but what he needs, down deep in his very marrow, is to get his hands into the earth, to establish communion with the rootbed of life.

Such participation is at once mildly humbling and exhilarating. You become partner of sun and wind and rain. You are somewhat master of a plot of earth. You encourage it to do your bidding and, if you are patient and fortunate, eventually you reap. You don't have to think of it that way. Few gardeners do. They merely work with the soil, and they feel a satisfaction in doing it. But what they are doing, really, is communing with the earth, cooperating with the elements. They are making contact with life down at its very roots.

The Belief *April 25*

By late April the countryman is thinking of June and haying, of summer and the growing season, even of September and golden October. The hillside birches still show only a gauzy green haze of leaftips, the swamp maples blush with half-opened blossoms, and mornings are still frosty; but he can see corn knee-high in his newly plowed fields, oats ripening on the lower forty, strawberries ripening in the kitchen garden. Today's weather, good or bad, can't greatly change this view of the world the countryman knows. Whether he is optimist or not, he has confidence in the soil and the seasons.

The closer one lives to the land, the less one distrusts time. It is only when one is alienated from the earth and its eternal sequences that doubt takes root. Few of the pat answers and instant solutions have validity when you are dealing with the soil. You see the slow but certain growth of trees, the persistence of grass, and you are aware of the tenacity of life. The earth's urgency is toward growth and renewal, and one season follows another despite man's diversions and interruptions. You can't hurry spring, and you can't interdict summer.

The countryman lives with these truths, no matter how they are phrased. He lives by them. They shape his life. So he looks about him now with confidence and with hope. Another growing season is at hand, deliberate as always, and he lays his plans, not for tomorrow but for June and July and next September.

Obvious as Sunlight

April 26

If spring were in the teaching business, which it isn't, we would now be hearing a basic lecture on philosophy. All the elements are there, spring after spring, and all we have to do is supply the words and attend their meaning.

It is essentially a philosophy of life, of sentient being. It deals with beginnings and with continuity, and if we look for meanings that is where we can turn. By the simple fact of being alive we particpate, for we are a part of the vast community of life which now responds. Spring is no accident. It is both a consequence and a reason, a quickening of forces as complex as a bud and as simple as flowing water.

If we are aware of the wonder of spring, we must also be conscious of the inevitability it demonstrates year after year. If we are aware of beauty, which is a human interpretation, we must also see the basic order of life grown out of winter's discard and lifeless litter. For spring is change and growth and pattern imposing themselves on what we too often think of as random disorder. And, perhaps most important of all, spring is achievement.

Here it is, spring, eternally new, eternally hopeful. And here are we, participating in a season which, year after year, gives the lie to all philosophies of chaos and futility.

The Digger

April 27

Some people are like ants. Give them a warm day and a piece of ground and they start digging. There the similarity ends. Ants keep on digging. Most people don't. They establish contact with the soil, absorb so much vernal vigor that they can't stay in one place, and desert the fork or spade to see how the rhubarb is coming and whether the asparagus is yet in sight.

Anyone knows that you can't just go out and work in a garden at this time of year the way a farmer does in his field. You have to woo a garden, from the very first day, testing its moods and giving your own moods a chance. There's no hurrying the relationship. When you've planted your first peas, you've done enough to start. After that you have to deliberate on where to put the next peas, and the spinach, and the lettuce. You need a warm afternoon for deliberating. And on cold days it's too cold to dig.

Rome wasn't built in a day, nor was Agricola's garden, or whoever it was that Horace wrote about. If you dig a garden all at once, you have no energy left to plant it. Do it bit by bit and you will have strength to pull the weeds later on.

There's no denying these truths once you stand with your feet on the soil and the spade in your hands. Such philosophy springs directly from the earth. The time will come when there's no other way out—you either dig and rake and plant or you give up. But on a warm afternoon in late April, well, let the ants do the hurrying. They don't know any better. Besides, they don't know rhubarb from pokeweed. A man does, if he's a gardener. And it's his duty to keep tabs on the rhubarb. The spade will be right where he left it when he gets back—if he ever does.

Catching Up

April 28

By the last week of April, whether spring's beginnings were early or late, the season commences to catch up with itself. May will complete the transition. Already the green and fragrant world of busy chlorophyll and bright-petaled blossoms is taking shape. The old saw about April showers and May flowers is more than a rhyme, yet somewhat less than complete truth. The showers help, but the blossoms were patterned in the seed and the shoot, not in the clouds. Spring is a consequence of the year itself, of the earth and the sun and their rhythms that defy man and his calendars.

Now come the surge and the insistence of growth. For a few weeks we will scarcely be able to keep up with change, which is everywhere. The miracle is not so much in budding and leafing and the opening of petals, but in the very magnitude of burgeoning and blossoming. Everything possessed of blood or sap, the life-juices of existence, is affected. And every day is another moment in the incredible, inevitable genesis of another year. Creation is taking place every hour. We are witness at vast emergences.

The pattern is set by now. The fertile urgencies are committed and another summer is in the making. We have known the early beginnings, felt the movings and the shakings, heard the summons, and felt the quickening. And, being both alive and sentient, we are both witness and participant, partaking of blood and sap and hemoglobin and chlorophyll. The season catches up with us as well as with itself.

The Miracle of the Bud

April 29

Spring is a time of miraculous happenings. The earth itself teems with new roots groping downward into the rich soil to feed and sustain new plants. Young shoots on bush and tree reach for light and sun, to foster growth and fruition. But all around us, in plain sight, is perhaps the greatest miracle of all, the buds themselves. Out of the buds, so countless and so commonplace, come this world's green leaves, its wealth of bloom, its surging growth of twig and branch and stem.

Who would think, seeing the brown twig-tipbuds of the lilac in December, that those winter-dormant buds were packed with such a freight of leaf and stem and blossom as now reveals itself? Who, glancing at a pear tree back in January, would believe that silvery leaf and milk-white blossom were stowed in those small brown knobs on the dormant branches? Who, passing a brook or a pond lined with swamp maples in ice-locked winter, would believe that the minute buds on those naked branches would turn the valley to a display of crimson blossom, then clothe it with summer-green shade?

Look at the dogwood, which defied the winter with twig-end buds like praying mantis heads and now is full of white-butterfly bloom and green leaves. See how the willows, which rattled their cold twigs, seemingly bare as bones, in the February blasts, came to kitten-soft catkin and then to whispery mist of slender leaves.

Everywhere you look, in the countryside, in the suburban dooryard, in the city's parks, the miraculous is at hand. It is happening with streetside trees and in rooftop planters for penthouse people, as well as in rural dooryards.

Probably the most astonishing example of what can come from one bud, in our area at least, is the hickory tree. When a hickory bud begins to unpack, it opens the big, pink-sheathed buds with a wealth of leaf, blossom and potential twig that would put a magician to shame if he tried to stow so much into so little space.

There they are, all around us, the wonder packets of green life, the miraculous buds, opening a whole new, green and flowery world.

April Summary

April 30

Before April is gone and the first flush of spring becomes the colorful wealth of May, we might pause for a moment of summing up.

April has its whims, but it always is marked by warm names for old truths newly seen: daffodil, anemone, violet, lamb, trillium, robin, oriole; and bud, blossom, flower, floret, bloom. April is color: pussy willow gray, pollen gold, violet purple, marsh marigold yellow, grass green. It is all the greens in the spectrum, of course, but before it is green it is an astonishment of pastels, leaves fresh from the bud, still soft as baby's skin, and glowing pink and blue and lavender and yellow and golden tan. It is the lowlands rouged with swamp maple bloom, the meadows frosted with bluets, the woodland margin dainty with anemones and waxen white with bloodroot.

April is a young world, new as sunrise, in which miracles can happen, and do happen every day before sundown. Nothing is newer than an April morning, nothing more full of wonders than a bud or a seed. April is an old world made new again, a tired, disillusioned world of frost and ice and snow made innocent once more. It is a tempered wind and a warming rain, and almost fourteen hours of daylight.

And in April, man is here only to see and listen and participate, not to manage or administer. April doesn't need him; it tolerates him.

May

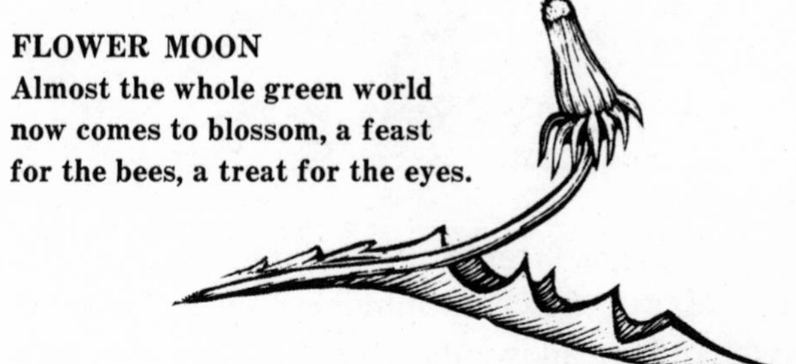

FLOWER MOON
Almost the whole green world
now comes to blossom, a feast
for the bees, a treat for the eyes.

May

May 1

April is promises and tentative beginnings, but May is achievement. May is dawn shimmering with dew and sunrise on lawn and meadow, dancing with young leaves in every woodland, jubilant with birdsong in every treetop. May is dogtooth violets beside brimming brooks, the first buttercups beyond the pasture fence, purple violets everywhere. May is apple blossoms and lilacs, and if any other month can surpass that combination we have yet to learn its name.

In the innocent years before May Day was declared ideologically significant it was festooned with May baskets and tokens of young love. The season itself still invites such sentiment and the world around us seems quite unaware of sophisticated change. May's skies are essentially guileless. May's sunny days still invite spring fever and the heart is still tempted by May's air of young ecstasy. May is full of gaiety and laughter.

May's full moon is sometimes called the Flower Moon, with ample reason. It might also be called the Gardener's Moon, since seeds are planted then and weeds are not yet of much consequence. Rabbits are still young, and woodchucks have not yet worked up an appetite. Lawns grow like mad in May, and the song of the mower is heard throughout the land.

May is altogether wonderful, once it comes.

The New Leaves *May 2*

The early flowers are bright in meadow and woodland, but the overwhelming beauty as May begins is in the new leaves on trees and bushes. We take leaves for granted; but when they are seen individually and fresh from the bud they are in no sense commonplace.

Is there a more beautiful sight than a pin oak fringed with the pink of freshly opening leaves? Or a sugar maple when its blossoms have begun to fade, its keys are forming, and its leaves are new and miniature? A willow leaf fully grown is a long, slender parcel of chlorophyll, but fresh from its bud it is a delicate spear of fragile fabric subtly colored. The big leaf of any tree is so familiar that the wonder of it is lost. See it young and that wonder is new again.

Most buds seem to infuse new leaves with some subtle coloring. When leaf and blossom come from the same terminal bud, as they often do, one can almost believe there was uncertainty until the last moment which would be which. Watch a lilac bud open and see the flower packet, each pinhead floret pale green, surrounded by infant leaves suffused by color that belongs to the flower itself. Watch the slow unfolding of a big hickory bud and you are half persuaded that some exotic flower of vast complexity is emerging from that pearl-pink bud sheath.

Even the texture of new leaves is new and strange—birch and poplar leaves soft as gauze, beech leaves delicate as a fluff of silk, pine needles soft as kitten fur. And all new leaves have a special touch, as though waxed and polished specially for the light of a May day.

The Truth of May

May 3

There are a dozen ways to define May. You can start with saying it is the summary of March and April. Or you can call it the foundation for June. Or you can summarize all the relevant answers by saying May surrounds you with all the elements of truth.

What is truth? That's an old, old question and it has had so many expedient answers that one should be doubly careful where it is asked. But in May you can go outdoors, out where there are trees and grass and open sky and wildflowers and wild birds, and know without asking that you are in the midst of truth. You don't even have to define it, because it is there, obvious.

There is the truth of grass, growing, restoring itself year after year. There is the truth of a tree, which couldn't falsify a leaf or a nut or a winged seed if it tried, and which sets down the record of each year, exactly as it is, in its growth rings. There is the truth of water flowing downhill, a brook sweet to begin with and with the urgency to remain clean if given half a chance. There is the truth of sunrise and moonset, of the sky, the dew, the thunderstorm. There is the gleaming truth of the buttercup, the echoing truth of a robin singing.

May is a special kind of verity, a testament to the reality of a live and sentient world. Define it as you will, it is all around us now, a reality that needs no explanation.

Orioles and Apple Blossoms

May 4

Spring can settle down and warm up any time now. The Baltimore orioles are back. They were just about on schedule, even though the season wasn't. They came, perched in apple trees still not in bloom, and began to sing. Basically, they were the usual oriole songs, but in them were phrases that seemed to ask what was going on, what had happened to May. But they did sing, and they made this a brighter, more colorful world; and somehow they warmed the raw, chill days just by being here.

You can count on the orioles. They arrive on schedule, seldom as much as a week early or late. They return, go to their favorite tall trees, tell the world they are here, and set about finding the right nest-tree. Then they go to work.

Orioles, of course, belong with apple blossoms and lilacs. Maybe that's why they come back when they do. But when, as this year, apple blossoms are late they make the best of it. Anyway, here they are, full of song and color. And just as soon as they can sing up a few warm sunny days we will have apple blossoms. They are doing their best to whistle May back into line with the season. More power to them!

The Baltimore Bird *May 5*

Fortunate is the householder, suburban or rural, with a tall tree and a Baltimore oriole. The two go together invariably, for the remarkable nest must be hung high, and the colorful male oriole seeks a high perch from which to sing by the hour while his mate weaves the nest, lays the eggs, and broods the hatch.

Despite the name, this oriole owes no debt to the Maryland metropolis. True, Baltimore has its orioles, but not as many as Hartford, say, or Albany, or New York City, or almost any area of the Northeast. The name comes from the orange and black which makes the male oriole spectacular. They were the family colors of the Calverts, of which one member, the second Baron Baltimore, was the patron of Maryland. When Linnaeus named this particular species he chose to honor Lord Baltimore, and thus the name still stands.

The oriole is a remarkable bird on several counts. Its nest is unique, a woven pouch suspended from a high, thin branch, often in an elm, sometimes in a sycamore or a maple. The female weaves this nest, and her skill at weaving has amazed man for generations. No other bird contrives to weave anything like such a fabric, or fashion such a safe and useful nest.

The male bird is no weaver. He may help gather material, but his special mission in life seems to be to make music. Hour after hour he sings, with one of the richest voices and from an infinitely varied repertoire. Between songs he displays his colorful plumage. There really isn't another bird like him. May and June would be drab indeed without the orioles.

Inevitable May *May 6*

Perhaps the most satisfying aspect of the turn from late April to early May is the sense of reassurance. It is essentially an inner feeling of order and rightness in this green and growing world in which we live. No matter what man may be doing with his own affairs, making unpredictable mischief or dreaming dreams of a better tomorrow, the season is going about fundamental and enduring matters as it has been doing for a long, long time. The season is predictable.

To walk along a country road and see a cloud of bloodroot in snowy bloom is to know this. To stop by the edge of a woodland and find dainty-flowered anemones nodding brightly in the breeze is to believe again. Visit a damp brookside and see the purple of violets in the fresh green grass, or pause in the damp margin of a bogland and marvel at the spread of marsh marigold in blossom, and you sense the surging inevitability of spring. Look across a meadow frosted at midday with bluets just opening bud and you know that there are achievements and consequences, most of them fortuitous in early May, that are beyond the will or hand of man.

May in the country is all these things, for it is natural force as simple as the opening of a bud and as complex as the vast spread of chlorophyll in the countless leaves, even in the infinite blades of grass. It is change and growth, blossoming and the buzzing bees, birdsong everywhere; sunlight and replenishing rain. It is life after dormancy, irrepressible life. And to know it, to participate in it even as a spectator, is to have some small part in inevitability.

Shadbush Shimmer *May 7*

Shadbush comes to bloom in the open woodland and along the river margins, filmy white against the haze of green. Member of the rose family and cousin of the apple, it is the earliest of the tribe to put forth flowers, and one of the daintiest.

Its early bloom gave it past importance still reflected in its common names. Here in the North it was called shadbush or shadblow because its blossoming signaled the run of spawning shad.

In the Southern mountains it was called serviceberry because when it came to blossom one could expect the circuit rider to make his rounds, to sanctify marriages, baptize babies, and renew the faith with religious services. Indians knew it as lancewood. And because its fruit ripened in June and provided the makings for the season's first jam, some called it Juneberry.

The names persist, though the naming is now largely

forgotten. Except in May, shadbush is now just another wild bush, a part of the expendable underbrush. But when it comes to blossom it still has its brief importance. It adds a special shimmer to the May morning.

Bluet Time *May 8*

The bluet is a blossom of no particular consequence individually, a tiny four-petaled flower with a golden eye, no noticeable fragrance, and a stem not much taller than the meadow grass among which it grows. But bluets grow in vast numbers in old pastures and on stony hillsides, and they bloom profusely. On a May morning they look like frost on the meadow, and by noontime they are almost foamy with their numbers.

Some call them Quaker-ladies, and some know them as Innocence, but botanists list them as "Houstonia," members of the Madder family and cousins of the partridgeberry and the inconspicuous bedstraw and goose grass.

Bluets are field companions of the deep purple meadow violets, and when they approach the woodland margin they are rivals of the anemones. By June they will be lost among the buttercups and early daisies. But in early May they are beautiful and insistent by their very numbers. They are the bright embroidery on the first green frock of the rural countryside.

The Shy Thrasher *May 9*

Some migrants arrive in flocks, but not the brown thrashers. When the robins come back you see them all over the meadow, and when the red-wings return they blacken the treetops along the bogland. But the thrashers seem to steal in, almost secretly. One morning at the end of April or early in May you waken to hear that wonderful, unmistakable voice repeating the bold, richly musical phrases as though proud of every one of them. Then you know that the thrashers have come back.

You usually hear them before you see them, but before the day is out one may reveal himself at the far side of the lawn, in the garden or the low shrubbery. There's no question who he is, that slim, graceful cinnamon-brown bird with a streaked breast, a long beak, and a long, eloquent tail. Built like an overgrown catbird, he is longer than a robin, big as a mockingbird. But he is twice as shy as a catbird, and twice as musical.

Actually, the thrasher is cousin of both catbird and mockingbird, all of them mimic thrushes. The thrasher can even imitate the call of the whippoorwill. But mimicry is a sideline with him; he has a long repertoire of original melody, wonderfully varied. By late May, when the nest-building is done and while his mate broods, he will spend hours in a tall treetop proclaiming the goodness of life, and he will go on singing even into July. But right now he is working for a living and singing mostly for fun. It is good to hear him announce that he is back. He makes the season seem in order.

Apple Blossoms

May 10

Don't let anyone tell you that the purpose of an apple tree is to grow apples. Not in May, it isn't. Purposes change somewhat with the season, and by the end of summer it may be important to have ripening apples on the bough. But that will be a bonus. In May the trees themselves proclaim that their reason for being is to achieve a special glory of blossom.

Of all the trees in this world, few others seem to bloom so whole-heartedly. In April an apple tree is just a tree, but in May it is a huge bouquet, exquisite in detail, magnificent as a whole. The individual blossoms are like beautiful little single roses, but the tree is so generous that the blossoms come in clusters, crowding upon each other, even hiding the young leaves that come with them. As buds they are deep, rich pink. Then the petals open and the whole tree looks snowy white, though there is still a faint, elusive pinkness to it, even less than a tint.

Bees know when apple blossoms open and swarm to fill the trees with sound. Their beating wings seem to concentrate the fragrance, waft it, so that while you can scarcely smell it with your nose in a blossom you are aware of that faintly spiced sweetness yards away. It is like an aura, the essences of sunlight, blue sky, and blossoms all combined, something you feel and know as well as smell.

But an apple tree in May needs no explanation, no excuse. It simply is there, in the orchard, in the backyard, or grown wild in the woods, prodigal with blossom and altogether beautiful.

May

May 11

May is a consequence of many things, many forces, and it never comes overnight, no matter what the calendar says. Its blossoms were established months ago, some in buds formed last summer. Its sprouting seeds matured their germs of life last fall. The roots that send up new growth in every meadow and woodland are fulfilling a destiny that reaches back to the beginning of living time.

May is a flowery month, a green time of rich fulfillment, of growth with its own purpose. It decks the earth. It warms the air. It makes this a sweet and habitable land. But it never happens at the turn of a knob or the flick of a switch, and it isn't a living room spectacle. There are commercials of course, but most of them are for the bees; and its theme songs are heard from the treetops. You don't have to lobby for it or wait for a Congressional appropriation. And it isn't selective about where it is on display; it comes to city and suburb, small town and open country, and anyone can watch it, even participate in it, from where he pleases. It isn't sponsored and it doesn't belong to anybody. May just is.

Perhaps that is one reason we all respond. Simple as sunrise, it is still a fundamental force that eludes our analysts and researchers, for it is a basic fact of life and the earth itself. It is the burgeoning, the resurgence, the promise fulfilled of life insistent. It is—well, it is May and altogether wonderful.

Change *May 12*

There is the temptation to say, as May spreads the leaves and opens the blossoms, that spring has come again just as it has come for untold eons. But the fact is that no two springs are exactly alike. Man contrives machines that turn out countless duplicates; but nature is not a machine. Change is the one constant in this living world, the essential element of life.

We go to the meadow to pick violets, but there are only a few where they were profuse a year ago; this year they are at their best a hundred yards away. We look for wild columbine on the rocky ledge, but the ledge itself has been split and diminished by winter's frost. We walk beside the familiar brook and see that the spate has filled one cove with silt, widened another. We cut across an abandoned hillside pasture, all grass five years ago, now dotted with seedling pines, a new woodland in the making.

Bloodroot still blooms beside the old stone wall, and

anemones. But the wall itself is tumbling and briars begin to overgrow the stones. Field mouse and chipmunk that sheltered there have had to find new homes. The ever-shifting balance has been changed again. The winds plant thistles and milkweed, the birds plant briars and wild grapes, the squirrels plant oaks.

Change, constant, unending change within the framework of the familiar, the enduring. Another May, another spring, eternal but unlike any other spring that ever was.

Scarlet Tanager *May 13*

He comes like a fiery flash, incredibly brilliant, even brighter than a cardinal, and one stares in awe as he perches in the top of an apple tree. Swaying against the blue sky of May, green leaves and flushed white blossoms around him, he sings. His voice may be hoarse and he may be lazily deliberate, but for a moment he is the most beautiful songster in the world, no matter what he sings or how.

Some call him the firebird, some call him the black-winged redbird, and both names are apt. No other bird alive can match his color, and jet-black wings and tail emphasize it. He could loaf all summer, as he seems to be doing there in the top of the apple tree, and still be a welcome neighbor. But he doesn't loaf, and that is why the casual observer so seldom sees him. He spends most of his time eating gypsy moths, tent caterpillars, and other sylvan pests. He is worth his weight ten times over in chemical insecticides.

But now and then he pauses between meals, perches in a high treetop, and acts as though he had all the time in the world. He is as deliberate, for a few minutes, as the season itself. He is a proud dandy, so casual he pauses between notes when he sings. And he really hasn't much of a repertoire or a really distinguished voice. But when he perches in a full-bloom apple tree on a May morning he could jeer like a jay and still have our admiration. Just the sight of him is song enough to last all day.

A Day Begins

May 14

Sunrise comes early now, before five-thirty as we read the clock; but the day begins still earlier, with first light, last winking star, and birdsong. Especially with song, for the dawn chorus of the birds makes the day's beginning a special occasion in city park, on suburban streets, or in the rural woodland.

There is neither scurry nor haste at that hour; haste awaits man's awakening. Stars slowly fade. The sky begins to brighten in the east. As the glow spreads, first birds awaken and call, tentatively, sleepily. Other birds awaken and answer. The calls become phrases of song as the light increases, deliberate as sunrise itself. The strengthening glow touches the treetops and there, on their high perches, the birds begin to sing as though they could already see the new day's dimensions.

The chorus rises and strengthens, filling the air. It continues until that crucial moment when the sun is about to appear. Then there is silence—incredible, awesome silence in the face of a great event, a miracle. The silence hangs in the air, almost palpable, until the sun's first rays appear. Then, like a great hallelujah, the chorus begins again, redoubled in volume. It is celebration, rejoicing, exultation in the new day.

Halfway to June

May 15

Halfway to June is a special time of the year, particularly here in the Northeast. It is neither late spring nor early summer, though it may partake of both from one day to the next. First green has begun to consolidate its patterns, but June's placid lushness is still to come. This is a comfortable time of new shade and tolerable temperatures and with an invitation from all outdoors.

Farmers back in the northern hills have planted their corn and are readying their machines for the approaching hay harvest. Cows are in the pastures, and so are first buttercups. Birds are nesting, and still making the dawns loud with song. Lawn mowers clatter in the suburbs and gardeners are on their knees to their early planting. City parks are green oases not yet hazed with hot summer dust.

It doesn't last long, this special season, which is one reason we so enjoy it. It can't stand still, for the urgency that began in March and April is driving it inexorably toward June and July. It is like the apple blossoms that came so swiftly and now have shed their petal-snow on the surging grass, like the lilacs that now perfume the air and will be only a remembered fragrance by the time first roses bloom. It is like the silver mist that shimmers over pond and stream at cool sunrise and is gone within an hour. But while it is here, halfway to June is a wonderful time to be alive.

A Boy and a Brook

May 16

Travel the country roads on a weekend, when school is not in session, particularly the hill roads beside the brooks, and you will see him. The boy beside the brook, the boy with a bait rod or a fly rod and a special light in his eye. Note that it isn't a willow pole he has, nor a twine string with a bent pin. Chances are you can look all season and never see that fictional young fisherman. If he ever did exist, which is doubtful, he is gone now. This boy beside the brook isn't being picturesque; he's fishing. He probably has a nylon line, and he knows his leaders, his wet flies and dry ones, and the way to use a worm. He also knows the water, the coves, the eddies, the ripples, and he knows fish.

Country boys have been fishing for a long, long time. It's a part of their growing up. Listen to a middle-aged man in waders and within five minutes he will say, "When I was a boy," or "Thirty years ago," and tell you the exciting things that happened right over at that bend or at the mouth of that brook. He has special memories, and now and then he will even share them. Not only of fish and fishing, but of sunlight on water, and shadblow in bloom, and misty dawns, and days that were full of April, or May, or June.

If you ever wondered why fishing is probably the most popular sport in this country, watch that boy beside the brook and you will learn. If you are really perceptive you will. For he already knows that fishing is only one part fish. Unless you too were a fisherman when you were young, you may never know the other components, but you can sense them a little, just watching. That boy probably won't tell you. He's a little bashful about such things. But he will remember, all his years. And so will you, just seeing him, seeing that look in his eyes.

May and Violets

May 17

They are not necessarily synonymous, but it is hard to think of May without violets. And May Day, back when it was sentimental rather than socially significant, was always marked by May baskets brimming with violets. Springtime, May, young love, and violets—they were all there, together, in those fragile paper baskets.

Spring brings earlier flowers, a few, but none better known or more widely distributed. More than eighty species of violets grow in the United States, in damp meadows, rich woodland, upland pastures, at rural roadsides, and on dry, sandy plains. In color they range from white through yellow to all shades of blue and purple; and their close cousins, the johnny-jump-ups or wild pansies, mingle these colors in the same blossom.

White violets have a rich, sweet fragrance. The blues and purples have only the woodsy, outdoors smell of spring. But all are rich with nectar, as the bees well know. Bumblebees are specially fond of the common blue violets that spread heart-shaped leaves and lift long-stemmed flowers almost everywhere. So are Saturday-free children. So are country grownups.

The old herbalists used violets for inflammations of the chest and lungs. Violets, they said, "specially comforteth the heart." They still do, as any Maytime wanderer will testify. Blue sky, warm sun, and roadside violets are as comforting a discovery as any heart could ask of the burgeoning countryside.

Jack, the Preacher *May 18*

Some call it Indian turnip, but most of us know it as Jack-in-the-pulpit. It comes to bloom now, with wild ginger and trilliums, in the damp edges of the woodland, as much a part of May as are the nesting robins. Botanically it is a cousin of the fetid skunk cabbage and the beautiful calla lily, and its blossoms are like nothing else in the woods. The green-and-purple striped sheath, reminding one of a quaint old lady with a corner of her shawl thrown up over her head, shelters a host of tiny flowers on a green thumb the botanists call the spadix. That spadix is Jack, the mythical preacher for whom the plant is named, and the sheath is his pulpit.

Gnats and small flies invade the sheath and pollinate the blossoms. In another month or so the leaves will wither and the sheath will shrivel to a twist of dry husk and Jack will have said his say. The grass will grow tall and summer will pass. But next September, when the grass withers there will be a tight cluster of lacquer-red berries where each Jack-in-the-pulpit stands today. Those berries, fruit of this May flowering, will be as fiery to the tongue as the root is now, the root that is the "turnip" that Indians are said to have roasted and eaten.

But for a few weeks in May, Jack stands in his pulpit, a congregation of wildlings around him and a choir of robins and orioles overhead. He conducts his annual revival meeting. And who can say that his voice isn't heard all through the woodland and across the meadow? Before he is through there is a veritable hallelujah of blossoming, a glory on all the hillsides of May.

The Sunrise Hour

May 19

The day starts early now, and with its own exultance. Soon after first light the birds begin to celebrate the dawn, and those who would know birdsong at its best are awake and listening. But the dawn chorus of the birds is only a part of this jubilation, as those know who are up and outdoors while the day is young and damp with dew.

Trees shimmer in the freshest of new leaves. Roadside grass is lush, hurrying toward June's ripeness. Buttercups gleam gold and wild geraniums turn pink faces toward the sunrise. The roadside meadow is frosty with great patches of bluets. At the first rocky ledge dew drips from the blue-green foliage of wild columbines and their crimson and gold bloom nods, heavy with trapped moisture. Ferns stand tall and brilliant green, fronds still showing a trace of the fiddlehead's curl. Chokecherries are hung with fat white tassels that in another hour will be loud with hungry bees.

Wisps of silver mist hug the hollows, memories of cool midnight. The busyness of the day hasn't yet intruded. You can even hear the breeze whispering in the treetops. Maybe that is what the robins are celebrating, this leisured hour, the robins, the orioles, the tanagers, the grosbeaks, even the doves. This is the sunrise hour, the day's beginnings, when all who know another dimension of time can, for a little while, participate in genesis itself.

The Green Canopy

May 20

Of all of May's swift changes, perhaps the most miraculous is the way the great green canopy is spread along every tree-lined street and in all the woodlands. Buds burst, inconspicuous blossoms hasten through their brief cycle, and the leaves appear. At first mere flecks of green (every shade of green there is), the tiny leaves droop on soft stems, still too young to hold up their heads. The stems strengthen, the leaves expand, and before we know it the trees are rustling in the breeze, dancing in the sunlight, pattering in the rain. The trees are in leaf again.

To us who live beneath them, leaves mean shade, ease to tired eyes, the pleasure of soft contours where a few weeks ago there were only stark skeletons of branches. But to the trees the leaves mean life and sustenance. Each leaf is a spread of chlorophyll, that green magic which traps sunlight, air, and moisture and converts them into starches and sugars. Every tree is a complex factory, yet the leafy process is completed with so little fuss that we are unaware of it. We pay the leaf less heed than an unfurling flower, yet it is the leaf that creates the basic food for everything alive.

There they stand, the miraculous trees, shimmering now in new leaf, already busier than man's huffing, puffing factories. We pay them passing tribute for their cool shade and green beauty, then resume our boasting about our own power and achievement, forgetting the mysterious, incalculable power of a leafy tree.

Salamander Weather *May 21*

Go into the woods on a rainy May day, when the air is warm and the rain is a comfortable rain and a leisurely one, and if you watch your path you will probably find a salamander or two exploring the complex world of grass-stem forests. Small creatures they are, not much longer than a man's finger, and a beautiful orange-red in color. Rain-washed, they have a bright, flowerlike hue, almost translucent. And they are leisurely in their movements.

Biologically speaking, they are of the ancients, related

to the amphibians, great and small, that crept from the waters of long ago and found the lands of this earth good. Around their cousins in Europe grew persistent legends. They were so cold-blooded, said casual observers a few centuries ago, that if they were tossed into a fire they could quench that fire at will, and they could emerge unharmed. And it was said also that they lived on air, and for that reason must have magical powers of health. Thus they came to have a place in the darker arts of healing and incantation.

Actually, they are neither mysterious nor fireproof. They are cold-blooded, true enough, but that is their quasi-reptilian nature. They live on the small insect life of their humble world and they hibernate through the cold season. They are harmless to humankind, as harmless as the little sand lizards that skitter at the roadside in the desert country of the American West. And as those small lizards are varicolored gems of animal life in the desert, so are the orange salamanders in the damp woodlands when violets bloom and warm May rains send rills down the hillsides.

The Busy Birds *May 22*

The "busy" birds, as some call them, are at work in the garden now, cramming their crops with insect fare, doing a better job of protecting plants from insect pests than any pesticide ever invented. You can see and hear them in almost any grassy dooryard, working at the job and not even whistling while they work. They haven't time to whistle.

The fox sparrow, one of the biggest and certainly the jauntiest of all our sparrows, is conspicuous in rich cinnamon-brown crown and tail, scratches like a Leghorn hen among the old leaves. There is no mistaking him.

The towhee is only a little bigger than a fox sparrow and he carries the same cinnamon brown, but on his sides.

His head is black and his belly is white, markings that catch any eye. He can make the dead leaves fly with his scratching, his search for insects. Some call the towhee a chewink, imitating his call notes, and some call him a ground robin.

The redstart, third of this trio, is a warbler, one of the few warblers with much black plumage. It has reddish-orange patches on tail and wings, it dives after insects the way a flycatcher does, and it also scratches and scatters old leaves.

All are especially busy in May, even a late May. All are friendly birds and seem to think people are good neighbors. They don't even ask for a handout or a fee for all the good they do.

The Ancients *May 23*

Green echoes of the remote past are all around us. On gravelly roadsides in sandy back lots, on damp margins of stream and pond, the horsetails, or scouring rushes, thrust up their primitive spore heads and their gritty, leafless stems and branches. Light yellowish-green, they come in two common forms, slim upright stems that look like miniature bamboo, and many-branched bushes of similar but smaller stems that look like upright witches' brooms.

These horsetails are remnants from vanished ages, direct descendants of the prehistoric Calimitales, those huge plants sometimes called tree-ferns of the Coal Age, some 300 million years ago. Those Calimitales forested the ancient marshlands and laid down the coal beds of today. They were so numerous that their spores, almost microscopic in size, created the huge deposits of cannel coal and jet. Their numbers are beyond easy comprehension. They were the earliest and most primitive of all the members of the fern family.

And here are their descendants among us today. Eons

have dwarfed them. The Calimitales towered high above the biggest of the dinosaurs, but few horsetails are more than three feet high. And time has humbled them. Until a few generations ago their stems, embedded with tiny grains of silica, were used for scouring pots and pans; today they are weeds, inheritors of the waste places, unwelcome even in the kitchen. But they persist, testimonials of time and change, far older than man, older than the trees we know today, older than many of our mountains, hoarding the secret of green life, perhaps of life itself.

Mister Mimic

May 24

Other migrants come and go, but the catbird comes with the violets and stays for the late asters, and virtually all the time he is here he contributes to the gaiety of his neighbors. He is here now and he is in fine form, celebrating the sunshine, jeering at the rain, demanding attention and deserving it.

He is our northern "mocker," cousin of the brash mockingbird of the more southerly regions, and he has almost all the real mockingbird's talents. He seldom uses them all, however, particularly the talent for sustained song. For he is a clown, an unregenerate mimic with what might be called a keen sense of the ridiculous. A phrase or two of sweet song and he must pause, as though to say, "Pretty, huh? But now listen!" And he will make a complete travesty of what he has just sung, finally jeering at it. He has an operatic voice, but he uses it for scat-singing.

And he likes an audience. He picks a nesting site near a house, by preference, and he will offer all kinds of vocal inducements to get human attention. Once he has it, he opens his bag of tricks. A show-off, no less: an adolescent with no self-consciousness whatever; a bird who seems to have the character of a party cut-up. He is as capricious as the weather, and that may be why we like him.

The robin is sedate, the oriole is a serious fellow, the blue jay is a blustering egocentric. But the catbird is a quick-witted entertainer who seems to find life a vastly amusing enterprise. Nothing completely dampens his spirit, and his world never seems to be going to pot. The only time we resent him is when we can't rise to match his mood, and that, after all, is our fault, not his.

The Rush Toward June *May 25*

The urgency is upon all of us and every growing thing around us. Daylight now approaches fifteen hours, but still there isn't enough time to do, to see, to participate as we would. The farmer hurries his planting to be ready for the hay crop swiftly maturing. The suburbanite mows his lawn and wages war with the dandelions and the crabgrass, hoping for an idle weekend or a free evening. The gardener is caught between spring bulbs and summer annuals, between peas and corn and beans and the annual crop of weeds.

Meanwhile, the trees spread their green canopy, hurry their blossoms to maturity and seedling, and the chlorophyll works overtime, feeding new shoots and old stems. Brooksides, purple with violets last week, begin to flush with wild geraniums. Meadows where the bluets were like frost two weeks ago are freckled with buttercups. Cool woodland margins have had their succession of hepatica, bloodroot, anemones, wild ginger, and trilliums and now are peopled with Jack-in-the-pulpits.

Sunrise comes early, with a chorus of birdsong, and dusk comes late, with wood thrushes calling and whippoorwills summoning the darkness. But the days are too short for the season's demands, too short to leave time for one to stand and look and feel and be a part of this surging rush toward June. Everything seems to be happening at once. Yesterday it was April, and tomorrow it will be summer.

The Persistent Mustards

May 26

Wild mustard blooms now at the roadside and in the meadow, yellow as buttercups, bright as a goldfinch. A nuisance to the farmer and the gardener, it delights the unprejudiced eye, for the color is one of May's delights. It is a weed only because it grows so plentifully and so persistently where it is unwanted.

The family name, *Crucifera,* comes from the Latin for "cross." The four petals of the mustard flower form the arms of a simple cross. The family includes the cresses, the peppergrass, and even horseradish, the largest member of all. Table mustard, the common condiment, is made from the ground seeds of domesticated cousins of those mustards now gone wild. The four common varieties of wild mustard—edge mustard, field mustard, black mustard, and white mustard—all were brought from Europe as field or garden crops originally. They liked our soil and climate and soon took off on their own. Even watercress will wander off down the brookside or across the lowland if given half a chance.

The mustards persist not only because of their adaptability but also because their seeds are so persistent of life. Black mustard and peppergrass seed will sprout and grow after lying dormant for forty years. Any countryman will vouch for this. He may fight mustard in his fields all his life, and still the yellow flowers will be there each May to taunt him. And to delight the eye of those who never tried to rid a field of mustard. But don't try to tell a farmer that mustard is beautiful. Not to him, it isn't.

June-Bugs

May 27

You hear them now, banging at window screens in the evening or fluttering and bumbling at the outdoor lights. They are called cockchafers in England, and June-bugs here in America. Or, more truly, May beetles, since they appear in late May in most areas.

They are beetles, members of the big scarab family and related to the sacred scarabs of Egypt. The family includes more than 30,000 species, and more are added each year as new members are identified. Those that bang our window screens grow from fat white grubs that live on the roots of plants. The grubs mature into brown beetles big as a man's fingernail that eat the leaves of trees and bushes. Having spent the day feeding in the trees, these beetles at dusk look for artificial lights. They are fascinated by light.

Their flight is awkward and bumbling, the wings inadequate for grace in the air. But they find a lighted window and bump and bang at the screen. Or they find an outside light and seem intent on getting inside the light bulb—they flutter and bang and flutter again. If one gets inside the house it usually falls on its back on the floor and lies there, legs waving, like a mechanical toy running down.

June-bugs don't bite people. They don't sting. They don't eat holes in clothing. They don't really like being indoors, no matter how they may try to reach an indoor light. Probably the Egyptian scarabs didn't really like being buried with royalty, either. But things like that happen when you are a May beetle called a June-bug.

Laughter on Wings

May 28

For sheer poetry of flight the barn swallows unquestionably deserve the laurel. Their mastery of the air is absolute and there isn't one motion of their wings and long, forked tail that lacks perfection. Theirs is a kind of lyric flight that makes one understand the meaning of exquisite grace. They give ultimate meaning to the feathered wing.

But for laughter in the air, for lilting song of motion that makes the heart rejoice, watch the swallows' cousins, the chimney swifts. The swifts are neither as beautiful nor as graceful as the swallows. Some have described them as "cigars on wings," and they are a kind of sooty-olive color, looking almost brown in the air. Their tails are short and rounded, their wings long and slim. But they fairly twinkle in flight, swooping, dodging, racing. And they often chitter as they fly, almost as though laughing at their astonishing performance.

A flight of chimney swifts is like a crowd of children, gay with freedom and dancing in delight. They make flight seem like a fresh discovery, a talent never before known. You can predict the patterns of the swallows, like a perfect ballet; but the swifts improvise from moment to moment as though too exuberant to be confined by patterns. They make up their flight-songs as they go along, exultant, practically jubilant at being alive and a-wing. They celebrate the miracle of flight.

The Golden Dust of Life

May 29

If the air of late May seems to have a strange, golden glint, particularly in the woodland, it is not only because the sunlight has its own aura. The air itself is dusted with the substance of life, the incredibly extravagant pollen crop from the trees.

The hickories, the oaks, the walnuts, and most of the conifers are in blossom and spreading clouds of sulphur-yellow pollen from their stamens in one of the oldest fertility rites on earth. Some of that pollen will reach the female flowers and produce the seeds that keep this a green and hospitable planet.

This golden dust of life, so minute that it dances in the sunbeams that filter through the woodland, hangs most heavily over the pines and spruces now, for they are the most generous of the sylvan producers. Pollen forms a yellow film on rain pools and makes them look like molten gold. It dusts the leaves of the underbrush, filters into houses, and mists polished table tops. It feels fine as talc between the fingers.

Yet this tree pollen is so nearly indestructible that deposits of it in old peat bogs can be identified centuries later; layers of prehistoric pollen show which trees grew there thousands of years ago. It is the very breath of beginnings. We probe and search and speculate, and all around us is life itself, finer than dust, insistent as time, simple as pollen.

Wild Strawberries *May 30*

They come to frosty white bloom when the first wild columbines are opening and the last of the wood anemones are still twinkling in the woodland margin. They come to fruit in late May and early June, first of the wild berries and, in the opinion of those who really know, the sweetest berries that grow. Why there aren't more of them is one of those tantalizing mysteries of the open fields.

Wild strawberries once were plentiful in sunny places almost everywhere. The first settlers picked them by the pailful and celebrated their flavor and abundance. They were "nuggets of wild sweetness" and "more pleasing than honey to the tongue." They made the finest jam that one could stow in the pantry. Still sun-warm and anointed with thick cream, they were very special fare. They were the reason for the first strawberry shortcake, beside which the modern counterpart is, if not actually a fraud, usually but a poor imitation.

Wild strawberries, when you can still find them, are prime examples of how much flavor can be stowed in a small package. They seldom are bigger than a fingertip but their seeds are inconsequential, their juice is blood-red, and their bit of flesh is all a concentrate of wild sweetness, so rich you smell their fragrance before you taste it. If there were wild strawberries in Eden, and there must have been, Adam was fool as well as sinner to taste any other fruit.

The Abounding Earth *May 31*

By May's end the urgency of spring begins to abate and the fecundity of summer is everywhere. The sprouting is done. The canopies of chlorophyll are spread and silently transforming the sun's energy into food for root and stem. Early blossoms fade, the ovules fertilized and fattening seeds. Eggs hatch. Nestlings appear and the insect buzz-and-hum makes the air vibrant. We live in a green world so filled with life that the very soil seems palpitant.

It is a teeming time. The earth abounds. Even the farmer's lush fields seem almost sparse in comparison with the wild meadows and the untended margins. Even the tepid water of the bogs is full of life, a primordial soup pregnant with squirming, wriggling, swimming creatures. Wasp and fly and beetle are busy in the garden. The night brings its bumbling June-bugs, its frantic moths at the lighted window, its mysterious fireflies winking their undecipherable messages.

May passes, and it is like the very springtime of life as we read it in the fossil rocks. The seed is but a symbol, for the urgency is toward proliferation, abundance, and variety beyond belief or understanding. Life not only persists but expands in all directions. No niche goes unoccupied. Chlorophyll and hemoglobin, green life and sentient flesh, are everywhere. And June and summer are at hand when time slows down and burgeoning is finished. June, and deliberate growth, the long, slow days that reach toward ripeness and maturity.

June

HOT MOON
Now comes first heat of summer, first cutting of hay, first of the garden harvest.

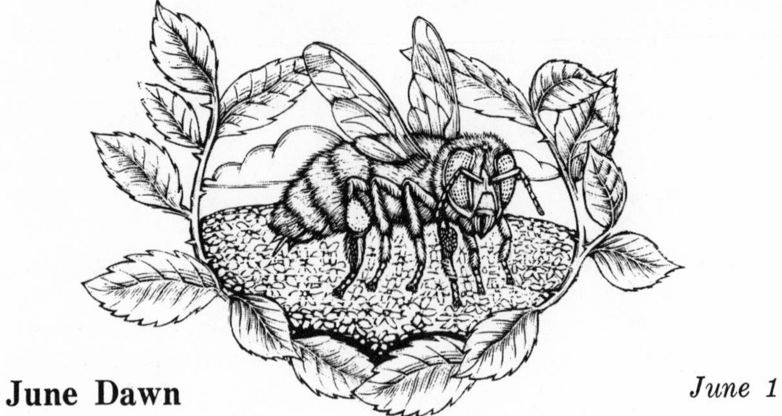

June Dawn

June 1

The world is new and young in the June dawn, fresh and sweet and almost innocent. It awakens slowly, to the swelling music of birdsong. The mists of night still lie in the valleys like the very mists of creation; and the riverbanks, the trees, the green meadows and hillsides are revealed with leisurely deliberation, bit by bit, as though newly created for this particular day.

There is no haste, no hurrying. The day begins at its own pace, unaltered by yesterday's confusions or tomorrow's uncertainties. This is another day, another blank page in the endless book of time, another chance. The wonder of new beginnings is everywhere, in the dew-wet grass, in the breeze-shaken leaves, in the shimmering spider web and the night-washed faces of buttercup and wild geranium. The world is hushed and waiting.

Even the sunrise is deliberate, when it comes. The first rays bathe the hilltops in a gentle glow and creep slowly down the hillside, jeweling the leaves and twinkling the grass, yard by yard. Robin and oriole and grosbeak sing as though their songs were newly discovered, written for this day alone, this dawning day. The mists swirl, in no haste to depart, and the river that inspired them is as leisurely as the sunrise, its sea-bound waters paced by the gentle fall of the land itself. Water and time refuse to be hurried by busy man's impatience.

A whole new day lies ahead, a day that never was before.

Generous June

June 2

June is a generous month. It is flowery June, a time of beauty and sweetness, spring come to its first great wealth of achievement. It is birds still singing, meadows and pastures lush, brooks still busy and chattering, trees in full leaf at last, cool shade, morning dew, the air fragrant with blossoms. We think of June as a special time for enjoyment.

And it is, of course. But we are the ones who find enjoyment. Nature has other purposes than to please mankind, and it is those purposes that are being fulfilled. The spreading leaf's purpose is to feed the parent plant, and the cool shade, the soothing green, are by-products, not designed for our pleasure. The blossom's purpose is to make and ripen seed, perpetuate the species. Its beauty may be a particular delight and make this a more beautiful world as we see it, but the blossom's destiny is to become a berry, a pome, a nut, a pod of seeds.

Generous June is a wonderful time to be alive and to know this sweet land. It is a time of extravagance, of more than the day demands. But it wasn't designed to warm a man's heart or delight his eye. It was here when man came along, and if he is wise he will count himself lucky to be here and enjoy it.

Chokecherries

June 3

This is the season when chokecherries make their presence known. These shrubby little members of the rose family, cousins of the haws, the apples, and even the pasture roses, now come to bloom in dangling clusters of dainty white flowers that look like fluffy kitten-tails. Walk a country lane on a cool morning and you can smell their faint, sharp fragrance.

Another month and they will be full of fruit, yellow turning red, then deep maroon as they ripen. True cherries they are, but with more seed than flesh, and with so sharp a tang that they pucker the mouth. Hence the name: they are so astringent they almost choke you if you try to eat them. But the birds love them, and that is why they are so widespread. The birds unwittingly plant them. Country folk used to make jelly from their juice, a pungent jelly that was the perfect accompaniment for venison or bear steak; but few folk bother to make such a wild-tanged sweet anymore.

As shrubs, or even as small trees, chokecherries have no distinction or use except as campfire wood. They are host to tent caterpillars. Even in October they aren't spectacular. But right now, in full bloom, they are beautiful. This is their time in the sun, their one brief span of glory.

June

June 4

May ends with a full moon and June comes with a bit more than fifteen hours of daylight. Dawn comes early, and with the cool, shimmering mist that fishermen know on inland lakes, mist that swirls and vanishes soon after sunup. Dusk lingers with long light on the hilltops and the night air stirring in the softness of new leaves in the treetops, air fragrant with the smell of cut grass and softly echoed with the throaty call of the wood thrush.

June invites tranquility, for it soothes the land and eases the haste of green and urgent growth. June is a month to live with, to relax, to appreciate life. Every field, every roadside, every woodland and meadow is evidence of the quiet abundance with which the earth clothes itself year after year. No matter what man may be doing, the fundamental earth is not a hostile place. It is a hospitable environment for life that would live in peace and know the essentials of existence.

June is a basic truth, the whole sustaining principle of change and growth and maturity, of seed and leaf, blossom and seed again. It is January brought to summer's fruition, winter given meaning in the whole of the year. It is those long, sweet days we bought and paid for with long, cold nights and short, bitter days at the dark turn of the year.

Wild Roses *June 5*

They grow in odd corners and uncut margins, sometimes on a stony hillside, often at the damp edge of a little bog. They bloom when robin fledglings first take wing and early daisies spread their white petals among the gold of fence-row buttercups. Some know them as pasture roses, some as swamp roses, some as sweetbrier, and all the names are true. There are half a dozen common species here in the Northeast. But all are wild roses, blush-pink and spicily fragrant in the cool of evening or at dew-damp dawn.

The sweetbrier came originally from Europe, where it was called eglantine; its small, round leaflets are unique, for when crushed they have the tantalizing smell of green apples. The others are natives, American as corn. Wild bees were gathering their rich pollen, a special feast, long before the white man first saw them. Bees still love them, and if a swarm could be confined to a wild rose tangle in June their honey would be ambrosial. But clover also comes to blossom now; for every rose there are a thousand heads of clover, and clover honey is the consequence.

As bushes, they make briery tangles. Cut and brought indoors, the blossoms soon wither and drop their petals. Their small, red autumn haws, bitter cousins of the apple, are rich fare for birds but acrid to the human tongue. But in June the wild roses are beautiful grace notes in the floral symphony that makes the forgotten corners of this well-trodden land echo with remembrance.

The Hayfields *June 6*

Now the sweet green grass smell is upon the air, one of the most haunting of all the fragrances of the countryside. In the suburbs it is the smell of fresh-cut lawns, but out in the rural valleys it is the age-old perfume of new hay curing in the sun, as seasonable as roses, as pervasive as the smell of corn pollen will be in August. It is rain and sunlight and earthy sweetness somehow brought to perfect combination in a grass blade, released there by the mowers, and refined by the air itself. Downwind, you can smell a hayfield half a mile away, as far as you can hear the clatter of the mower.

It is a special sweetness, like nothing else in the world. Old journals speak of it from the days when farmers cut their hay with a scythe, for hay was one of the first cured crops man gathered after he domesticated the horse and the cow. It is an insistent fragrance, lingering in old barns whose mows haven't held a harvest of hay in a generation. Climb to any barn's hay mow even in icy January and you can smell early June all around you. It is a ripeness, a richness from the soil, an open-air spiciness mild as a late spring morning. It is dew and buttercups, high noon and clover, lingering dusk and fence-row daisies.

It is the essence not only of grass and hay, but of the season itself, and of the land. It is the sweetness of a green world, a hospitable world whose basic urgencies are growth and plenty.

Not Forever *June 7*

The first cutting of hay is baled and under cover, out where the farms begin, and the corn is up and reaching for the sun. Only two more weeks of spring remain. The year moves swiftly toward its midpoint, a year of four seasons, four spans of time not dependent on machines that go tick-tick-tick. Despite the urgencies of man's own follies, there is a kind of time that doesn't have to be measured in seconds and microseconds. For those who would stop long enough to look for it, June, which is the turn from spring to summer, provides the essential pause that should restore perspective.

June makes few demands, even on the countryman. It is the time when hay is first ready to cut, true; but if a man doesn't cut his hay it simply goes to seed, the basic purpose of grass after all. What a countryman does in June is really for his own comfort and convenience, not a matter of compulsion. If he wants security and plenty he will take in his hay and other harvest when it is ready. If he would rather loaf in the shade he probably won't starve, though he will have hungry days come February. But his fields won't care. Nature won't even notice.

The June world has its own business, and man can participate or not, as he will. The urgencies now are of his own making. It is his calendar and clocks that drive, not the seasons. The trees and the grass and even the water could do very well without hurrying man and his machines. That's one thing June means. Another is that no season, not even spring and summer, lasts forever.

June Days Begin Early

June 8

The sun now rises soon after five o'clock, daylight time. June days begin early, possibly because there is so much for June to accomplish. The leaves are spread, the early flowers have bloomed, and now comes the surge of growth that makes July and August. Tree and vine, bush and grass now need a full fifteen hours of daylight to complete their annual assignments.

But even a June day begins with a sense of peace and leisure. Night is gone, the stars have faded, yet the day itself takes its own time in rousing. The insects are quiet, still sluggish with the night's chill. A few birds sing, but even the chattering brown thrasher is somewhat restrained, waiting for full sunlight. The night's mist lingers in the hollows, shimmering like remnants of vanished starlight, reluctant to go.

The trees, lush with fresh green, seem to shiver and stretch as a breath of breeze touches them. They shed a fine shower of dew from their night-washed leaves and almost catch their breath, as though newly wakened. Beneath them the grass twinkles. Buttercups nod at the edge of the hay meadow, and yesterday's cutting of hay, awaiting the day's sun for further curing, breathes the essence of June in the dampness of first sunlight.

A robin scolds, then flies to the tall elm and begins to sing. A grosbeak takes the cue and whistles from the nearest maple. The thrasher stops chattering. The mist rises and the day begins, but still unhurried, still peaceful, still full of that sense of unending time, of long-day June.

The Flags of June

June 9

The iris comes to blossom, the iris named for the rainbow that once spanned a springtime in Greece. The yellow iris, sometimes called corn flag, and the purple iris, sometimes called the blue flag, and all the other early irises that have been dear to the hearts of country folk for generations. And in the meadows and pastures, and down along the brooks, the wild irises, large and small, come into their own, from the big blue fleur-de-lis to the miniature blue-eyed grass, which is probably the least of all the irises and one of the daintiest.

It's a venerable flower, the iris. Some say it was the "hyacinth" of ancient mythology. The Saracens long ago grew it in their cemeteries as a symbol of their grief. In early French art the white iris was an emblem of the Virgin. It supplied the pattern for France's heraldic fleur-de-lis. For more than five centuries the iris was a part of the royal emblem of England.

Several species are native to America, including a few which were used by the Indians as a foodstuff. Orrisroot comes from the iris, for the perfumer and the pharmacist. And the bees love all the irises that bloom.

But for most of us the irises are garden flowers, simple and old-fashioned or hybridized and complex and exotically beautiful. They grow beside old garden walls and along old dooryard fences and in special beds of their own. To an older generation the simple ones were always "flags," and they bloomed when the tulips began to fade. Flags and lilacs and "pineys" all belonged to early June.

The Green Leaves

June 10

Green leaves are so plentiful from April till October that we take them for granted. Every tree and bush has leaves and every grassy place is a mass of leafage. Even the geranium on a window sill is a part of the green miracle, spreading its leaves to catch the sunlight. Even the weeds among the rubble in a vacant lot.

The leaf is commonplace, but without the green leaf we would perish, all of us. The mysterious green chlorophyll within the leaf manufactures the basic foodstuff for all animal life on earth and does it without a sound, without one wisp of smoke or fumes. And beyond this fundamental creation of sugars and starches, this mysterious process which is at the heart of all our harvests, the leaves cool and refresh the whole atmosphere around us. They absorb carbon dioxide, a waste product of our bodies and our machines, and give off oxygen, our very breath of life. They cool the air by evaporation and renew the moisture that falls as replenishing rain. One average oak tree will give off 150 gallons of water on a hot summer day.

That is one reason the green countryside lures us in summer. It not only looks cooler, it is cooler, and its air is fresher. That is one reason for parks in the city, open spaces of grass and trees. We need the leaves almost as much as the trees themselves need them. They are fundamental to life. We destroy the trees and banish the grass at our own peril.

Five Crimson Doves *June 11*

Wild columbines nod in the thin woodland and on rocky hillsides with a flash of crimson and a golden yellow gleam. They were in bloom before the bloodroot faded and in more shaded places they will still be in bloom for another month or more.

It is hard to believe, but the columbines are cousins of the buttercups now glinting in the meadows. They both belong to the big botanical family called *Ranunculaceae*, or crowfoot. So do the dainty little anemones of April, and so does hepatica. The columbine's botanical name, *Aquilegia*, has its riddles: but so do the plant's common names. The botanical name may have come from the Latin for eagle and refer to the claw-shaped spurs on the flower, or it may come from the Latin words meaning to collect water and refer to the way dew gathers in those floral spurs.

The common name, columbine, comes from the Latin word for dove, apparently from a fancied resemblance of the spurs to the birds. Another common name, Five Crimson Doves, comes directly from the same source. Still another name, honeysuckle, is a kind of generic name once given to almost any flower with sweet nectar, one of the old folk names that preceded Linnaeus and our present-day system of organized botany. And, for some obscure reason, the columbine now and then is called "Meetinghouse."

Whatever the name, it is one of early summer's special wild adornments. In the field, that is; it is not a "picking flower."

The Wheelbarrow

June 12

Consider the wheelbarrow. It may lack the grace of an airplane, the speed of an automobile, the initial capacity of a freight car, but its humble wheel marked out the path of what civilization we still have. Particularly that phase of civilization which leads down Main Street, through the front gate, around the house, and into the back garden. It also led the way up Broadway, across State Street, and even through Piccadilly Circus; but that's another story.

The story we prefer is a simpler one. It deals with rocks and roots and hunks of sod and bags of lime. It includes dead leaves and lively onions, old compost and new potatoes, seedling flats and spades and rakes, squash and pumpkins and outsize heads of cabbage. And two hardwood handles, two callused hands. It makes the rounds of March mud and May rains, July sun and August thunderstorms, October harvest and November frost. It goes places without ever getting far from home.

Like faith, the wheelbarrow can move mountains. A few drops of oil can silence its loudest complaint. In spring it is a thing of beauty, particularly if it is both new and red. In summer it is a challenge to human endurance. In fall it is—sometimes—a cornucopia. Always it is there, needing only human companionship and cooperation to get things done.

Best of all, it is shaped to its purpose. When the sun is at its height, the garden bench is far away, and human energy has dwindled to the very neap, the wheelbarrow waits with welcoming arms and recumbent seat. No rock, no bag of lime, no harvest from the fertile earth ever fitted the contours of the wheelbarrow as well as the weary frame of its owner.

The Thrush Still Sings *June 13*

Dusk approaches, on a June evening, and you sit and rest after a day in the sun at the shore, in the country, in a lawn-and-garden suburb. You sit and sense the evening without really looking or listening, sense birdsong back of and beyond the sound of cars or trucks or children shouting. You sense the evening chorus of robins and orioles and thrashers and wrens and catbirds. A pleasant sound in a somewhat less than ideal world. And no need to try to sort out the singers, even if you can. Birds.

You listen with only half your attention, still aware of the day's worries. Then another voice is there, a voice you have waited to hear without quite knowing you waited. *Ay-oleee. Olee-ay. Ay-olee.* Up at the edge of the woods, but somehow dominant over the birds in the nearby trees. The wood thrush, the bird with that superb contralto voice, first cousin of the hermit thrush, and one of the two or three best singers we have.

You listen now to this thrush's song, deliberate and almost serene. The phrases are clear, precise, and with casual pauses between them. There is no rush about this singing, nor even any sense of effort. It is like a breeze in the woods, like the flow of a brook. *Ay-oleee.* And after a pause, *Olee-ay.* Not exultant, as the singing of an oriole, nor effusive as the wrens, but announcing that life itself deserves a song. You listen and your pulse begins to slacken. The thrush still sings.

The Chattering Popples *June 14*

They are the talkative trees of the woodland, chattering in every breeze, whispering in every breath of air. Countrymen here in the Northeast call them popples, a term that can include aspens and cottonwoods as well as poplars. Lumbermen have little use for them, preferring pine or oak or maple; when they are harvested it usually is for pulp for the paper mills. They are too common to belong to the sylvan peerage. But they have their own distinction.

Popples are friendly trees. They mingle with gray birches on rocky hillsides, persist at the pasture margins, cluster at the river's bank. They take over neglected knolls, populate weedy wastelands, possess the brinks of the boglands. Cut a grove of popples and in five years the roots will have sprouted a whole new thicket.

When buds open in April they shimmer with silver leaflets and are tasseled with catkins. In May they fill the air with cottony fluff bearing their seeds to far places. All summer they twinkle in the sunlight, spangle in the moonlight, as their leaves twist and turn, fairly dancing. In the rain they really dance to the special music of raindrops on their thick leaves. In October they are briefly golden before the brittle leaves skip and rustle down the country roads.

And all summer they chatter and prattle, perhaps with no meaning at all beyond the meaning of wind and green leaf, the chitter-chatter of sun and air and countryside, and plebeian popples.

The Bumblebee *June 15*

Behold the bumblebee, that big, improbable black and gold insect that shouldn't be able to fly but does, that could be a model of industry but isn't, and that is neither meek nor mild though Englishmen call it the humblebee. It is a hummer and bumbler, noisy as a locust, colorful as a butterfly, and as much a part of the sunny June day as a pasture rose or a wild strawberry.

The bumblebee is an exponent of the easy life and an example of moderation in most matters. Like most bees, it has social instincts, but not to excess; its communities are mere villages, so to speak. Not liking to waste energy, it often nests in field-mouse dens in or near clover fields. Able to make wax, it sometimes fills small waxen jugs with honey for a rainy day or two, but it doesn't seem to think the world will end if it fails to hoard honey by the bucketful. Armed like a whiteface hornet, it seldom goes looking for trouble. Its kind has been here on earth a long, long time.

Bumblebees tolerate man, up to a point, but they refuse to be domesticated. They eat when hungry, rest when tired, and are neither thieves nor killers. They even sleep at night—which is more than can be said for some insects—often sweetly couched in an aster blossom or a zinnia. They aren't as improvident as grasshoppers, but they don't work themselves to death in six weeks, either, as honeybees do. Man could do worse than ponder the bumblebees, especially on a sunny June afternoon.

The Nestlings

June 16

Now the nestlings appear, robins on the lawn, ducklings on the pond, baby partridges in the thin woodland. The new generation is hatched and feathered and beginning to learn a few things about life.

Young robins, trailing their mothers as they search the grass for worms, cheep like spoiled brats and stand agape, waiting to be fed. They don't yet know they will have to forage for themselves in a few more weeks. Ducklings, swimmers from the day they were hatched, trail their mother along the shore, learning early lessons about shallow water and its insect fare. And scattering frantically at the splash of a frog or the sudden appearance of a turtle. Innate wariness is the price of life.

In the edge of the woodland a mother partridge sees a human intruder, clucks an alarm, and feigns a broken wing. Her brood of chicks, each no bigger than a dandelion's ball of fluff, scatter and vanish. The mother limps and flutters, trying to lure the intruder away. Stand still two minutes and you probably will see a tiny eye wink where there seemed to be nothing but a leaf shadow. Perfectly color-protected, the chicks hide by squatting motionless among the woodland litter. Turn and walk away and the mother partridge will return.

It is mid-June, the time when nestlings learn to fly and face the hazards of this unpredictable world.

Wild Strawberries *June 17*

In their journals, the earliest white settlers here hailed wild strawberries as "so plentiful and so sweet they make this a land of especiall delight." Sometimes they called them strew-berries or stray-berries, but the naming didn't matter. They were familiar fruit, common in England but never in such plenty or with such flavor as those that brightened whole New England hillsides and scented whole valleys.

The berries they gathered and ate with such satisfaction were meadow berries, sweetest of all our native kinds, and eventually they provided the stock for our first cultivated strawberries. But the old stock persists, untamed, in upland pasture and even along rural roadsides, to the particular pleasure of rural wanderers.

Mid-June is their time of ripeness, but you need no calendar to know their season. They reveal their presence early, with snow-white bloom at bloodroot time. Apples come to blossom, the scent of lilacs fades, wild geraniums blush, and young robins leave the nest. Then you look for ripe strawberries. If your nose is not too much dulled, you even smell them out, for there is too much tang and sweetness to be confined.

You search them out, with eye and nose, and you eat them, sun-warm and dew-sweet; and maybe you take a few home to share. Not often, though, for they no longer cover whole hillsides. So you pluck and eat, and feel triumphant, for you too have found "a place of especiall delight."

Knee-Deep in June

June 18

We are knee-deep in June, as James Whitcomb Riley put it. A good many birds are still singing, at least morning and evening, and the drone of the cicadas is yet to come. Bees do the droning now, bees in clover. And farmers with their tractors, at work in the hayfields. June is haytime, and anyone with a nose to smell can tell you that if he has been out in the country. There's no other smell in the world quite like fresh-cut hay seasoning in the June sun.

Knee-deep in June, which means roses both in the garden and along the fence rows. The pasture roses didn't winterkill, as so many of the garden roses did, and they are pink as dawn just now, flushed and sweet and almost as much a lure to the bees as is the clover. June without roses, all kinds of roses, just wouldn't be June.

And strawberries, of which Riley also spoke in celebrating June. Strawberries, also both wild and tame, come to their ripeness now. And in those berries is the sweetness of early summer, June's own concentrate. The wild ones hide in the meadow grass, but the tame ones are there in the garden for anyone, preferably the owner, to savor, sun-warm and full of juice. Raspberries approach ripeness now, too, including the little wild blackcaps, which are a treasure to anyone abroad in June. But give the blackcaps another week to sweeten.

Knee-deep in June. A wonderful time to be alive and sentient. A time of richness, of early ripeness, of summer at its very best.

No Time to Sing

June 19

The chorus of birdsong diminishes, as always when hot days come, though it still is heard in the cool of morning and evening. There are various theories about the reasons birds sing, but beyond all speculation is the fact that most of them are now too busy to sing. Their nestlings need a protein-rich diet, chiefly insects, and most of the parent birds' daylight hours are spent gathering food for them.

This phase of bird life is too often ignored in arguments about poisonous insecticides. When it is shown that the organic poisons kill birds as well as insects, the stock answer is, "What do a few birds matter?" Actually, every dead bird is a major ally lost in the war with the insects.

A brown thrasher feeds its nestlings as many as 6,000 insects a day. A pair of barn swallows catches and feeds 1,000 leafhoppers to its young in one day. A house wren feeds 500 spiders and small caterpillars to her nestful in one afternoon. A Baltimore oriole takes as many as 100 caterpillars to her woven pouch of a nest in one hour. A yellow-shafted flicker will dispose of 5,000 ants between noon and sundown. Even the noisy starlings and the messy English sparrows eat Japanese beetles by the thousand and feed as many more to their young.

The wonder is not that the birds sing so little now, but that they have time to sing at all.

Summer Solstice

June 20

Tomorrow brings the summer solstice, another marker on the endless cord of time. In original meaning, the solstice is that moment when the sun stands still; and perhaps we cling to the old name because we wish this might be so, though we know it never happens. We would have summer, the lush, warm days of sweet luxuriance and green achievement, for weeks and months on end. At the year's meridian, we would linger and have the sun, and time itself, stand still.

But we know the solstice is only a notation in the inevitable progression of the seasons. In everyday terms, the sun has now achieved its greatest northing and now turns back. Tomorrow marks the turn and from here on the hours of daylight, as a consequence of the earth's own motions, not the sun's, will slowly, subtly diminish into autumn and winter. Bee-drone days and firefly nights will pass. Time has no resting place.

So we listen to the bees, we cherish June's roses, we smell the hayfield's fragrance, and we watch the swallows in their evening flight, welcoming summer. Ripening berries are sweet to the tongue. Brooks are languid, rivers are leisurely, bogs team with brief amphibian and insect life. And the day's dimensions are as hospitable as the green earth itself. Summer is briefly ours, a season that dims the memory of inclement March and holds no hint of raw November. The solstice comes, and all about us is the sense of summer's foreverness, like glowing starlight, like clear, cool dawn, like the midday drone of the July harvest fly.

Summer and Time

June 21

Now it is summer by the almanac. Summer came with the solstice this morning when, to give "solstice" its literal meaning, the sun stood still. It was turning the corner of the seasons and now it begins to move south again, as we say, toward fall and winter. We are at the time of longest daylight, earliest sunrise and latest sunset, which will continue with only a few seconds of change for another week. Time, if we would only pause and let it flow over us, for a little while partakes of the deliberation that is the mark of summer in almost everything except man's affairs.

Spring has its own haste. Spring is sprouting and burgeoning, the opening of the leaf and the blossom. It is mating and birthing, the hatching of the egg, the spreading wing, the urgency of the bee and the wasp, the surge of green across the earth. Then the first rush is over, the trees are vast canopies of chlorophyll, the meadows tall with grass, the fields thick-bladed with corn and oats. June matures into summer and the quiet process of growth for which April and May were a time of preparation. Summer becomes a summary of spring's achievement, a totaling of sun and rain and fertile soil added to the substance of the seed and the root.

The urgency of spring is past. The berries ripen in their own time. The bees replenish the hive. Clover comes to sweet blossom, then to seed. Daisies whiten the roadsides. Fireflies sparkle the evening. Time flows like the brooks that must have leisured through Eden when summer blessed a young and innocent earth.

Whippoorwill

June 22

Few birds are more seldom seen or better known by call and reputation than the whippoorwill here in the Northeast. The bird's call is fascinating to the uninitiate; it is also one of the most insistently repetitious birdcalls ever uttered, and two whippoorwills challenging each other vocally can disrupt sleep for hours. Yet those who heard the whippoorwill's call in youth will go miles to hear it again. It isn't a song; it is a memory, a legend.

Even in name the whippoorwill is a legend. It belongs to the scientific family called *Caprimulgidae,* and *caprimulgus* is Latin for "goatsucker." Because members of the family haunted herds of goats at dusk, they long ago were believed to milk the goats and live on milk. Later it was learned that they lived on flying insects and followed the goats because they attracted such insects. But the name persisted, finally outranked the English common name, nightjar, which at least had truth to back it up, for if any bird can jar and jolt the night, this one can. But the family name is goatsucker, even to ornithologists.

There are other members of the family in the South, chuck-will's-widow and poorwill, and there is the nighthawk, the least vocal one of all. But we know best and remember longest the whippoorwill, which comes north in mid-spring, summers here, and goes south again for the winter. It builds no nest worthy of the name, it hatches two eggs on a pile of dead leaves, and it sleeps all day. It is seldom seen. But its call, which sometimes is repeated several hundred times almost without pause, is seldom forgotten. Old men who haven't heard a whippoorwill in years will smile with remembering at the very name—whippoorwill—and wish to hear it again.

Fishing

June 23

There is a common and accepted fiction that fishermen go fishing to catch fish. Some do, of course; but more don't. The fish caught are only a lesser part of the catch. The greater part is the day in the open, the little things that feed the eyes, the ears, and the soul, though we are so perverse and so practical that we seldom talk about them.

How many of us would get up to see an early summer dawn without the excuse that fish bite better then? Yet it's really the dawn world that a man goes out to see, a sunrise full of the golden green of trees spangled with brand new leaves, full of robin song, full of mist from the lake or river, full of the strange, thin echoes of man's world just coming awake. It's the sudden flight of a nesting duck, startled into whirring wings and beaten water and gleaming light on swift ripples. It's the sight of wild geranium bowing under the weight of dew, and the red and gold and blue-silver leaf of wild columbine. It's the smell of wood smoke from a farmhouse chimney, and the taste of vacuum coffee on a sunlit bank or sand bar.

It's the fishing, yes. The way a fly follows a riffle, the way a plug plops, the way a wormed hook goes down into a deep pool. The strike, the rush, the play of line, the sound of reel, the catch, or the lost fish. But it's also the gleam of a dragonfly, the rattling cry of a kingfisher, the stark awkwardness verging on grace and beauty of a heron. It's the slow climb of the sun, the slow travel of the shadows, the drift of a cloud.

Fish? Oh, yes, one must have a reason and the day must have a purpose. But it's the fishing, really, the dawn and the morning and the day, and man's knowing that it's still there, still real.

Firefly Nights *June 24*

In daylight they are small, drab, soft-bodied beetles that annoy nobody and are seldom noticed. Then darkness comes and the warm summer night is filled with winking lights of mystery. Those inconspicuous little beetles take to the air over suburban lawns and rural meadows and the darkness comes alive and glowing with a special kind of fantasy.

Man has known and marveled at the fireflies for centuries, but their essential secrets still elude us. We can now name the chemicals that seem to create their heatless fire, and we can say the process is something like an enzyme action. We can talk about it in learned language, and we even speculate on its reasons. But the fact remains that we don't know why or precisely how the firefly creates light. We don't even know why some South American fireflies flash green and red, though those we know best seem limited to a phosphorescent yellow gleam.

All we really know is that fireflies make a special magic of the warm summer night. We go out in the darkness and there they are, like a host of winking stars come down to spangle the night and create that incredible ballet of soft light. That is enough, really—to see, to know, to marvel. The night should have its own secrets, even such a haunting one as the luminous mystery of the firefly.

Wings in the Dusk *June 25*

These are firefly nights, when urban parks, suburban lawns, and rural meadows twinkle at dusk with the mysterious signals of those harmless little beetles that possess the secret of "cold" fire. But theirs are by no means the only wings in the summer dusk.

High overhead are the nighthawks, swooping, gliding, diving, seining the air for gnats, and mosquitoes. Once rural as their cousins, the whippoorwills, now they often nest on city rooftops and they even course the city's canyons at dusk. Out in the open, and often over the water, are the swallows for whom the feathered wing must have evolved to perfection.

Nearer the ground are the dark wings of bats and moths. The bats are fluttery, shadowy; they trick the eye, deceive the watcher, as they swoop into sight and vanish utterly. Children of dusk, they play hide and seek with the darkness. But the big moths, the dark brown ones that live on nectar, make no secret of their presence. They hover at the deep-throated flowers, like hummingbirds, and they stay in the garden till dusk has deepened into night.

And out beyond the busy streets, out where the meadows are rural, late dusk brings the whippoorwills. Not always and by no means everywhere; but when and where the whippoorwills call, the firefly nights are full of magic and memories and the lore of other days and nights.

The Exodus *June 26*

Now comes the exodus, the annual change of scene. Vacation time, freedom from the job, and the going from city to country, to the seashore, to the wooded hills and lakes, to the mountains. The search for or return to another scene than the close, familiar streets and their summer swelter, their artifacts and machines.

Why quit the cities merely for rest and refreshment? Why seek the green of trees, the ebb and flow of ocean tides, the stubborn stand of mountains? Fresh air, of course, and relaxation, a chance to let down. But something more, too, something as subtle as a breeze, as obvious as a lighthouse. Because the ocean's slow, incessant beat still speaks of the beginnings of life, all life, and of the endless flow of time. Because a mountain has its own enduring identity as well as firm reality. Because a tree in a hillside pasture is a living thing grown from a seed, an achievement that cannot be duplicated by man's most ingenious machines.

One needn't renounce the cities or the machines to know these things, even briefly. But without at least an awareness that they do persist, a dimension of life is lacking. That is the basic reason for the annual exodus—to know again, if only by brief contact and subconsciously, that there is a fundamental world that does not depend on the artifacts and the factories for existence; to sense, however vaguely, that there is a source, a basic environment, that gave rise to life and still sustains it. That there is an ocean, a tree, a mountain, as well as a city street.

Rubythroat *June 27*

Seen in sunlight, it is a blur of wings, an iridescent flash of bronzed green and a touch of ruby red. At dusk it may be mistaken for a hovering sphinx moth. Actually, it is the hummer, the ruby-throated hummingbird, the smallest bird we have and one of the most remarkable. We see it now in the flower gardens, on high terraces in the city, in side yards in the suburbs, at the old-fashioned flowers in the country dooryard.

There are only a few varieties of hummingbirds, all native to the Western Hemisphere, and the only one we know here in the Northeast is the rubythroat. All the dimensions of its life except its migratory flight are on a miniature scale. Its body is not much bigger than a bumblebee, its nest is the size of half a walnut shell, and its eggs are no bigger than fat garden peas. It lives on nectar and miniature insects. But it can run away from a hurrying bee, it can outmaneuver a swallow, and on its annual migration to Mexico it crosses the Gulf of Mexico, flying some 500 miles nonstop.

This brilliant little atom of bird life, however, is full of everyday energy and self-confidence that sometimes amounts to truculence. It seems to fear nothing on wings. It will attack a hawk, a crow, even a rambunctious kingbird, and put any one of them to flight. A strange bundle of paradoxes, this little winged jewel. It loves flowers, couldn't live without them. Its chief competitors are bees and moths. But bird it is, every milligram of it, and soon it will be haunting the bergamot and the jewelweed, a gem on wings, a little demon dressed like a miniature dandy.

The Moths and the Birds *June 28*

Now comes the time of the big, spectacular moths, the time when the Polyphemus and the Sphinx haunt the flower garden at dusk and the Luna beats its frail wings at the window screen, trying to reach the light inside. Luna, the light green moth, often four inches in wingspan, sometimes is called the most beautiful insect in America.

It is also the time of the less spectacular moths and their more voracious caterpillars, the coddling moth, the tent caterpillar, the gypsy moth. They are busy in the orchards, in the wild cherry trees, in the hardwood forests, and their caterpillars are among the major economic pests in the woodland areas of America.

Fortunately, it is also the season when many wild birds have fledglings about to leave the nests. More than half the food of our 1,400 species and varieties of birds consists of insects, and virtually all the food for nestlings is insects, provided by the parent birds. This diet affords natural control of the caterpillars as long as man doesn't upset the natural balance by using pesticides that kill birds as well as insects or by destroying natural protective cover for the birds.

In Washington, D.C., it was found that robins fed their nestlings with tussock caterpillars. Elsewhere English sparrows and hairy woodpeckers did the same thing. A New Hampshire survey showed that eighty-seven percent of coddling moth larvae was eaten by birds over the winter. And the late E. H. Forbush, in charge of a campaign to control gypsy moths in Massachusetts, found that in at least one area the birds ate so many gypsy moth caterpillars that artificial control measures were not needed.

Corn

June 29

Whenever modern man gets to thinking too much of himself, he would do well to go out in the garden and look around. And if he thinks of himself as the sum of all intelligence, he should take a particularly long look at the stalks of corn growing there. That corn is a plant developed by men whose name and origin are lost in the misty past. But those simple men knew, somehow, how to hybridize plants. In a method we have still to learn, and over a period of time we cannot even calculate, they developed corn as we know it from a wild grass.

Look at the stalk, sturdy, economical, efficient. It stands braced on its roots. It is of quick growth. Its long, broad leaves are so arranged that they catch rain and dew and funnel it down where it is needed. As a plant, it is very near to perfection. It silks out, as we say, with vastly more silk than is needed, just so each kernel on the incipient ear can be properly fertilized. It tassels out, with a pollen-bearing apparatus that is ideal for its purpose.

And it concentrates its yield, a big quantity of useful grain in compact form. It ripens and is an almost perfect storage crop. It is packed with nutriment for man or beast. It comes in varieties which suit almost all climates and long or short seasons.

Look at the corn, and pause for a moment and wonder how it was evolved, and by what simple men. We are wise, and we have improved the corn we inherited, but nobody has yet found out how to evolve a corn plant in the first place. That was done before man became "civilized."

June-Becoming-July

June 30

The calendar is a reminder but not a necessity. You know it is June-becoming-July, even with your eyes closed, when you smell the too-sweet milkweed blossom at the country roadside. You know what time it is by the season's clock when you hear the first harvest fly buzz to its shrilling climax and run down to a hiss and a dull drone. You listen to the oriole and the tanager and the exuberant robin at dawn and again at dusk, but seldom in the warm hours between.

Walk the open fields before the heat of the day has settled on them and you smell the old, old tang of mint and bee balm and yarrow. Stand at the garden fence before the bees have gathered for their day's work and the spiced fragrance of old-fashioned pinks is a sweet reminder of the season. Stand there at dusk and you will know the perfume of nicotiana and the soft flight of dark moths hovering at the nectary blossoms. Linger as the first stars appear and you will be in the midst of a firefly galaxy.

It is a sensible time, in the root-sense of that word. The

senses are piqued and quickened by the smells and sounds and subtle presences of early summer. It is a lively, teeming world, too busy to watch any calendar except that of the sun and the long, lingering daylight hours of summer growth and summer abundance.

July

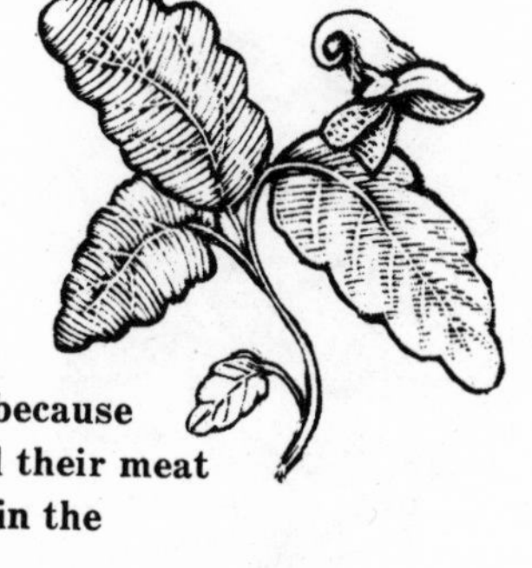

BUCK MOON

A baffler, but perhaps because buck deer were fat and their meat could be quickly dried in the hot July sun.

July

July 1

July is the first real month of summer, the pause toward which all the haste and energy of spring were hurrying us. Days are long, dusk comes late, nights bring a sense of leisure. Country roadsides are sweet with clover and the drone of bees no longer has the frenzy of May and apple blossoms. Daisies and black-eyed Susans decorate but don't yet dominate hillside pastures. Fence-rows are pink with sweetbrier, aromatic in leaf as well as blossom.

July dawns on lake or river can be gauzy with mist and glowing beauty, a special bonus for quiet fishermen. July afternoons can roar and rumble with thunderstorms that slash the sky, shake the hills, and drench the valleys. July nights can be as cool as May, as sultry as late August, and they are lit with more fireflies than stars.

The pressure eases, now, in all growing things; and man is invited to ease his pressures too, beneath a tree, on the deck of a sailboat, on the sand where the surf sets its own rhythm. August will come soon enough, and September, and autumn. Here is July, and summer.

Honey-Sweet July

July 2

You can smell the season now, a special sweetness that marks the mists of dawn and the cool of dusk and is even there in the heat of a July afternoon. If it has a reminder of honey, that is no illusion, for it is the fragrance of clover and milkweed in bloom; and the essence of both is being stowed in the waxen comb. You smell it now on the summer air. You will taste it next winter on the breakfast plate.

The clovers are both wild and tame and range from the small white clover of suburban lawns to the big red clover of the hayfield and the tall sweet clover, both white and yellow, of the rural roadside. All are sweet of blossom. But clover fragrance makes no demands. It is a presence in the air, a gentle sweetness faintly spiced.

Milkweed, however, cannot be ignored. Its fragrance is like the essence of honeysuckle added to the heavy scent of the tuberose. It is almost too sweet, too insistent. Come on a patch of milkweed in full flower and you first wonder what careless perfumer has been at work. The warm summer air becomes almost heavy with milkweed aroma. Few other blossoms, wild or tame, are so full of such fragrance, and few flowers bloom more generously in July.

So you walk the roads and fields. The bees hum. The hot air shimmers. Grass heads ripen. Summer possesses the land. And you can smell July, honey-sweet, on every breath of air.

Bee Balm

July 3

Some call it bee balm or Oswego tea, some know it as wild bergamot, and botanists list it as *Monarda didyma*. Butterflies, bumblebees, and hummingbirds call it their own and add a lively touch of color to every patch of it that blooms. It is their candy store, their special trove of midsummer sweets, and anyone who would have hummingbirds as daily visitors should have a garden corner of bee balm.

Its lure for the nectar gatherers, however, is only one aspect of this tousle-headed member of the mint family. Its blossom is ragged as a tatter, utterly disheveled, but it flaunts the finest scarlet red in the floral spectrum. Wild or tame, it is spectacular; but it never really forfeits its wild ways, even in a garden, spreading insistently, overwhelming lesser plants, sturdy and exuberant.

As a plant, even in the wild, it is equally insistent, for every part of it, leaf, stem, even the dry seed head in autumn, is rich with an aroma that is mint and spice and lemon, all intermingled. Touch a leaf and it perfumes your whole hand. Brush a plant in passing and your clothes are fragrant for hours. Compared to its assertive essence, the fragrances of wild roses and honeysuckle are mere wafts of fugitive sweetness.

There are other bergamots, pink flowered and magenta, but none with the brash beauty or the pervasive fragrance of bee balm. It is the scarlet tanager of the wildflowers, its song transmuted into bold, unequivocal perfume.

Independence

July 4

Even without a national holiday, the first week in July would be a festival of independence in any year, if there only was time to be festive. But out where independence really begins, on the land, this is a very busy time. Between the demands of the season and the imperatives of the weather, the countryman is too busy now growing and harvesting the fundamentals of independence to do much celebrating.

Maybe July's long, hot days weren't actually designed

to give a man time and opportunity to prepare for a plentiful tomorrow, but that is the way it works out. There is an abundance on the land, and there is a beauty and a luxuriance of growth both wild and tame, that makes arguments about ideologies seem absurd. Basic to all is the urgency of the seed to grow, the need of the stem to bud and blossom and make seed again. And there is independence, root, branch, and ripened fruit, which is a way of life as well as a way of thinking.

So here is July, busy as the summer bees in roadside clover, growing the substance of independence in every field and meadow and woodland, and inviting man to cooperate. Not to sit down and bask, but to work and sweat and make the most of it before it turns sere with frosty autumn; to do the harvesting and prepare for tomorrow and next year and the years to come. It looks so easy now, this July independence, and it is so hard to hold, come winter. But without it we have only the husks, the dry and tasteless husks, when we need the food of freedom.

Summer in Blossom *July 5*

By the first week in July the day lilies at the roadside and the brown-eyed Susans in the old pastures splash the countryside with van Gogh orange. The hot, tropical shades leave no doubt about the season. Tawny hawkweed might have been imported from a Mexican landscape, and even its rather pale yellow cousin, Canada hawkweed, has a hot-climate look about it.

The elderberry bushes are frothed with white blossoms, to be sure, and the daisies that still claim their share of the waste places are white and gold, a cool combination against the lush green of trees. But that sun-color, that warm weather yellow, is everywhere. The evening primroses spread their petals in late afternoon, to lure the moths. Butter-and-eggs, the wild snapdragon, combines the yellow and orange in blooms that lure the bumblebees. Jewelweed, both the pale yellow and the red-spotted, lifts its succulent stem and opens its pouched flowers for bumblebees and hummingbirds. Moth mullein, the common giant mullein, Saint-John's-wort, golden ragwort, and half a dozen cinquefoils make the back roads and the old meadows sparkle with their variety of hot-sun yellows.

And now the sunflowers, big and little, tick-seed and plain, tuber-rooted and everyday, come to bloom, the apotheosis of that yellow response to July, that mid-spectrum color which is like the midday sun itself, summer come to full flower.

The Hordes *July 6*

They hum, they buzz, they flit and flutter and creep and crawl, and the warmer the day the more active they are. Insects, the vast and varied world of insect life, revel in summer. The bumblebee's broods of sterile daughters haunt the clover and the hidden nectaries of the garden. The honey bees, gone wild and hived in a hollow maple, work themselves to death in six hot midsummer weeks. The wasp builds her mud nest or her paper apartment house and the hotter the day the more fretful her temper and activity. The ants dig, harvest, stow, enslave, march, make war, and tend their hatchlings beside the paths where we walk unseeing.

There are almost 90,000 species of insects in North America and 25,000 of them are beetles. Beetles are everywhere, clicking, creeping, gnawing, pillaging, scavenging, even lighting the night; dragonflies, little changed in 300 million years, clatter in flight, stare you down, and live on still smaller insects. The ubiquitous flies and the insatiable mosquitoes thrive everywhere in heat and humidity. Butterflies spangle the hot afternoon and big, dusky moths haunt the garden in the cool of the evening.

The myriad insects outnumber mankind a billionfold and summer is not only their heyday but, for most of them, their whole span of life. Man fights them for his mastery of the earth, and they outbreed all his efforts. Only the cold of hard frost can quiet them, and even then they leave egg and pupae as their legacy to another summer.

Ox's Eye and Farmer's Curse *July 7*

Summer wouldn't be summer without daisies, though the common field daisy, known to almost every man, woman, and child, is sometimes called Farmer's Curse. Ask any farmer and he'll tell you why. Daisies beautify rural roadsides, but they invade meadows, pastures, and all kinds of cultivated fields. Most farmers smile at picnicking youngsters who gather handfuls of daisies, but they gasp in utter bafflement at summer visitors who actually pick them to arrange in vases.

The daisy is kin to the chrysanthemum. The blossom's golden center consists of a mass of botanically perfect miniature blossoms, each complete with stamens and a pistil. The white petals actually are rays, each one the single petal of a miniature pistillate flower. When the petals wither and the flower head ripens it produces a whole packet of seeds. These seeds have vigorous vitality. Hence the persistence of the daisy.

The name comes from "day's eye" and refers to the yellow center of the flower, which in folklore represented the sun. Sometimes the common field daisy is called the oxeye daisy. There is no real reason for this, since most oxen's eyes are brown, not yellow. But the name daisy is loosely used for black-eyed Susans and even for asters, by some, so the naming doesn't too much matter.

Daisies grow in vacant lots and even in the city's concrete gutters, if they can find a crack. They are tough as urchins, persistent as beggars. And to the unbiased eye they are beautiful, even in a meadow. Unless you happen to be a farmer.

The Succulent Bean

July 8

The bean is a strange vegetable. It provides food for man and beast and, like all members of the legume family, it enriches the soil in which it grows. It is edible both green and dried. Just now it comes to the table in green form, the snap bean fresh from the garden. Properly cooked and buttered, it is one of the most satisfying of all early garden yield. Later it will be a challenge to every gardener alive—every neighbor, every weekender, every casual visitor, will be begged to take beans, just to be rid of them. But that's for later. Just now it is a treasure and a gustatory delight.

The bean is such a simple thing to grow, and it can be such a trial to the gardener! It sprouts easily—unless cold, wet weather attends the planting. It grows quickly—unless cutworms attack. Or unless rabbits or woodchucks find it. Or unless any of a dozen voracious beetles descend. Or unless mildew attacks. It blossoms profusely, and the blossoms turn into pods overnight—unless blight sets in on a damp, chill day. It thrives with pampering, with weeding, with hoeing. Yet on occasion a stray bean will grow like mad despite total neglect in the midst of a weed patch. The bean is unpredictable. But satisfying.

The bean has been grown since prehistoric times. Indians grew it here long before the white man came. It probably will be grown as long as man grows anything. But if it grows another ten thousand years, it will never taste better than it does right now, young and green and tender.

It won't taste half as good in August. And in October it will be just another shelled bean. But right now—well, right now the bean is a wonderful achievement.

Hot-Season Color

July 9

Strong color now catches the eye at the country roadside and along the meadow margins, colors that we think of as hot-country hues, tropical in their insistent vigor. The deep orange-yellow of the black-eyed Susans, the even stronger red-orange of tawny hawkweed, demand attention, and the day lilies with shades that run from russet red through vivid yellow catch the eye and hold it.

They are our height-of-summer colors, matching the green lushness of field and woodland. It almost seems that the wildflowers are trying to match the oriole, the goldfinch, and the scarlet tanager for attention. They make the softer colors of May and early June seem pallid by comparison, though perhaps we forget how sun-hot could be a massed show of dandelions in full bloom. But most of spring's colors were young, the flowers of a new season still gathering strength. These are an expression of summer at its prime, fiery with sunlight, vicious with lightning, surging toward maturity. These are the colors of bold July swaggering toward August.

There are other colors, less insistent, to be sure. Milkweed's too-fragrant pink-and-purple bloom is here, and evening primrose shows a delicate yellow; wild chicory is warm blue, and Queen Anne's lace is a white cloud at the roadside. But it is those hot colors, those touched with flaming orange, that really mark the season. They tell us, whether we listen or not, that our July was born in the hot countries and still has their colorful mark on it.

Jewelweed

July 10

Give it half a chance and jewelweed will take over almost any damp, woodsy spot. Its tall, bright green stems and leaves, almost translucent in the sunlight, make a small jungle; but walk through it and you leave a clear path, for those stems have all the brittle frailty of any succulent plant. Break them and they ooze a juice which country boys declare is a cure for poison ivy.

Seen in the morning sunlight, a patch of jewelweed seems to gleam with orange-yellow spangles. Look more closely and you find the flowers that give the plant its common name. Strange flowers with a deep saclike base and the petals joined in a bell-shaped form with divided lobes, the whole a rich golden yellow, almost a bronze, and speckled as a robin's egg, the speckles a browning red. The flowers are small and fragile, and they hang from slender stems. Bees seek them out, and now and then a hummingbird comes to explore their depths.

Touch-me-not, the plant is sometimes called, because when the flowers are gone and the seed pods ripen, some inner tension is established which pops those seeds as from a miniature catapult if any passerby should brush against them. Thus does the jewelweed spread so swiftly—it hurls its seeds in all directions, profligate and persistent. Botanically the plant belongs to the family called *Balsaminaceae*, and it is close kin to the cultivated flower known as balsam or, erroneously, lady's slipper, which adds its fragrance and varicolored beauty to the old-fashioned garden. But jewelweed is no cutting flower, even for those who would bring the wildlings indoors. It is largely foliage anyway. Its jewels are small and are best seen in the damp woodland by those who are willing to go there before the morning dew has dried.

The Beetles *July 11*

July is the month of the beetles. You see and hear them everywhere, fireflies in the dusk, whirligigs on tepid ponds, rose beetles, bean beetles, squash beetles, potato bugs, ladybugs, and literally thousands of others in park and garden. At the latest count there were 275,000 known species in the world, more than 27,000 in the United States; and the numbers rise each year as new species are identified.

Most beetles—the firefly is a notable exception—are hard-shelled, bumbling insects with inadequate wings, active legs, big appetites, and aggressive natures. Generally considered an economic nuisance, they still have their purpose in the world's ecology. Without them many birds would starve, forest litter would clutter the woodland, carrion would taint the air.

Some species eat dead wood, some destroy weeds, some eat or bury dead birds and small animals. Some help keep other insects in check; ladybug beetles are the chief scourge of the incredibly fecund aphids. Eons ago the beetles made adaptations whereby one species or another lives and thrives in almost every niche in nature. Thus they persist, in a way justifying the ancient Egyptian belief that the scarab beetles represented immortality.

You hear them now, the larval grubs now grown to chitin-armored maturity, making a day-long undertone of summer sound, clicking, rustling, rattling, bumbling in flight. They scurry at the grass roots, gnaw at the tree leaves, eat the blossoms, full of midsummer energy, the countless, ubiquitous beetles that possess July.

Rain

July 12

We fret over a rainy day, resent a rainy weekend or vacation. Rain makes us miserable. Rain is wet. We prefer sunshine, for a rainy day is dull and damp and uncomfortable.

Yet without rain we perish, not only the countryman whose crops must have it but the urbanite as well, for rain supplies all the clean, fresh water there is on earth. Water covers seventy percent of this planet's surface, but the oceans are salt and briny. Mother of life, the sea must be distilled before we can drink it, and rain is the product of that distillation. The sun draws water vapor from the ocean, clouds of that vapor cool and freshen the air and temper the sun's own heat, and from them comes the sweet source of all the flowing water we know. Sweet water, in the form of rain or snow or fog or dew or mist—the indispensable moisture of the living leaf, the living tissue, the fluid of our own flesh and blood.

We talk of water shortages, yet water is one of the enduring constants of our environment. Man, not water, is the variable; and man himself has created the growing scarcity of clean water by his careless poisoning and pollution.

Yet, rain is water; rain is wet. But, like it or not, a rainy day is a blessing to the earth and everything that lives upon it.

Bouncing Bet

July 13

The pink family doesn't really possess the midsummer roadside, but its members make a showing that can't be overlooked. They range from the ubiquitous chickweed to the bold campions, from the dainty crimson maiden pinks to the flaunting banks of bouncing Bet that now are like pink and white drifts of bloom.

Bouncing Bet came originally from Europe, where it was known as soapwort and bruisewort. My Lady's Washbowl. It was planted in early gardens in part for its flowers, which have the sharp fragrance of the garden's spice pinks, and in part for its roots. Those roots have a soapy element, which gave the plant its Latin name, *Saponaria,* and were used by pioneer women for washing their hair. And an infusion from its roots and stems was believed to ease the pain of bruises. It was a useful plant to have at hand.

But it escaped from the garden to the roadside, and there it is today, hardy friend of bee and butterfly, no longer valued as an herb but still often picked for country bouquets. On a damp morning a bank of bouncing Bet can perfume a whole roadside, and its generosity of bloom is unfailing. The Bet who gave the flower her name is long forgotten, but the simple beauty and the tang of its fragrance make her memorable though anonymous. She probably wore these blossoms in her well-washed hair.

The Pause *July 14*

If time ever stands still, even for an hour, it is on a mid-July day along a rural road with a leisurely stream on one side and fields and a wooded hillside on the other. It is early afternoon and the air is warm and quiet, even among the top leaves of the roadside trees. The sky is clean and clear except for a few huge white cumulus clouds that make cool shade patterns as they slowly drift across the sun.

The loudest sound is the drone of a half-sated bumblebee lazily going from a fat head of red clover to explore the heavy sweetness of a milkweed's lavender blossoms. Over the stream's slow current is the metallic shimmer of two dragonflies in drifting flight. A painted turtle drowses on a half-submerged log like a black knot edged in scarlet, the colors matching those in the raspberries on the nearby bank, one ripe black berry surrounded by unripe red ones.

Black-eyed Susans outshine the roadside daisies, and the first few heads of Queen Anne's lace make flat-topped clusters of yarrow look pewter-gray. A song sparrow sings, pausing between phrases but still sounding out of season. A catbird somewhere in the trees mimics two phrases of the sparrow's song.

Out in the stream a fish surfaces, slaps the water, and the circling ripples spread, gleaming in the sunlight, ripples like time itself.

The Dragonflies *July 15*

We libel their kind by calling them dragonflies, and we compound the libel with myths and old wives' tales, describing them as horse-stingers, devil's darning needles, snake feeders, and snake doctors. No dragonfly ever stung a horse, sewed up small boys' ears, or fed or ministered to any snake. They are not only harmless to mankind; they are among our most helpful insects, feeding almost entirely on gnats, flies, and mosquitoes.

They are abroad now, over ponds and streams, coursing meadows and rural roadsides, their strangely metallic-looking wings shimmering in the hot summer sunlight. They are eternally busy, eternally curious, and their big compound eyes—perhaps the most efficient eyes in the whole insect world—make them look grimly hostile. Something about them speaks of remote times when there were dragons, even flying dragons, of millennia past when the whole teeming life of this earth included none of our own kind.

We watch them, and perhaps we sense those countless ages on those metallic wings today as they hover and wheel in swift flight. And they watch us, we know not why. But we are uneasy, and we recall the myths even as we watch in wonder while they seine the air. We named them dragons because we remember, in the race memory, a time of dragons. But we watch them warily because, knowing so much of the past, their kind may know something of the future, too.

Summer's Song

July 16

By midsummer the songbirds are less jubilant, though they still join in a dawn chorus; and at dusk the wood thrush and the brown thrasher remind us that July itself is a song. But the enduring themes are so quietly sung that we need all our senses to know them.

Growth and fruiting and change are the insistent melodies now, and all are of more than aural meaning. Growth is everywhere, in the roadside weed patch, the grassy meadow, the brushy margin, and the woodland itself. Twig and stem have their own rhythms, their own subtle melodies. So does fruiting, the opening of the bud, the spread of petal, the insistence of pollen, the ripening of the fertile seed which is the plant's particular song of endless tomorrows. Silent songs of growth and fruiting, yet fundamental and as true to rhythm as was the ecstatic song of the oriole in June.

Change is less obvious, since it is essentially a song of time, and time flows in a steady, silent stream. But there is the song of change in every sunrise, every noontime, every dusk that creeps down from the hills. It is a song sung by light striking through green leaves, by cool shadows on the grass, by moonlight on dark water, by starlight in the night. The endless song of change.

The rhythms endure and the days pass, each hour another note in the eternal song. The solstice is now three weeks past and already the quiet, fundamental songs have a few notes of August's theme, and even September's. Looking, listening, sensing, we know that this is summer's song; but we also know that no summer's song lasts forever.

Milkweed

July 17

Rural roadsides now are fragrant with summer essences ranging from the sunny sweetness of curing, new-cut hay to the sharp tang of wild mint crushed underfoot. But most persistent of all, and the one often mistaken by the passer-by for the smell of clover, is the heavy perfume of common milkweed, which can sweeten a whole hillside. Trace it to its source, the clusters of brownish-lavender blossoms that later will produce those big silvery-green pods, and milkweed fragrance is like a blend of honeysuckle and tuberose, both at their most intense.

The milkweeds have a whole volume of legend and lore in their background. The botanical name, *Asclepias,* honors the legendary god of healing, who was a pupil of Charon, the centaur. Aesculapius the healer became so skillful he could revive the dead, at which point Zeus became jealous of his power and killed him. The legends fail to say whether Aesculapius used milkweed in his potions, but the herb healers of more recent times certainly did. The orange-flowered milkweed, commonly called butterfly weed, is also known as pleurisy root and had a highly respected place in the old herbals.

Milkweed has no commercial importance. Its latex-like juice doesn't make good rubber and its silky floss can't be spun. But there isn't another roadside plant that can compete with it in fragrance.

Midsummer *July 18*

Dusk comes a few minutes earlier now, and sunrise a few minutes later, than they did a month ago. Summer divides the twenty-four-hour day to its own dimensions, and off there in the distance, a few miles away, lies autumn. Change, the eternal constant, subtly shapes days.

You sense the change in the way the shadows fall. The pool of shade beneath a big maple moves slightly back from its farthest reach to the north. The beam of sunlight slanting through a north window in the morning now has narrowed. And at the roadside are clouds of Queen Anne's lace. Daisies begin to fade. Wild raspberries ripen. On the oak trees young acorns are in plain sight.

Field corn, beyond the suburbs, begins to tassle out and the tang of corn pollen hangs in the air of a hot afternoon. Garden tomatoes fatten, still grass-green, toward August ripeness. Last spring's early mildness brings summer squash by the bushel to roadside markets and baby beets to the farmer's table.

You hear the change in the birdcalls, fewer songs of ecstasy, more parental alarms and scoldings. The wood thrush is heard in the evening, and the dove and the whippoorwill. The insects drone, afternoon and night, proclaiming life even though theirs is a one-season lifetime. Bees are busier. Wasps are more spiteful. Harvest flies buzz and shrill in the heat of midafternoon. Dragonflies seem to hurry on rattling wings.

It is midsummer and the beat of time is like the throb of a healthy heart, strong, steady, and reassuring.

The Wings of Summer

July 19

This is the season of swift, fragile wings, the oldest means of flight on earth. They flutter and buzz, they click and rattle, as the insects go about their brief span of life. According to fossil evidence these wings, some thin as tissue, some tough as horn, have been here 250 million years, 100 million years longer than the feathered wings of the birds.

They are everywhere we look, on the city street, in the rural meadow, at the seashore and on the mountaintop, far toward the poles and deep in the tropics. The dragonfly's glittering wings flash in the sunlight over pond and stream. The bright butterfly's wings hover among the roadside weeds. The dusty wings of the night moths haunt the garden and the lighted window. The midges dance on the long rays of evening light, and the flying gleam of the firefly is borne on wings softer than the thinnest silk. Fly-buzz, bee-hum, mosquito-whine, all are the sound of thrumming wings.

Some are incredibly swift wings. The bee and the housefly beat their wings 200 times or more per second. The mosquito's wings make 600 strokes per second, and some midges beat their wings almost twice that fast. Yet there are leisurely wings, too. The big butterflies beat their wings only 10 or 20 times per second and the dragonflies about twice that number.

How these wings evolved we still do not know. But here they are, glinting, shimmering, making the air tremble and pulsate with life. Wings, incredible and beyond number, the very wings of summer.

Elderberries

July 20

The elderberry bushes are in bloom, and seeing them from the roadside one thinks that they deserve a better fate than to be regarded as weeds and grubbed out. Many a cherished lawn shrub isn't much prettier than an elderberry bush in full bloom.

Time was when the elderberry was respected. The white flower head which now covers the bush and is a lure for bees by the hundred matures into a lush panicle of purplish-black berries. Those berries are full of sweet juice, so sweet it refuses to turn into jelly without the help of apples or some other pectin-rich components. But that juice, when properly handled, makes elderberry wine. There was a time when most rural cellars included at least a jug and often a keg of elderberry wine. Elderberry wine had certain indisputable medicinal qualities, as well as a kick and a tongue-tantalizing flavor. It was surprising how many countrymen felt a bit puny as long as the elderberry wine lasted, puny enough to need a glass of it every day. But where can you find real, homemade elderberry wine today, no matter how puny you feel?

Elderberries also made many a tasty pie in country kitchens. In upstate New York the elderberry pie was so much esteemed that the berries were gathered and dried at the height of the season for pie-making during the winter. But who today dries elderberries, and who but those with long memories even makes fresh elderberry pies?

So today the elderberry bushes bloom, and they bow with their load of fruit, and the birds flock to them with delight. And all the old pleasure that sprang from those humble bushes in the past is little more than a memory. But while they bloom they are a delight to the eye. And, as we say, the bees love them.

Summer Songster

July 21

Now, when most of the other birds have almost stopped singing, the house wren sounds twice as loud as he did a month ago. Though one of the smallest of all our dooryard birds, even smaller than a chickadee, the wren's outstanding energy gushes, bubbles, and sputters out of him both in song and action. Even when he is building needless nests or being a truculent spitfire, he pauses to sing. He will fight at the flick of a feather, with his mate if no enemy is in sight.

Exemplary folktales have long surrounded the house wrens. Except when they emphasize domestic harmony, most of them are true. Mrs. Wren, known as Jenny in most of the folklore, is a good homemaker and mother, she is neat and tidy, she is dressed demurely, and she seems properly modest. But her home life often is turbulent, full of noisy squabbles with her temperamental mate who is a show-off and has decidedly fickle tendencies.

Perhaps it was the need for an audience that drew the wrens out of the woods and into the dooryards long ago. They like the company of people. And most people like wrens. Otherwise they wouldn't put up wren houses to welcome them back each spring or listen with so much pleasure to their effervescent song on hot July days.

Chicory

July 22

Chicory is in blossom at the roadsides and in neglected fields, one of the few wildlings of the season that have a color to match the July sky. Chicory bloom is one of the warmest blues on the rural landscape, and the individual flowers are big as silver dollars, big as the field daisies that always seem to be near neighbors. In fact, some call it the blue daisy. Others know it as blue sailors, or succory, or coffee-weed.

Like so many other roadside weeds, chicory is an immigrant. But it came from Europe as a cultivated plant, not as an unwanted invader. Abroad it is grown for its flowers, for its foliage, and for its roots. Young, the leaves are salad fare; and with reason, for it is close kin to the endive of our own gardens. Older, the leaves and stems make satisfactory forage for cattle and are cut for hay in Europe. The dried roots are used, particularly in France, as a substitute or adulterant for coffee. Where the plant came from originally is not known. Perhaps from Egypt, or maybe from Arabia.

But here it is now, tall, sparse-leafed, deep-rooted, and beautiful with those big blue flowers. It consorts with thistles. It prefers a sandy, lime-rich soil. It endures drought, seems to thrive in the July heat. It is bright as a summer morning, generous as July itself. But only on sunny days. On gray days or rainy days the blossoms refuse to open. They wait for sunshine and a clear sky, a blue sky to match their own eye-catching color.

Midsummer

July 23

Midsummer is the power and the glory of the earth. Anyone can live with summer; you don't have to wall yourself in or shield yourself from it. You are a partner, of sorts, in summer's achievements, whether you are a countryman with a meadow and a cornfield or a suburbanite with a lawn and a flower bed. But if you become too arrogant, forgetting that you are a junior partner, a thunderstorm may box your ears or a tornado may make you think twice about human omnipotence.

Roadsides are white with daisies, orange-splashed with

black-eyed Susans. Queen Anne's lace begins to show its frothy furbelows. Oaks are committed to acorns and the nuts on hickory, walnut, and hazel bush are established, deliberately maturing toward autumn and ripeness.

Already a month past the summer solstice, the sun, as we see it, has begun edging south and daylight has lessened by half an hour. The inclination is toward autumn, though we are reluctant to admit it. Now, midsummer, is winter's dream of perfection; it is April's hopes and May's promises come true; it is the richness and the ripeness of the earth again made manifest. And man participates, if he will, not as proprietor but as a participant in life itself.

The Fiddlers *July 24*

The long-legged, rasp-winged insects now come into their own and we won't hear the last of them until hard frost arrives. They are the leaping fiddlers, the grasshoppers, the crickets, and the katydids.

Grasshoppers are spoken of in the Bible as "locusts," and their hordes have contributed in many lands, including our own West, to the long history of insect devastation and human famine. Walk through any meadow, or along any weedy roadside, and you will see them leaping ahead of you, hear the rasping rattle of their harsh wings in brief flight. But they do little real fiddling. The fiddlers now are the crickets.

Listen on any hot afternoon or warm evening, particularly in the country, and you will hear the crickets even though you seldom see them. In the afternoon you will hear the black field crickets chirping, as we say, and often into the warm evening. But in the evening, from dusk on through the warm night, the more insistent sound will be the trilling of the pale green tree crickets. Individually the tree cricket's trill is not so loud, but because all those in the neighborhood synchronize their trills the sound can be as insistent as were the calls of the spring peepers back in April.

The loudest fiddlers of all are the katydids, which look like green, hunchbacked grasshoppers. Night after night they rasp wing on wing and make that monotonous call, shrill and seemingly endless. But the katydids won't be heard for another two weeks or so. Meanwhile the crickets possess late July, chirping and trilling the warm hours away as though summer endured forever.

Beyond the Fact

July 25

Relentless, inquiring man has factual answers to a multitude of matters, but there are countless others that seem, especially on a summer morning, to transcend cold fact and invite the warmth of understanding. Yet how can their meaning, which is something felt and sensed, be translated into the language of our common speech?

We see the mist rising from a lake or a river, like incense to the creation of a new day. We hear the throb of a wood thrush's song in the distance. We see the glint of first sunlight on a lawn still wet with dew, the amazing whiteness of a daisy petal, and the sharp orange contrast of a tawny hawkweed bloom. We smell the incredible sweetness of a milkweed's brownish-lavender blossom tuft. We hear the crisp, secret rustle of a whispering breeze in a cornfield and catch one swift glimpse of a scarlet tanager against the clean, clear blue of the sky.

We see the way a bindweed's twining stem climbs and the way its blossom twists out of its bud and becomes a white trumpet. We listen to the scolding of a mother robin and the remote, sad call of a mourning dove. We smell a hay field, watch a barn swallow in flight, hear a bumblebee humming in search of breakfast. We feel the sting of a nettle on an unwary hand reaching to pick a few seedy, tang-sweet blackcap berries. We sense the day, the pungent, busy morning world that needs no human hand to shape it. And we know that factual answers are not enough.

The Untamed

July 26

Farm crops and garden plants may suffer from prolonged drought, but weeds and wildflowers survive and even flourish. Just now the bright blue of wild chicory and the lightly flushed white bloom of bouncing Bet mark the roadsides. Queen Anne's lace lifts its fluffy white heads at the pasture's edge. Bindweed, the wild morning glory, uncurls its trumpets in the weedy margin. Mullein and evening primrose, fleabane and daisy, milkweed and vervain, all bloom as usual.

All of them have a wild vitality, a kind of plant patience and persistence, that has brought their kind through countless weather cycles. Most of them are profligate with seed. A single milkweed pod will spill 200 winged seeds to the wind. One purslane plant, cousin of the garden portulaca, scatters 200,000 seeds in a summer; and such a minor flowering plant as the hedge mustard ripens twice that many. Most of the wild seeds have remarkable vitality. Those of some species can lie dormant, awaiting a favorable season, thirty or forty years.

It is their nature, all of them, to grow and multiply when the season favors. They are a part of the green urgency of this earth, one of the strongest forces we know. Long ago they learned to live with passing vicissitudes of time and weather. Thus they survive, unpampered and asking no quarter, some of them beautiful, all of them tough, insistent, and full of untamed hardihood.

The Byway *July 27*

There was a time when it led from farm to village, not directly but passing other farms along the way. It wandered, following the valleys, avoiding the hills, because teamsters chose the longer, easier way for their draft animals—first oxen and later horses. It once crossed the brook at a shallow ford, later on a wooden bridge. It was a dirt road, grass-grown between the wagon tracks and with overhanging trees, and later it was graveled in the boggy places.

But still it was a narrow, winding back road with curves that demanded caution and old trees that were a hazard to careless drivers. But partridges nested nearby and orioles hung their pouch-nests in elms that overhung the brook. Deer came down to feed and drink at dusk. Foxes taught their kits to hunt mice in the roadside tangle.

The new highway, ruler-straight, cutting through hills and striding across valleys, took its traffic. It became a byway whose upkeep was debated in town meeting every year. But some insisted that we need the byways too, so it was not abandoned. And there it is today, like other byways here and there, a place to know and visit when one would ease the tensions and the tempo. To know that life is being as well as going, that there are times when the byways are more important than the highways of this world.

Queen of the Night *July 28*

No matter what they bring back from the moon, the men who arrive there today will not alter the moonlight that has fascinated man and warmed his dreams since he first took shelter in a cave. It is still Queen of the Night, out there in the darkness. It is still the goddess that a dozen civilizations have named to their pantheons—Diana, Phoebe, Cynthia, Artemis, Hecate, Selene, Luna, Astarte. No rocket or module or chemical formula or equation can destroy it.

There it is, a gleaming, golden crescent in the western sky; then through its phase of waxing till it rises in the east at sundown, a great coppery disk that becomes the silvery full-moon sentinel of the whole night; then waning, a wasted half-moon high in the sky at dawn, a last-quarter crescent low in the east, and gone again in that dark phase which ends with a new moon in the west again.

Long before he calculated the earth's seasonal relationship to the sun, man based his calendar on the moon's predictable phases. We still recognize the Harvest Moon and the Hunter's Moon. For generations, farmers and gardeners planted and reaped by the moon's phases, believing that it influenced growth and yield. Now we know that the moon is responsible not only for the ocean's tides but for an earth tide that also ebbs and flows.

June moon, October moon, January moon, March moon—moon of visions and poems, of love and dreams, of tides and the throbbing pulse—still in its orbit, unchanged through the eons, predictable as today's sunset.

The Everlasting Hills *July 29*

Since time immemorial the hilltops have been special places. The old gods dwelt there, and only those who were favored by the gods could even visit their sacred precincts. Rain and lightning came down from the hills. Eagles nested there. Men lived in the valleys and looked up unto the hills in awe.

Later, much later, it was said that only the natives of any land were familiar with the hilltops. Outlanders stayed in the valleys where the old roads ran and where the towns and villages had grown up close beside the watercourses. It took a long time to learn that without hills there would be no valleys, that for every valley there were two hills and beyond those hills were other valleys.

But the hills still stood, stubborn and remote, and those who climbed them learned what the hillmen had always known—that gods still dwelt there, gods of trees and rocks and clean, sweet air. They learned that the blue bowl of sky was vastly bigger from a hilltop and that the earth itself was far wider than any valley they had ever known.

We are not a hill people. Our towns and cities are still centered in the valleys, and the gods who rule our lives are the gods of statistics and machines. But when we would find peace and relaxation we turn to the hills, the green and everlasting hills where the old gods are still remembered.

Dog Days

July 30

Back in Roman times the Dog Days ran from early July till the second week in August. That was a direful season when ponds stagnated, snakes were blind, and dogs went mad. But the time was called the Dog Days because of the Dog Star, Canicula, not the cur dogs in the streets. The stargazers, searching for the cause of seasonal troubles, found that Canicula was at that time in conjunction with the sun. There was nothing they could do about the movement of the stars, so they simply said Canicula was to blame and urged the people to make sacrifices to the star and watch out for dogs and snakes.

The gradual movement of the stars has somewhat shifted the dates of Canicula's conjunction, and now the Dog Days come in late July and August. We now know that pollution, not stagnation, makes water poisonous, we know the truth about rabies and mad dogs, and country folk, at least, know that snakes often shed their skins about now and are briefly blind and sometimes truculent during the molt. Dog Days have nothing to do with these things except in the coincidence of timing.

And Dog Days beliefs do persist. Ponds grow stagnant and scummy, and we are told that the water is "unhealthy" if not actually poisonous. Mosquitoes are supposed to be more bloodthirsty now, and to leave bigger welts. Poison ivy thrives. Baneberries ripen, red and juicy—and poisonous. Snakes are short of temper. Blame the Dog Star, if you wish, but don't blame the dogs. They don't like Dog Days either.

The Chromatic Harvest *July 31*

As summer advances the colors change, slowly, subtly, but unmistakably. Spring is a time of new greens, pale greens of all degrees that warm and deepen week by week, and for the most part of whites and pinks and thin yellows in the blossoms. Early summer strengthens the spectrum with blue-green in the treetops, stronger yellow in the flowers, occasional orange and light blue, and here and there a touch of red. But by July's end the strong colors have begun to appear, sign of the season's chromatic harvest.

Wild chicory has already forecast the change with its rich blue blossoms. Now comes the great lobelia with another blue entirely, and along the damp margins the blue vervain comes to bloom, not blue at all but deep purple. Thistles top their thorny selves wth reddish-purple cockades. Rank-smelling burdock is arrayed in warm magenta. Joe-pye weed is so full of urgency that its upper leaves are wind-stained before the red-magenta flowers appear, and ironweed is generously tufted with madder-purple blossoms.

Soon the country roadside will gleam with goldenrod,

late summer's answer to June's buttercups. Then will come the New England asters, royal purple and a fitting climax to the summer's color. Gentians will come, a treasured accent; but it is the purple and gold that will dominate, the whole season's richness come to magnificent completion.

August

STURGEON MOON

Probably sturgeon, too, were fat and prime about now, and right to catch and dry for winter.

August

August 1

August comes with hot days, warm nights, a brassy sun, and something in the air, perhaps the season itself, that begins to rust the high-hung leaves of the elms. The listless leaves of the maples have a dusty look and the sycamores and basswoods are hung with seedy fruits. Sumac holds its candle-flame clusters, red as the sumac leaves will be in September.

First goldenrod comes to bloom along the roadsides, and early asters appear, lost in the clouds of Queen Anne's lace. In damp places the purple vervain leads the parade of darker color that already begins to show in the first flower heads of joe-pye weed. Thistles flaunt their thorny tufts of deep lavender, and tick trefoil is in weedy bloom, its small lilac flowers preparing stick-tight pods. Bur marigolds, masquerading as roadside sunflowers, come to blossom, and great lobelia lifts its blue spikes above the podding milkweeds.

Brooks languish in their stony beds. Only the grandfather frogs groan and rumble in the dusk. The whippoorwills are less insistent, and now a barred owl is heard questioning the night. The big, dark moths haunt the flower garden's deep-throated flowers, gleaning nectar the August-lazy bumblebees overlooked. The night still twinkles with fireflies but the day's heat lingers and the air has a dusty

August scent, the smell of languid summer. And overhead the warm air touches the treetops, rustles the rustling leaves in the broad-topped elms.

Feast of the Green Corn *August 2*

Indians called it the Moon of the Green Corn and it was a time of feasting from the fields. We know it as the eighth month and name it for a Roman emperor who never even dreamed of roasting-ears; but we, too, feast from the fields when sweet corn comes to market and table.

The early European explorers found corn—maize, to give it its native name—being grown almost everywhere from Nova Scotia to Florida, from Minnesota to Texas, even in the desert canyons of the Southwest. The Indians of New England were famous for their corn and grew at least four varieties, one for roasting-ears, or green corn, one for succotash, one for meal, and one to parch and pop. Corn festivals were common. Corn pollen was holy. Corn meal was a symbol of plenty and favor from the gods. We abandoned the ritual but preserved and improved the corn, made it our major grain crop.

Field corn slowly ripens, but sweet corn's succulent ears now come to table and plate, and we still indulge in the feast if not the festival. And, when we think about it, we thank the Indians. The corn was theirs in the beginning; we came late to the feast. But, thank all the gods, we knew a good thing when we saw it. Sweet corn!

Serenity

August 3

Out where time sets its own pace, a kind of sweet serenity now possesses the land. The early rush for a place in the sun is over. The trend now is toward maturity. Grapes fatten on the vine. Early apples begin to blush. Wild blackberries ripen.

The frantic frog chorus that was so loud a little while ago has relaxed to the slow rumble of the frog grandfathers whose voices echo in the night. On ponds and quiet backwaters appear large patches of green algae. Cattails lift green bayonetted ranks from the mucky margins. Dragonflies in the hot afternoon, swallows in the cool of evening, seine the air for mosquitoes.

The heat of midday throbs with the cicada's shrill drone, one of the drowsiest of all summer sounds. When the cicadas rasp you know the last of the insect hordes is out of egg and pupa and moving toward that stage again. Beetles swarm in the grass. Grasshoppers rattle into the air ahead as you walk the pasture path. Green hornworms gnaw at the tomatoes, strange creatures that will become broad-winged sphinx moths and haunt the flower beds at dusk.

The struggle for life goes on, but the great haste of the green world is past. Even in the insect world a kind of balance is struck. It is as though we were bidden to watch and listen and understand, relax the little worries, know the big ones for what they are, and strike our own balance on serenity.

Goldenrod Surf *August 4*

Goldenrod comes to bloom along rural roadsides with one of the brightest yellows in the floral spectrum. It brightens dusty August even as it brings a reminder that September lies just ahead, though actually it is a late summer flower and is past its prime by the time autumn creeps in. But when the goldenrod flaunts its yellow plumes the asters are not far behind.

Most of the goldenrods are native to America. We have almost a hundred species. England has only one and all Europe only ten. But the Latin name, *solidago,* reaches far back and means to strenghen; it came from the old belief that a tea made from goldenrod leaves was an effective tonic. Goldenrod was a common item in the fragrant stock-in-trade of the old herbalists. The nectar also has its virtues, as the bees well know; late summer honey seldom lacks the tang of goldenrod, and even now the bees are busy at the yellow blossoms.

Pioneers made one of their few bright colors from the goldenrod, a strong and cheerful yellow. On occasion they used the fibers in its stems like hemp, for cordage. But the virtues of the plant are largely forgotten now. It is a roadside weed, an invader of neglected gardens and unkempt meadows. Its graceful sprays and glowing color are commonplace. Folk belief once blamed it for hay fever, but that was disproved years ago, so it lacks even the notoriety of ragweed. It is just the golden surf of late summer, graceful, nectar-laden, and still a tonic, a visual tonic for the jaded eyes of August.

Summer's Maturity

August 5

Call these the Dog Days, if you will, or the doldrums of summer, or the last few weeks of the vacation season. In the country it is the time when the haste of growth has slackened, when maturity has begun. The cornfield has silk-blond ears. The hayfield has its second crop of bales. April and May now lean toward September and October, and meadow and margin are rank and nearing ripeness.

You see it everywhere. Roadside daisies fade. Early asters take their places. Milkweed shows green, young pods. Oak leaves can no longer hide the acorns. Grapes, both wild and tame, have clustered fruit waiting only a few more weeks of sunlight to turn purple. Elderberries are heavy-headed with fruit that will soon be oozing juice and sweetness. Green cones hang heavy and resinous on the pines. Early apples redden.

You hear it, in the more insistent cawing of the crows as they discuss the morning, in the shrill sibilance of the cicadas in the heat of the afternoon. The brook, shrunken in its stony bed, whispers instead of chattering. There is a crisper rustle among the poplars. The elms, almost as silken as the maples a month ago, now make a papery sound in the evening air. The dusk-time twittering of the swallows is ended and the whippoorwill is not so insistent. Robins scold more, sing less.

The ripeness comes. Summer itself matures. Shadows fall in a new dimension and the sun shifts in its course, halfway now from the solstice toward the equinox. August make its own season.

Catfish

August 6

Those who fish for bass and trout loftily ignore the existence of the catfish, and perhaps properly so; he is not for them. But the countryman, the man who knows a channel cat from a mud cat or a bullhead, knows that there's fun as well as food in catfish water. You fish for cats either day or night, but country boys, and men too, like to go in the evening. There's something about a deepening night on a pond or a streambank that gets into a country fisherman's emotions and settles there most pleasantly. For such an evening you take a lantern, a can of worms, a light pole, and, if you are fishing from a boat, a hand line. And take a congenial companion, a quiet conversationalist, not a chatterer.

Once on the water, or beside it, bait the hook generously with worms. Night crawlers, the big fellows that abound in soft earth at the edge of the barnyard, are best of all. Let the bait sink in promising water and keep an attentive finger on the line. If catfish are there, one will find your worm; and if he is of respectable size you will know it, particularly if you fish with light tackle. But you'll soon bring him in. Experienced hands know how to handle him, how to avoid the sharp horns with which he is armed, how to disengage the hook; inexperienced hands soon learn—or decide catfishing is not for them.

Dusk deepens and soon the night is there to enjoy. This is what you came for, as much as the fish themselves—the starlight, the wind in the willows, the night call of a heron, the gleaming wake of a muskrat in the water. But you don't talk much about these things, not to outsiders. You tell them, if they ask, that you had a mess of catfish by midnight, that you skinned them, soaked them in salt water, and had them fried for breakfast. Good? Well, a catfish fisherman enjoys them. That's about all you can say—to an outsider.

Queen Anne's Year

August 7

There are population explosions in the plant world, too, mysterious and often spectacular. This year we have had a Queen Anne's Lace summer. This fluffy, white-flowered member of the carrot family has outdone itself and great fields and banks of it have marked roadside and pastureland. But this doesn't mean that next summer will again be white with it. Some other wildflower may take its place.

A year ago the roads and waste places were brilliant with black-eyed Susans. They made an orange spectacle of the countryside. But this year they fell back to their usual numbers. A few years ago the wild cucumber proliferated, draping trees and bushes everywhere, and its shimmering little white flowers and spiny green pods seemed about to possess the world. Then it, too, returned to normal. And before the wild cucumber year was the summer of the giant mullein. Its towering stalks, velvety gray-green leaves and small yellow blooms crowded the roadsides and meadows. But the mullein, too, was back to normal by the next summer.

We don't know the reasons for such explosions. The weather may have something to do with it. Or there may be something in the air or the soil that fosters one plant for a season and is mysteriously exhausted. Perhaps some natural control is relaxed for a season, or perhaps an unknown combination of circumstances makes one plant's seeds abnormally fertile for a year. All we really know is that such cycles occur, sometimes with spectacular results, and that they almost never are repeated in successive years.

The Katydid's Clock *August 8*

The lights of the fireflies begin to dim, the buzz of the annual cicadas passes its shrill crescendo, the crickets stridulate, and after the crickets we hear the first katydids. You can time the season by the insect sequence. Crickets now are fiddling in the long, hot afternoons, katydids will soon be scratching at the night.

If haphazard folklore hadn't endowed the katydid with the dubious power of prophecy, this noisy green cousin of the grasshopper would be just another insistent sound in the August night. It hatches from an egg like a miniature lentil, spends weeks in a wingless stage, and begins to rasp its wings only when it reaches maturity and seeks a mate. Tradition says first frost will come six weeks after the first katydid is heard.

The katydid no doubt has its own clock and calendar somewhere in its compulsions, but it is not the clock or calendar we know. As for most insects, summer is a lifetime to a katydid—birth and growth and maturity, which ends in old age and death. Summer, to a katydid, is egg to egg again, and the scratching of the katydids means only that the urgency of time is now upon the insect world.

So the katydids will soon begin to stridulate, for summer and time are passing far faster than we know. Insect time ticks madly now, setting the tempo for buzz and scratch and hum that mark not a season but a lifetime.

The Worts *August 9*

Ragwort still shows its rather dusty yellow flowers at the roadside, and soapwort makes a display of pink in the waste places. They are only two of the dozens of worts that thrive and bloom without particular notice or acclaim, since the old-time gatherers of wild herbs have largely vanished. For the worts were among the prime items on the "yarb" list. The very fact that the syllable "wort" is incorporated in the common name is testimony to their past. "Wort" goes back to the Gothic word for root, and to the Anglo-Saxon *wyrt,* meaning "herb."

Any casual list of worts will run to at least 150 plants, running the alphabetic scale from adderwort to yellowwort. Go through such a list and you will find the whole range of human ailments set forth, or at least so much of the range as was known and denominated a hundred years ago. Take cankerwort. Go on down to gutwort, which might have lacked elegance but probably reduced many an ache. Nettlewort may have assuaged the sting of the nettle, and if so it surely was potent. Quinzywort certainly was used as a hot infusion for a very sore throat.

There was even a rupturewort. We still recognize soapwort, mentioned above, which is nothing more than bouncing Bet, a pleasant flower with a root that can substitute for soap. And there is toothwort, there is navelwort, there is sneezewort, there is the generic woundwort, and there is wartwort. The worts, the persistent herbs of the old backcountry apothecary, constitute a kind of folk poetry of human ills and aches, of pain and hope and trust, and inevitably of occasional cure.

August Moon

August 10

There's warmth to an August moon, and the fullness of mid-summer. It isn't a harvest moon that seems about to fill the sky when it first climbs over the horizon; but it is a generous moon that lights the green hills with a kind of ripening-apple glow. There is a mellowness about a moonlit night in August that is a sweet antidote for the cicada heat and the dusty glare of an August afternoon.

An October moon is a moon of maturity and harvest, taking to itself something of the crisp corn yellow of the fields and the deepening crimson of the maple hilltops. But an August moon is a moon of growing plenty still upon the vine. In it you can see the richness of that venerable symbol of fertility, the squash blossom; and the sweet golden kernel of new corn, the pollen fragrance, is in August moonlight. There is a sense of completion, of earth bounty come to its mid-August peak.

Katydids scratch the night, but there is also the silent beat of moth wings. And on a distant hill is the tentative bark of a fox, testing the air for some faint hint of autumn. Summer it still is; but summer passing the peak, reluctantly starting the long, leisurely glide toward frost and November. Early windfalls scent the breeze from the orchard, not quite a cider tang but the promise of cider to come.

And there is the August moon rising in the east, a late midyear moon over a northern hemisphere of midsummer plenty and midsummer peace.

Tam-o'-shantered Acorns *August 11*

Green acorns hang heavy in the oaks, ripening toward October when their tam-o'-shantered nuts will be a harvest for every squirrel in the woods. From that harvest, since a squirrel's industry always surpasses its memory, will sprout tomorrow's oak groves. Thus, oak to nut to squirrel to oak again, have these noble trees spread and persisted.

There are about fifty species of oak native to this continent, and the acorn is the insignia of every one of them. They fall into two big groups, white oaks and black, and within each group is a variety of species. White oaks have light-colored bark and rounded leaf tips. Black oaks have darker bark and sharp-tipped leaves.

The acorns of most of the white oaks are edible and moderately sweet. Indians often used them for food. Most black oak acorns are bitter with tannin.

The old name for acorns, mast, came from an Anglo-Saxon word for meat. They are rich in fat and protein and in the old days swine were herded into oak woods to fatten on them. Both animals and birds still eat them. Green as they are, the squirrels already are sampling them. Another month and they will be feasting; and planting acorns, unwittingly, in every woodland where oaks can find a foothold.

Askutasquash *August 12*

The Indians of the Southwest had an eye for beauty as well as meaning when they chose the squash blossom as a symbol of fertility and plenty. It has a generous grace of form as well as a richness of color ranging from golden orange to sun yellow. In some plants the bloom is a hand's breadth across, so big it is almost rank. Yet the petal texture is tissue thin, easily crushed by a careless touch.

The modern botanist speaks of the family as *Cucurbita* and includes in it the gardener's pumpkin, his muskmelon, his cucumber, and his squashes of various shapes and sizes. The Indian called it *askutasquash* and contributed the syllable that we have applied to one branch of the family. The Indian's *askutasquash* were primarily the tough-shelled pumpkins and the tough-skinned squash that mature late and keep well into the winter. He usually grew them in the same field with his corn; the squash blossom and the corn tassel were twin symbols of fertility in many of the old Indian ceremonies.

Look at a classic Navaho silver necklace and you will

find the squash blossom, symbolized in the white metal, the open petals and, the round fertile ovary beneath, for it is the female flower. In silver it is conventionalized to a fine simplicity; but there it is, the August blossom of the squash vine which crept along the sandy soil and opened its petals to the sun, the rain, and the four-winged bee. Look at the garden today and there it is in live color, still open to sun and rain and bees, *Cucurbita* or *askutasquash* as you will, symbol of the soil's fertile plenty.

The Meteors *August 13*

Meteors will be flashing across the sky tonight and for a couple more nights to come, for now is the time of the Perseids. They are the "shooting stars" whose orbit the earth crosses now. They are called Perseids because they seem to radiate from the constellation called Perseus, which rises in the northeastern sky around midnight. Those who watch meteors regularly say close to seventy light-streaking Perseids an hour can be seen. The casual amateur may easily see twenty or twenty-five in an hour of watching.

There are several showers of meteors at various times of the year, but the Perseids are probably the easiest to watch. Most famous are the Leonids, but they occur in mid-November, often on sharply cold nights when only enthusiasts enjoy star-watching. The Perseids come when the stargazer's chief hazards are mosquitoes.

A meteor is a particle of matter moving rapidly from outer space and heated to incandescence by friction of the earth's atmosphere. Most meteors burn up and vanish. Now and then one survives the burning and strikes the earth. Then it is called a meteorite. A few times, large meteorites have fallen and blasted huge craters, as the well-known one in Arizona and in Siberia. But the annual meteor showers, such as the Perseids, are mere reminders that we are not alone in the universe, that the stars themselves are made of such stone as this earth we live on.

Tomatoes

August 14

Tomatoes ripen, and there is rejoicing among those who know good garden food when they taste it. There is private celebration, which might very well be made public. If it were, perhaps we would be able, once and for all, to scotch that nonsense about tomatoes being long considered poisonous. Every now and then the old tale comes up. Not long ago a radio announcer said they were considered poisonous fifty years ago. Why, fifty years ago tomatoes were sold all over America, canned and succulent the year around! One encyclopedia says they weren't considered edible until "well within the last century." That also is nonsense.

The tomato is a native American. It was grown and eaten by Aztecs and Incas when the white man first arrived. The name comes from the Aztec word *tomatl.* The Spaniards took tomato seeds back to Spain early in the sixteenth century, and the tomato has been grown, eaten, and improved there ever since. Gardeners in England knew and grew the tomato in the seventeenth century. The tomato was grown here in the colonies before 1750, from seed imported from England and Spain.

Thomas Jefferson grew tomatoes. Among his garden records is mention of the "Spanish tomato (very much larger than the common kind)," which indicates that there was a "common kind." Jefferson grew them in his salad garden, and they were neither exotic nor a curiosity. In fact, they were on sale in the Washington markets long, long ago, by Jefferson's own account. So let's be through with the "poisonous tomato" nonsense.

The Pause *August 15*

Mid-August comes with misty dawns and more deliberate days, sunrise now three-quarters of an hour later than it was at summer's turn. Tomatoes ripen and hot afternoons are tanged and golden with field corn pollen. Crickets fiddle in the warm dusk and a lopsided moon hangs in the evening sky. The next full moon will be the harvest moon. Summer eases down the long slope toward the autumn equinox, October, and the fallen leaves.

Now comes the ripeness, the maturing for which the seed of April sprouted and the bud of May unfolded leaf and petal. The milkweed is fat and silvery green, packed with a cargo waiting for September's wind. Fat acorns hang in the white oak, slowly maturing toward the squirrels' hoarding-time. Wild grapes sag the high festoons, green promise of purple plenty in the frosted days to come. Rank meadow grass ripens bronze panicles of seed. Sumac darkens its close-packed berries and flaunts a scarlet feather of leaves, a taunt to the season.

The green haste begins to abate, the urgency of sap and silent industry of chlorophyll past their peak. Ripeness is a consolidation of time and achievement, and what has not already been accomplished must await another year, another summer. The last full moon of summer wanes and time seems to pause a little while as the season slowly mellows toward completion.

The Little Lakes *August 16*

Big pond, small lake, the naming doesn't matter. It is water, fresh water cupped in a hollow among the green hills, cool haven from summer's heat and hurry, a priceless heritage.

All over America we have been rediscovering the little lakes, and with care and wisdom we can save them from the fouling that has made sewers of our rivers and has ruined so many of our ocean beaches.

What is such a lake? It is a green shore lapped by clean, clear water. At night it is filled with stars and moonlight. Dawn and it is gauzed with mist. Sunrise begins to lift the mist and the water dances and glitters as the morning breeze begins to clear the air. Noon and it is lazy as the damselflies along its shore. Warm afternoon brings swimmers to its beaches, and small sailboats make their quiet, leisurely way like exotic butterflies. Evening and fishermen are out for a last cast or troll. Sunset fades, but dusk lingers, shimmery with reflected light. Then darkness, starlight again, moonlight, and the slow lap of water at the moored boats.

Man is not an aquatic animal, but set him down on the shore of such a lake and he becomes amphibious, a leisurely swimmer or sailor or fisherman. His tensions begin to ease and wash away. Clean, clear water is a solvent for worries and problems. Perhaps we have begun to learn this, at last, as we have come to know the shimmering retreats from beleaguering pressures.

Poisonous Pokeberry *August 17*

Late summer comes to ripeness in a multitude of ways. Consider the pokeweed, a flourishing wayside plant that looks good enough to eat, stem, leaf, and berry. It is a strange and beautiful wildling, sometimes eight feet tall, with big green leaves and with fat stems and stalks splashed with red as though its dark, ripe berries overflowed with juice. Yet both leaves and berries are poisonous if eaten, though the birds gorge on them with no ill effect.

The name pokeweed or pokeberry comes from the

Indian word *pocan,* meaning a dye-plant. Some call it garget or scoke or coakum, all strange-sounding names of obscure origin. And some, who see the doves feast on its berries, call it pigeonberry. The dark purplish-red juice of the berries was once used as a dye, hence the Indian name. In the spring its first shoots are as harmless as dandelions and are often eaten as boiled greens.

Pokeweed flourishes like the green bay tree. By now its stems are two inches and more in diameter and it branches like a maple. It blooms profusely in long racemes of small white flowers that ripen into berries shaped like miniature pumpkins, smaller in diameter than a lead pencil. Strange plant that it is, it has blossoms, green berries, and berries fully ripe at the same time. But the first hard frost will kill those fat red stems and leave only the bleaching skeleton to shred away through the winter. Just now it is lush with late summer ripeness—juicily inviting, yet nauseatingly poisonous.

Milkweed *August 18*

Botanically it is *Asclepias,* in honor of Aesculapius, the Greek god of healing. The everyday name is milkweed, and the two best known members of the family, butterfly weed and common milkweed, are now in bloom. The bright orange flower of butterfly weed is found only in favored places, but common milkweed grows almost everywhere, with its fragrant lavender and white florets.

This milkweed is a common roadside plant, too common for its own good, but it does have virtues beyond a pretty flower and a sweet odor. Its milky sap contains the raw material for rubber and has periodically attracted researchers. The silky fluff from its pods would make beautiful yarn or thread, but it lacks the necessary natural twist. But generations of herbalists have used both root and juice, particularly for respiratory ills. And young milkweed shoots make excellent greens.

The milkweed's florets are fertilized primarily by ants and bees. The florets occur in tufts of seventy or more, each less than a quarter of an inch in diameter. And each, by one of those quirks of nature, is an insect trap. One misstep and the ant or bee sipping nectar and unwittingly fertilizing the floret is caught by the leg and doomed to a starving death. But for centuries the ants and the bees have gathered milkweed nectar and fertilized the florets. They never learn—they live by instinct. And the milkweed survives and multiplies, making the world a somewhat sweeter place.

Fiddlers in the Night *August 19*

Late August nights always are insect-loud, but this year they seem louder than usual. Probably this is because so many of the stridulators, the insect fiddlers, were late, their schedules thrown off balance by the weather. Few harvestflies were shrilling in July, and until about three weeks ago the crickets didn't achieve much of a chorus. The katydids, loudest and most insistent of them all, didn't begin to rasp at the night until ten days ago. Now all these fiddlers are out and making the darkness echo as though driven by a special frenzy.

They are, of course. Their lives are swiftly passing and the species must be perpetuated before deep frost puts an end to them. Their clocks tick to a far faster beat than ours and they begin to run down by mid-September. Life must be committed to the fertile egg before then. So the warm nights echo, mate to mate, with the oldest mating call on earth.

What we really hear is summer passing. We heard spring come in the shrilling call of the hylas, the spring peepers. We heard summer in the dooryard in the familiar song of the robin and the ecstatic improvisations of the brown thrasher. Now we hear summer passing and autumn just beyond the hilltop in the trill of the field cricket and the harsh scratching of the katydid. Now, in the insect-loud night, we know that October will come, and November, when only the scuffle of sere leaves will scratch the night.

The Overlap *August 20*

Goldenrod is an autumn flower, but it blooms in August. You see it everywhere now, along rural roadsides, in old pastures, in suburban back streets. Ironweed comes to bloom, and joe-pye weed, and quite a few of the asters. What we have is the late summer overlap of the seasons, with black-eyed Susans flaunting their brilliant orange here and there, with wild lavender bergamot fading but still full of busy bees, with burdock in pretty purple bloom, not yet hook-spined and audacious. Pasture thistles still bloom, but the early blossoms have gone to floss which the goldfinches rag out and strew to the afternoon breezes.

You walk down a country road and see wild grapes hanging green as leaves, and just beyond them is the scarlet flash of woodbine already turned to October color. Bouncing Bet, the roadside pink that blooms into November, has taken the place of the daisies. Queen Anne's lace hasn't yet begun to curl into its bird's-nest shape. Pokeweed, as always, has blossoms, green berries, and ripe purple berries even on the same stem. Evening primroses still open their brilliant yellow petals in late afternoon.

Berries redden on the pimbina, but acorns are still tight-capped and green. Pears ripen. Sumac berries and sumac leaves here and there turn burgundy and crimson. The warblers have gone south, the swallows are leaving at noon tomorrow, and the mosquitoes are still here.

Sumac Flame

August 21

The sumac is unpredictable. You go down a country road, still green and peacefully occupied with late summer, and see a flash of crimson bright as a maple in October. It is startling, that flash of flame that shouldn't be there now. Then you see that it is a lone sumac, often one of an otherwise green clump, already standing like a huge Sioux war bonnet, every leaf in full color, red as a stormy sunset.

Other trees and shrubs wait at least till mid-September, but there is always a sumac that has lost track of time. Wet summer or dry, hot season or cool, it happens; and the one that burst into color early last year may remain properly green this year while another turns blaze-red in mid-August. Perhaps there's something in the parent sap that prompts such strange behavior. It sometimes seems that lots may be drawn to choose the shrub that will first flare and flame and eventually set fire to the whole autumn woodland.

Its color is the sumac's distinction. In autumn it achieves not only crimson but a bright, clean yellow, a brilliant orange, and even a reddish-purple. It can be beautiful. But when it bursts into flame in August it makes you wonder what happened to summer.

Festival

August 22

If August had no other reason for being, we would celebrate it as the time of the ripe tomato and the ready roasting-ear. Both come to the table now in flavor and abundance that would make Lucullus envious. One reason August has no holidays as such is that sweet corn and garden-ripe tomatoes make every day a festival.

So thank the Indians, thank Columbus, thank the gardener and the farmer. Don't make the list too long or the thanks too detailed, because the corn won't wait and the tomatoes ripen by the minute. But do give fleeting thought to the fact that corn and tomatoes are among the enduring treasures native to this land. The Indians grew and ate them long before Europeans knew there was an America. The colonists came late to the feast, but their descendants have enjoyed it every August since. Feast, and be grateful.

Corn is maize, if it really matters, and the tomato is the *tomatl,* in the old Indian tongue. But in August corn is the sweet ear at its prime, like no other flavor in this world; and the tomato is rich, red, juicy succulence unmatched. Boil or roast the corn, hurry it to the table, butter it well, salt it judicially, and fleck it with pepper. Chill the tomato or, if you are the fortunate gardener himself, pluck it sun-warm, slice, give it just a hint of salt and a breath of pepper. Then eat, feast, for forget the gods who sipped nectar. If the gods had ever tasted sweet corn at its prime or garden-ripe tomatoes, nectar would have gone begging.

Crab Apples *August 23*

Crab apples are ripe. They hang like scarlet jewels in the late August sun on a thousand hills and in the dooryards and along the green borders; and beneath the trees the windfalls are like a froth of red and green bubbles in the grass. And on ten thousand shelves are glasses of fresh honey-amber crab apple jelly.

The crab apple is a venerable fruit still full of the tang of the wild. It is the native apple of the north, sturdy and persistent, and it still represents a concentration of elementally sturdy qualities. The fruit itself is small, for quick growth and ripening. The flesh is firm and crisp and full of juice. The flavor has something of late frost and stony hillsides, a concentration that has a kind of acid independence; it has enough flavor for an apple three times its size.

It's that flavor which makes crab apple jelly so well worth the making. Jelly made from the juice of the crab apple's big cousins may have the same body, the same general color, but never the same taste. Who ever distinguishes by name among jellies made from winesaps or russets or northern spies? And who ever fails to give crab apple jelly its full title?

Crab apples also make a rather special cider, though you'll almost never find it in the market. Only those with their own trees and their own press ever make it and then only if they have a discerning palate and the patience to gather a few bushels of crab apples at a proper time and put them through the mill.

You'll find that tang, too, in springtime, when the crab apple tree is in bloom. But the blossom fragrance is only a promise; here's performance, here's the fruit itself in full red ripeness on the bough.

Mist at Sunrise

August 24

The misty dawns of late summer are as much a part of the season as are daisies and goldenrod. The mist fills the valleys and settles over the ponds and streams like smoke before sunrise, and with dawn's first light there is a curling and wreathing with mysterious little air currents playing tag. Then the sun rises and the whole filmy curtain begins to lift.

This isn't the murk of high humidity that makes a midsummer morning so sultry. This is the shimmer and the glow of a changing season. It is the heavy dew that washes the dusty, tired leaves and keeps the valleys green well into autumn. This is autumn itself before it has gathered its forces, the breath of autumn that we see long before there is even a hint of frost.

It comes on a morning when the sky is clean and clear, a morning bright with blue and green. The long shadows of dawn lie cool across the land, and this filmy gauze of whiteness is there, so thin it shivers when the first sunlight strikes it. It glows and gleams. Wave a hand and it swirls with silvery glints. It is the very essence of impermanence.

It is even less substantial than the haze of Indian summer, that thin, far haze on the autumn hilltops. This is morning mist, nothing more, a brief glimpse of days to come, of late September around the bend and just over the hills.

Zinnias *August 25*

One thing about the zinnia: It doesn't need pampering. Give it a rootbed, sunlight, and a start, and it will make its own way. It responds to care and cultivation, but it makes few demands. And with half a chance a bed of zinnias will brighten the end of August as few other flowers. Zinnias will brighten the forepart of August too, but there is more competition then.

The zinnia's colors are strong, old-fashioned colors with little subtlety. Botanists and breeders have done things to its shape, twisting its petals and quilling and even fringing them, but it remains a zinnia for all that. Not even the specialist can alter its zinnia scent, which an old-fashioned gardener can recognize in the dark of the moon. And its generosity is magnificent; cut one bloom and two will take its place.

Some call it a rank and weedy plant and liken it to the sunflower. But no matter. There's a relationship, all right; there's kinship, too, with the big daisies and, in lesser degree, with the asters. But the zinnia needs no apologies. It holds its bright head high, in the garden or in the decorator's bowl, and speaks for itself.

Its name is touched with German, in honor of the German botanist Johann Gottfried Zinn. But it is as native to this continent as the pumpkin. Mexico and our own Southwest cradled it and the early Aztecs honored its beauty. Cortez found it flourishing in the legendary gardens of Montezuma when he captured the City of Mexico. It still has the glow of the southern sun on its petals. Particularly in late August.

Still August

August 26

It always seems to catch us by surprise, that day when we know that summer is not endless, that autumn is just over the hill or up the valley. It follows a night of unexpected coolness, and we hear the katydids scratching at the dark. First katydids, and they miss a few notes; but they persist, and the old saying echoes once more in our memory: Six weeks from first katydid to first frost.

After the cool night comes a chilly dawn. But it is the light, not the temperature, that marks the change. The clean blue sky, the sharp shadows, the way they fall. The setting for a brand new season. A blue jay calls and looks almost gray against the sky as he flies away. Not another bird makes a sound until a crow caws in the distance.

We look at the trees, half surprised to see the maples still in green leaves. So is the Virginia creeper on the dead elm. The goldenrod at the roadside is yellow, moon-gold yellow; but it always blooms in August. A cluster of day lilies is still in flower, but they look completely out of season. We have had a glimpse of autumn, heard its whisper, smelled its breath in the cidery odor of windfalls from the apple trees at the garden's edge. But it was like meeting an old friend at an unexpected time and place, out of context.

It takes a day or two to adjust. Then we remember that it's still August, and we get time in perspective again. August, not autumn.

"A" Is for Apple *August 27*

Consider the apple. Forget for the moment that there are early apples and late apples, orchard apples and dooryard apples, even wild apples. Forget Adam and William Tell and Johnny Appleseed. Note in passing that the apple is a rose, and vice versa, and remember apple trees in May. But concentrate on the apple itself, which is the roundness of the earth, the red and gold of the sunrise, and the summary of the fruitful season's sweet ripeness.

The apple is juicy crispness to the tooth and tongue. It is the tang of wildness tempered to the appreciative palate. It is jelly for the morning toast, amber touched with rose, ambrosia tinged with wild honey. It is sauce for the roast as well as for goose and gander. It is pie, if the cook knows the nature of an apple and the function of a crust; it is an abomination if the cook is ignorant of either. It is a confection when baked by a genius, though the genius must know which apple to bake as well as how to bake it. Those who know brown betty at its best marvel at the inspiration of the unknown Elizabeth who did such service to the apple.

And the apple is cider, at a proper time. Cider, with all its potential. Take apple cider as it comes, or leave it to its own devices, it remains the apotheosis of the apple. True, it turns to vinegar in time. But vinegar has its sharp virtues. And along the way the apple makes the wine look pale and taste insipid.

Consider the apple and thank the tree, where the apple reddens now. Few seeds sprout and grow for such an achievement.

Time to Go

August 28

Regardless of the calendar, there is no mistaking the season when the flickers begin to gather in small flocks and discuss air routes south and the state of the weather. Discuss something, anyway, and since they start their migration soon afterward the routes and the weather would be logical topics.

Usually the flickers wait till mid-September to prepare for the trip, but this has been one of those summers when not even a flicker could outguess the weather. From extremes of heat and humidity the days have turned to typical autumn chill, then back again. It must have been quite confusing to birds accustomed to timing their lives and their actions by day-to-day weather. The swallows gave up on the weather several weeks ago, held their conference on rural telephone lines and headed south. Even some of the robins have quit their usual haunts and gone away.

A few flickers winter over this far north, but not many. They need a certain amount of insect fare, mostly ants, to go with the berries on their diet, primarily bayberries and the berries of poison ivy. But most of them migrate. They gather in large flocks along the coast—near Cape May, New Jersey, and Cape Charles, Virginia, for instance—and travel south together. In the spring they will return about the time the first robins get here.

But this is autumn, by the weather, time to go; and the flickers aren't going to stand on ceremony about it.

Berries for the Birds

August 29

Say whatever else you will about the summer now waning, it has been a good season for wild berries and the birds that feed on them. Beginning with wild strawberries in June, which were bigger and more numerous than usual, it progressed through a big crop of blackcaps and wild blackberries, both bigger and juicier than usual. And now the late berries are ripening.

Wild grapes hang in bigger bunches than usual, to the special delight of the blackbirds. Chokecherries are gone, but they were lush and plentiful and the waxwings gorged on them. High-bush cranberry bushes are loaded and now ripening. The viburnums are full of fruit. The red osier dogwoods had loaded clusters which had little chance to come to full ripeness, for the birds made a feast of them early.

Sumac always seems to bear full heads, but the berries in those heads are fatter than usual this year. Woodbine berries darken, twice their usual size, it seems. Poison ivy berries are large and plentiful, and they will be a painful temptation to strangers in the woods looking for colorful leaves and berries. In the deep woods the partridgeberries already glisten on their trailing vines; they will be a benison for the grouse back in the hills, come snow time. Even the scarlet berry clusters on the Jack-in-the-pulpit are fatter than usual. And the spicebushes begin to sparkle with their generous crop of red-orange fruit.

The birds have lived high this year, and the migrants will go south well fed. Those who stay out the winter will have a full larder, at least to start with.

The Monarchs *August 30*

The newest generation of monarch butterflies is now emerging from chrysalises on milkweed plants. From now till late September they will brighten fields and roadsides with their black and orange wings. Then they will disappear from the Northeast, not because they die with summer, as most butterflies do, but because they migrate. Incredible as it seems, these fragile creatures migrate to Florida and return next spring, when they find young milkweed plants, lay their eggs, and complete their cycle. The eggs hatch into green caterpillars with black and yellow stripes, pupate, become chrysalises, and emerge as butterflies once more, ready for migration.

All butterflies are remarkable, going through the incredible stages of egg, caterpillar, pupa, chrysalis, and butterfly again. But the monarchs are unique. American monarchs never lay eggs on anything but a milkweed plant, and the caterpillars feed only on milkweed leaves. Long ago they appeared in Hawaii, but they never stayed till the milkweed was established there. Yet when they reached New Zealand and Australia, almost a century ago, they chose another plant and settled there. They have even been known to cross the Atlantic, though they are rare in Europe.

Here the monarchs are among our most numerous late-summer butterflies, spectacular in color and pristine in beauty because they hatch so late. They come with the goldenrod and the asters, special spangles for late-summer days, and they stay until the maples have begun to turn to gold and crimson.

Purple Majesty

August 31

Now come the days of rich purple in fields and meadows, denoting not only a time of year but a stage of maturity. It is as though the whole summer had been building toward this deep, strong color to match the gold of late sunlight and early goldenrod.

Flower colors are mysterious in origin, but it is generally thought the full, hot sun of the tropics produces the brilliant yellows, deep oranges, full-bodied scarlets. And it is understood that the lesser sunlight of the temperate zones produces lesser colors. Early spring brings us, except in the violets, the weaker shades, whites, pinks, thin yellows, light blues. Early summer warms the landscape with deeper yellows, stronger blues, some orange, and a variety of reds. But it takes August and the accumulation of warmth and sunlight to produce the strength of purple in showy masses.

The thistles flaunt it. Burdock achieves rich purple flower tufts that will ripen into hook-spined burs. Ironweed, standing tall in the lowlands, lifts massed heads of purplish-blue to the sun. But it is the asters, those strikingly beautiful ones that carry New York's and New England's names, that demand attention. They bear the purple of royalty, rivaled only by that of the gentians which will appear in their own deliberate time.

Summer begins to fray away, but where the purple asters bloom it does so in unchallenged majesty.

September

HARVEST MOON

This may reflect the white man's influence. The Indians didn't have to work overtime at harvest.

September

September 1

September comes, and with it a sense of autumn. Not autumn itself quite yet, but the year now definitely has turned toward color in the woodland, ripeness in the fields, frost in the moonlight. Summer thins away. The sun now clearly moves toward the equinox, only three weeks away.

Few summers have given such a sense of impatience with tradition. When August dawn finds the temperature in the low forties back in the hills, as it did several times in the last few weeks, there is no denying that change is close upon us. The trees recognize it; patches of color came early, here and there, in the cooler valleys. Roadside goldenrod bloomed early. Queen Anne's Lace passed its prime almost two weeks ahead of schedule. Birds that should be content to stay till mid-September are already gathering in restless flocks, migration on their minds.

So September comes with a few more harbingers than usual, some of the outriders early with their message. But autumn never comes overnight. It creeps in on a misty dawn and vanishes in the hot afternoon. It tiptoes through the treetops, rouging a few leaves, then rides a tuft of thistledown across the valley and away. It sits on a hilltop and hoots like an October owl in the dusk. It plays tag with the wind. Autumn is a changeling, busy as a squirrel in a hickory tree, idle as the languid brook. It is August ended, October inevitable, summer's ripeness and richness fulfilled in sweet September.

September's Spectacle *September 2*

The color comes day by day and week by week, always deliberate; but before it really possesses the woodlands there is another spectacle, almost like another spring, at the roadsides and in the meadows. Now come the autumn flowers, less varied than those of May but so abundant that they make September another flowery month.

Some of them are holdovers, late summer's bloom persisting. Goldenrod always comes by mid-August, but it seems to rise to a peak of golden abundance in early September. Vervain persists, its purple making the lavender and ruddy pink of joe-pye weed and ironweed look pale. Late thistles make spectacular purple accents. And bouncing Bet seems to come to special bloom as the equinox approaches, with drifts of pink and white where Queen Anne's Lace is worn and faded.

But the particular spectacle of September is the asters. They almost seem to have been biding their time, waiting for a less crowded stage on which to display their finery. New England asters, deep purple and rich gold, stand tall and proud. Smooth asters lift their generous heads of blue-violet ray flowers and heart-leafed asters open violet bloom.

The color comes, but first it comes to the roadsides as a prelude to the great symphony in the woodlands. September prepares the setting for October.

Deliberate September

September 3

September is more than a month, really; it is a season, an achievement in itself. It begins with August's leftovers and it ends with October's preparations, but along the way it achieves special certainties and satisfactions. After summer's heat and haste, it even brings a sense of quiet and leisure as the year consolidates itself and its achievements.

In the goldenrod's gleaming glory is the certainty of greater glory in birch and maple and aspen. Scattered bursts of flame in the sumac light fires that will spread to woodbine and swamp maple and dogwood and chokecherry. Asters frost the roadsides, reminder of frosty mornings ahead, and milkweed floss and thistledown are glinting reminders of chill, misty dawns to come.

Fireflies are gone, but the stars begin to glitter in the deepening dusk. The cicada is stilled, but cricket and katydid are loud in the lengthening night. Bees are busy with a final honey-hoard. The chipmunk lines his winter bedroom and stocks his granary. Squirrels harvest and hide the nut trees' bounty.

But the green urgency is past, its ripeness almost complete. Even the days and nights near their time of balance as we approach equinox and harvest moon. Deliberate September, in its own time and tempo, begins to sum up another summer.

The Trees

September 4

Summer passes and the trees begin to mark the season, elm and oak and maple. They have begun to draw their sap of life down to the roots again, hoarding their resources for the long rest through the short, cold days at the same time that they form the buds for next summer's leaves, buds that will lie dormant till the magic kiss of another spring. And this summer's leaves are slowly being drained and sealed off, to color and fall and molder into earth again.

If there is fulfillment and perfection, surely it is among the trees, the oldest living things we know. A maple seed ripens, twirls downward into the grass, sprouts, sends a root down, a shoot up, opens a few leaves to catch the sun. It grows, in its own urgency, strengthening year by year. The sapling becomes a tree that shades man and beast, harbors songbird and squirrel, feeds bee and looping worm. Aided only by sun, rain, and earth itself, it lives with the seasons, heals its own wounds, and outlasts its human neighbor. And each spring it is a fountain of sweet sap, each autumn it is a golden magnificence.

A man can plant a tree or a woodland, but he must start with a seed or a sapling. He can live with trees, or he can cut them and destroy them. A tree is a living thing, but a firelog is only heat and smoke, and a board weathers and wears away. Trees endure, marking each season as it comes, each tree a vital pattern of growth and strength and beauty. Eternal truths abide in living trees.

The Ripeness *September 5*

The dipper hangs low in the north and Cassiopeia is off to the east of the Pole Star. High overhead is the moon, in its first quarter tonight, which means a half-moon as we see it. It is moving down the sky westward, a waxing moon that will be this year's Harvest Moon when it comes to the full a week from tomorrow night. Already the glow is there. Dusk melts into moonlight.

September nights have the ripeness of the season in them, and moonlight makes them special. Orchard and vineyard scent the night with cidery fragrance and the bouquet of uncasked wine. Meadow and roadside still smell of hay, the sweetness of cut grass, and of mint and bergamot and daisy and goldenrod that were mowed as trespassers. Cornfields, rustling in the night air, still have a trace of that pervading smell of pollen that made the summer air shimmer in a golden haze.

On the oozy margin of the pond are cattail ranks at stiff attention in the moonlight, and the pond, rippling and glinting, has a damp, clean smell quite different from the pond smell of Dog Days. The breeze from the hilltop is soft to the cheek and tells of nut hulls and ripe haws and hemlocks full of small green cones. A barred owl hoots from the pine grove.

Another month and color will flood the woodland, frost will come swaggering across the land. But this is the gentle sweetness, the ripeness of the land, before the Harvest Moon matures.

The Aster Season

September 6

Their name comes from the stars, but the wild asters spangle our landscape in such profusion that they make even the most starry September night seem underpopulated. Before this month is out they will be in blossom everywhere, along the roadsides, in fence-rows and meadows, in the lowlands, in the woods, on the hilltops, even in vacant city lots and suburban backyard margins.

The asters are a far-ranging family, but America is specially rich with them. All Europe hasn't one aster that can compare with ours, which range from the size of a dime to that of a half-dollar and in color from pure white through all degrees of lavender to the royal purple of the family's queen, the big New England aster.

The early ones come to bloom in August, but autumn is their season. They frost our mild September days, mingle with the glory of October's woodland color, make Indian summer bright as June, and often linger into chill November. They make us forget midsummer's daisies and they seem to laugh at the departing birds. Harvests are reaped, farms are snugged, fireplace smoke scents the evenings, and still the asters hold high their yellow-centered heads. They are still here when the milkweed seeds have flown and the thistledown has wafted away.

They are a hardy tribe, the wild asters. Without them our autumn would lack a bright dimension and have a lonely look.

Autumn Miracle *September 7*

We think of spring as the miracle time, when opening bud and new leaf proclaim the persistence of life. But autumn is the season when the abiding wonder makes itself known in a subtler way. Autumn is achievement, and September is the time when purpose and the endless continuity are evident in the seed.

Spring's rooting and leafing and summer's blossoming were obvious steps in the endless process, which is growth and reproduction and endless repetition. Now growth comes to annual fruition and preparations are completed for another year, another generation. The acorn ripens and the hickory nut matures. The milkweed pod opens its packet of winged seeds.

Grass ripens its head of minute grain. Sumac lifts its clustered red fruits, fertile with seeds, at the roadside. Box elder is thickly hung with tassels of samara, winged seeds that will cling to the twigs after the leaves have fallen. Burs and stick-tights ripen ingenious pods, ready to hitch rides to new seedbeds. Green life, pregnant with root and leaf and growth, is now encapsulated in the seed to await another spring, another round in the endless cycle.

September

The visible, green prime of life is passing. The trees begin to proclaim the change. Soon the leaves will be discarded, the seeds will scatter, the grass will sere. Another season of growth will be completed. But the miracle of life persists, the mysterious germ of growth and renewal that is the seed itself.

The Pulse of Autumn

September 8

If the season calls for little journeys, it is autumn. Summer, by habit and custom, is our time for travel to far places, to know the exotic and the unfamiliar. Then come September and early autumn, and a whole new tempo. Then comes the time to travel afoot and know again the world just down the road or across the nearest hilltop.

You walk, and this world just beyond your doorstep has new dimensions. So have you. Your pace, your pulse, your whole awareness begin to match the basic rhythms. There is no haste, no scurry, no racing the clock. The roadside maples count the years, not the days and hours. Milkweed pods take their time about opening, awaiting a proper day and breeze to spill their silken cargo. As the fading plumes of goldenrod slowly grizzle, the bees haunt the deliberate asters for a late hoarding of honey. Tam-o'-shantered acorns hang heavy on the red oaks, waiting wind and squirrels to plant the groves of a remote tomorrow.

Crows are muted, jays are wary, as they watch the restless migrants, knowing that by November they will own the woodlands. The flames of woodbine creep up the popple, deliberate as the sun. Gentians come to bloom. The bumblebee waits for midday warmth to seek his breakfast and crickets chirp all afternoon in the roadside grass with its bronze-ripe heads. Wild grapes ripen, grape by grape.

The season's slow change is all around you. You walk

with the measured rhythm of the year, unhurried, and you become a part of it. Your pulse, your pace, become the pulse and pace of autumn.

Gossamer Season

September 9

This is gossamer season, when a dozen different strands glint and glimmer in the sunlight.

Dawn shimmers with spider filaments, proof that late hatches of spiderlings have the instinct to travel. On such gossamer strands, strong as steel, light as feathers, tiny spiders have traveled into the Arctic and almost to the summits of the Himalayas. But most of them merely ride a breeze to the next pasture. And when the stillness of night becalms them, the dampness of night air brings them down to earth. You see them at sunrise, a lacing of silver threads over grass and bushes, glinting with dewdrops, not spiderwebs but merely spider gossamer, the vehicles on which young spiders launched themselves into a vague, instinctive tomorrow.

Noontime glistens with the floss of pasture thistles, their big, purple flowers now ripened into big tufts of airy filaments. Down in those tufts are thistle seeds, very small and very sweet to the taste of goldfinches. The birds are at them, tearing the heads apart to reach those seeds. You look across the pasture and see a gleaming cloud around each thistle plant, and in each cloud a bright black and yellow goldfinch. A thistle, a breeze, and a goldfinch can make a whole pasture gleam.

Soon milkweed pods will open, with their silver floss. Fluff from hawkweeds, from fall dandelions, even from early goldenrod will soon shimmer the air, September's early autumn celebration.

Harvest Moon

September 10

This is the week of the harvest moon which, regardless of calendar or equinox, is autumnal as a corn shock. With reasonably clear skies, it will be a moonlit week, for the Harvest Moon is not a hasty moon. It comes early and stays late.

There was a time when the Harvest Moon gave the busy farmer the equivalent of an extra day or two. He could return to the fields after supper and evening milking and continue his harvest by moonlight. That was when corn was cut by hand and husked by hand, when shocks tepeed the fields and fodder was stacked in the barnyard, when the song of the bangboard echoed and the husking peg was familiar to the hand.

But times change, and schedules. Now most of the farmer's long days come at plowing time, or planting, or at haytime. Corn is cut by machine and chopped by machine and stowed in the silo; or it is left standing in the field till a few fine late fall days, then picked by the mechanical picker, which can outstrip a dozen men.

There's harvesting to be done, of course, but much of it now centers on the kitchen rather than the barns. The last bountiful yield comes from the garden, the late sweet corn, the tomatoes, the root vegetables, the dozen and one kinds of pickles and relishes. The canning, the preserving, the freezing, the kitchen harvest in all its variety, reaches its busy peak, the last rush of the season.

It's still the Harvest Moon, but the farmer with his field harvest well in hand is looking forward to the next full moon, the one in October. So is his dog. That will be the Hunter's Moon, and the coons will be busy in the cornfields by then.

The Migrant Hawks *September 11*

The hawks are migrating. Find one of their migration routes, which usually follow the great valleys of this country, and with any luck at all you will see the big birds moving slowly but steadily south. Most of the migrants are broad-winged hawks, but with them will probably be a few falcons and pigeon hawks.

The broad-wings are the last of the hawks to arrive here in the spring and the first to leave in the fall. And they are notorious for their group habit of migration. As many as 2,500 have been seen passing a lookout point in western Massachusetts in one mid-September day. Lookouts in western Connecticut have reported seeing as many as 2,000 broad-wings traveling southwest at a leisurely pace in two separate flights within an hour.

For a long time all hawks were commonly called "chicken hawks" and were believed to kill domestic fowl as preferred food. Slowly the truth has become known, that most hawks live on rats, mice, rabbits, and insects. Only three or four out of a dozen eat small birds, and only Cooper's hawk commonly eats chickens. The others have a fixed place in the balance of nature. Today they are protected, at least to some degree, in more than thirty-five states.

The flights coming through New England and the Northeast now are summer residents in New England and eastern Canada. Those that summer in the upper Great Lakes area follow a migration route down the broad valley of the Mississippi.

The Trend

September 12

The color comes slowly, but by the second week of September there is no mistaking the trend. The woodlands are still green, but now with subtle shadings that already forecast October. And roadside trees, particularly the maples, begin to show flashes of red and yellow, a few leaves here, a whole branch on down the road. Some may be victims of salt-sickness or drought, but even back in the cool, damp woods well away from the roads a few maples show early color. Elms look worn and tired and have a russet cast.

As always, first vivid color came in the sumacs. But now the fiery red begins to creep up the climbing woodbine, leaf by leaf. Birches are turning pale and popples come to that yellowish-green which means their chlorophyll has begun to fade. Hickories, still bountiful with ripening nuts, look almost as tired as the elms; their leaves droop and seem to be rusting out like old tin cans. Down on the woodland floor the viburnums darken toward October's reddish-purple.

The color doesn't come overnight. It creeps in, day by day, as the goldenrod fades and the asters whiten the roadsides. It comes like a deepening, bluish shadow in the ash trees, like strengthening sunlight in the aspens and the maples. It comes like a growing flame in the red oaks and the gum trees. But now, in September, it is still a subtlety, a trend, a still-whispered promise of autumn glory.

First Frost

September 13

First frost comes in the night, a clear, scant-starred night when the moon is near its fullness. It comes without a whisper, quiet as thistledown, quiet as mist; but the countryman senses its approach in the late afternoon look of the sky, in the hush of dusk, in the smell of night air drifting down from the hills.

It comes like a traveler returning, uncertain of its welcome. It follows the swales and hollows down from the ridges as though its feet knew the way even in darkness. It touches a bush here, a vine yonder, brushes the corner of a hillside garden, and finally it walks through the lower valleys. Dawn comes, and daylight, and you see its path—the glistening leaf, the gleaming stem, the crystalled spiderweb, the limp, blackening garden vine, and blighted blossoms.

Another night or two the frost walks the valleys in the moonlight. Then it goes back beyond the northern hills to wait a little longer, and the golden mildness of early autumn comforts the land. Crickets, briefly silenced by first frost, trill the warm afternoons toward the dusk when the last, loud katydids join the chorus. Color begins to brighten the treetops. Some talk of Indian summer and some merely say it's a good time of year to be alive.

Then the frost returns and walks boldly, hilltop and valley, at dusk and dawn as well as in the darkness of the night. Later, in October and November, after the golden days.

Woodbine Flames

September 14

If any one color can be said to set off the fires of autumn that will sweep through the woodlands in a few more weeks surely it is the crimson of the Virginia creeper. Impatient sumac showed a few scarlet feathers in August, as always, but they were vivid feathers, no incendiary coals. Now, however, the creeper that we also know as woodbine has begun to send its deep red flame up the trees and through the roadside bushes, burning color that has no smoke but the morning mist, no heat but the south-swinging sunlight.

Virginia creeper is a cousin of the wild grape, though one would never guess it from the five-fold leaves. Its fruit, however, is like small clusters of miniature grapes that ripen to the deep purple of Concords. And the vine is as ubiquitous as the insidious poison ivy, for which it is sometimes mistaken. But even if one forgets to count—the creeper is five-leafed, the ivy three-leafed—the color is the clue; Virginia creeper turns a deep crimson, sometimes almost Burgundy, but the poison ivy turns scarlet and orange and yellow.

The creeper always colors early, while the maples are still deliberating. It comes to full flame, then seems to scorch the briars and kindle the bush dogwood leaves. Finally it sets off the swamp maples and the autumn fires are really blazing. That spectacle is still to come, but there's no turning back now. Virginia creeper has begun to show its flames.

Fulfillment

September 15

The words that come most readily to mind just now have their origins in this earth's plenty. "Ripe" goes back to early Germanic words for "reap," meaning harvest; and "harvest" is rooted in early Greek for "fruit" and "to pluck." Even the word "plenty" goes back through old English and French to venerable Latin for "full." So when we think of ripeness and harvest we are in the long tradition of the earth's plenty, the season's fullness in every sense.

This ripeness is by no means limited to the farmer's tilled fields or the gardener's ripening rows. It is everywhere that knows autumn now. Summer's growth comes to completion. The trees ripen their nuts and fruits. The grasses mature their seed heads. The blossoms of June and July become the fat pod and the fleshy pome of September. Last spring's birthing and hatching have forgotten the womb and the egg; next year's parents, now furred and fledged, fatten for the trials of winter.

The surge is almost over. Life now begins to relax into the annual pause that is a kind of biological Indian summer, a time of relative ease and quiet. The plant commits its future to the seed and the root. The insect stows its tomorrow in the egg and the pupa. And, as the urgency begins to abate, man, close to the land and surrounded by his own harvest, knows again the old, old truths of the season. It is, even today, the time of ripeness, of reaping, of plenty, of summer come to fulfillment.

The Hoarders *September 16*

Now come the hoarding days, not only for the traditional bee and ant but for all provident creatures. Field mice have been harvesting and stowing seeds for weeks. So have chipmunks, stocking their winter granaries with everything from grass seed to acorns. Squirrels put even the ants to shame with their scurrying industry, stowing nuts by the bushel, at least a third of which they probably never will find again; that is the way the woodland spreads. And the woodchucks, gorging on grass and clover and fruit and laying up their harvest in body fat, hoarding their winter reserves under their own skins.

The bees are summer-busy every sunny afternoon, bringing in a late harvest from goldenrod and aster, stocking the hive with rich winter fare. Other insects do their hoarding in egg and pupa, from which another generation will emerge next spring. Still others, like the Isia isabella moth's caterpillar, the black and red-brown woolly bear, eat their fill and hurry off to a hiding place where they can hibernate, frozen stiff as an icicle.

Man, in some ways the least provident of all, digs his

carrots, if he is a gardening suburbanite or a countryman, plucks and cans his tomatoes, brings in his winter squash. He has picked his beans, pickled his beets, chopped his cabbage and peppers into relish. His cold pantry is his hostage to winter. Now he wishes he had grown potatoes, too, and he envies farmers who grow sugar beets and keep bees. Sometimes, after a trip to the market, he wishes he too could hibernate.

Floral Heritage *September 17*

Wild asters now begin to take over the country roadside with bright abundance, frosty white and lavender and deep purple. Soon the restless gentians, bluer than the autumn skies, will be in spectacular bloom in unexpected places. Goldenrod fades, Queen Anne's lace is worn and tattered, the gleam of evening primroses is almost gone, but bouncing Bet and yellow toadflax take their places. The wildflower beauty will persist another month or more, reminder of how nature bedecks and glorifies this scarred old earth.

With a greater wealth of wildflowers than any other land on earth, this country could be a floral Eden. Only man's thoughtlessness can check the flowers. Give them a chance and they make the wastelands gleam, glorify the hillsides, and adorn the roadsides.

Who can forget an expanse of Texas bluebonnets? Or a New England pasture full of bluets, or a Kansas roadside gleaming with sunflowers? Who would forfeit the memory of a whole swale of violets? Or of a shoreline marsh dazzling with rose mallows, a Connecticut roadside vivid with wild bergamot—and hummingbirds? Who could forget a Colorado mountain road lined with mariposa lilies and blue columbines?

The asters come to blossom, countless as the stars for which they were named. They glorify our autumn. They are reminders, too, of the floral abundance that is ours, not for the taking but simply for the keeping, for the cherishing of what we have.

The Flickers' Holiday *September 18*

The flickers begin to gather for migration and their actions add another facet to the mystery of the birds. All summer these big woodpeckers were resolutely individual, busy with family life and wanting no company, even of their own kind. Now they become gregarious. You see them in flocks of a dozen or more in the edge of the woodland, in the ripening meadow, along the brushy roadside. They feed on the season's ripe berries, but food obviously is not their major interest. They seem to have time for tribal gossip and even for community play.

Other migrants follow the same pattern. A few weeks ago the swallows were gathering in premigration flocks, and before the swallows the warblers were doing it. Soon the robins will be gathering. But the flickers are rather special examples because they are so insistently individual except at this particular season.

There is general reluctance to grant birds such emotions as we know as human beings, but what would be more natural than that they, too, should enjoy September? Nesting is completed, fledglings are on their own, the weather is favorable, and there is food in plenty. In the pattern of their lives this should be a kind of vacation time and tribal gatherings would be understandable, even among flickers. Who knows but that they discuss the summer's events and the trip ahead, in whatever way they can? In any case, the flickers are flocking, and they are obviously having a holiday.

The Clocks Run Down

September 19

To warm-blooded creatures, such as people, the crisp, cool days of autumn are invigorating. The step quickens, the eye brightens, and life takes on new vigor. But to the cold-blooded ones, such as insects, who are at the mercy of the sun rather than their own inner fires for life and energy, time begins to run out when nights turn frosty. With the short days, their clocks begin to run down.

You may hear it in the evening, in the slow tempo of the stridulent ones, the katydids and the crickets that were so insistent only a few weeks ago. Now their chorus diminishes. When they rasp at all it is with the deliberate tempo of a fiddler drawing a worn bow across the fraying strings.

You see it in the morning, before a late sun has warmed the day. The bumblebee that sought haven in a bedraggled blossom crawls painfully out to warm his joints and renew his sluggish vitality before seeking a belated breakfast. You watch a slowly lumbering beetle, arthritic with the cold, making his painful way among the withering garden weeds. The stiff-legged ant is a sluggard, the wasp is almost tractable, and the grasshopper has no hop in him till almost noon.

Briefly, when the sun has asserted itself by early afternoon, life is almost normal. For a few hours flies buzz, ants hurry, and late gnats dance like lively motes in the mild air. Then evening nears and the buzz, the haste, and the dancing are at an end. We, warm-blooded and invigorated by the season, welcome the change and even celebrate it. But the cold-blooded children of summer, the insect hordes, have had their day in the sun.

Beyond the Equinox

September 20

The sun now rises almost due east, sets almost due west. This is the week of the autumn equinox when, briefly, daylight and darkness are almost equal. Then the nights begin to lengthen in a steady progression that leads to the winter solstice, to official winter, to January.

Summer ends with a little more color than usual, perhaps because of the August drought. But all summers end with the scarlet feathers of sumac showing in roadside thickets, symbols of the Indian summer to come, and with soft maples in the lowland beginning to show the same red tones they had last April when their blossoms burst bud. You don't have to be an astronomer or even a mathematician to recognize the change. The precise time, perhaps, can be calculated by the relative positions of earth and sun; but autumn really is change at the root, in the air, and in the earth itself, not in the stars, and the precise moment is not important.

The obvious truth is that summer is past, that the year's season in the sun has run its course. Now comes the recapitulation, the summing up of the summer's growth. Nature begins to prepare for winter. After the color in the woodlands, the leaves will blanket the soil. The litter of autumn becomes the mulch and then the humus for the root and the tender seed. The urgency of growth is ended for another year, but life itself is hoarded, in root and bulb and seed and egg. Now comes autumn, and rest, and time to see beyond the nearest hilltop, beyond the equinox to the reality of the earth.

Sumac Fire

September 21

Some day that sumac's color signals the autumnal equinox, though they cannot readily explain why an occasional branch or even a whole clump turns color in late August. In any case, by now most of the sumacs at the roadside and in the corner of the back pasture begin to look like Sioux war bonnets and are ready to lead the parade right into Indian summer. They are full of the most brilliant reds one will see until the maples take over.

Sumac is native to almost every area of the world except the polar regions, and the name comes almost unchanged from the Arabic down through Old French. The wild species are outcasts in most places, but in earlier times people found many uses for them, in tanning, in dyeing, in cabinet work, as condiments, as a varnish base, even as an oil for candles. And everywhere the birds continue to feast on the generous seed heads of the common staghorn sumac. There is a poisonous species, whose leaves are as dangerous to the unwary as those of poison ivy; but it is rare in our area. Its leaves too are compound, but they are short and rounded, not long and feathery.

Sumac is stubborn and persistent. Give it an inch at the edge of a pasture or along a back road and it will take the proverbial mile. But it does have its own beauty, particularly when autumn turns the equinoctial corner. Crimson is its basic color, but it also achieves a fine, clean yellow, a rich orange, and, at times, a splendid purple. One wonders why the legend-makers never gave it credit for lighting the autumn flame in the forest, setting off the whole blaze of color. Legendary or not, there it stands now, full of cool autumn fire, ready to set the whole woodland aflame.

Autumn

September 22

Another equinox occurs and, by those charts and markers we use to divide time and measure our lives, today is autumn. For a little while now, days and nights will be almost equal, dawn to dusk, dusk to dawn, and the sun will rise and set almost true east and west. Then it will be October, tenth month of our twelve-month year, and moving toward the winter solstice.

So much for the arbitrary boundaries, which are for the almanacs and the record books, even less imperative than the figures on a sundial. The autumn with which we live is as variable as the wind, the weather, the land itself. Its schedule is that of the woodland trees, the wild grasses, the migrant birds. Go to northern Maine and you can walk with frost. Go to Carolina and you can bask in late summer sun. Travel north or south and you touch the year in another place. Stay where you are and it comes to you in its own time.

Essentially, autumn is the quiet completion of spring and summer. Spring was all eagerness and beginnings, summer was growth and flowering. Autumn is the achievement summarized, the harvested grain, the ripened apple, the grape in the wine press. Autumn is the bright leaf in the woodland, the opened husk on the bittersweet berry, the froth of asters at the roadside.

Leave the equinox to the record-keepers and know autumn where you find it, when it comes. See it, smell it, taste it, and forget the time of day or year. Autumn needs no clock or calendar.

That Cricket

September 23

The cricket is a small, black, ambulatory noise surrounded by a sentimental aura. On occasion it lives in the open fields, but its favorite habitat is behind a couch or under a bookcase in a room where somebody is trying to read. It has six legs, which make it an insect; two antennae, which make it a creature of sensitive feelings; two wings that can be scraped together, which make it a nuisance.

Only the male cricket scrapes its wings together to make its characteristic noise—or song, as some insist on calling it. The female has more important matters to attend to. Houses where people wish to read are chiefly inhabited by male crickets. S. H. Scudder, the entomologist, found a good many years ago that the common black cricket's notes are pitched in E natural, two octaves above middle C. We have found that many house crickets are flat, and persistently so. We have also found that while the cricket's customary tempo is eighty beats to the minute, it occasionally skips half a beat. Perhaps it has a bad heart.

Few adult crickets are supposed to survive the winter in cold climates such as ours. But few adult crickets in this latitude know when winter begins; they start scratching wing on wing in August and keep at it until the wings are quite worn out. Their wings are very durable. And a new crop of crickets is hatched each spring.

In China they used to hold cricket fights, pitting cricket against cricket and wagering on the outcome. Or they did until more important fighting engulfed their land. Such a custom had the particular virtue of eliminating one cricket each time a fight was held. The "song" of a Chinese cricket was not considered cozy or sweet or even domestic. The Chinese were wise.

September Morn

September 24

The chill of dawn seems even colder when one remembers the hot days of only a month ago. Then one remembers the past week's warm noons, hot, lazy afternoons, and one thinks that, after all, it now is September. One watches the mist over the water, gauze of the day's wakening.

It is quiet. No dawn chorus of songbirds. In the distance two crows caw, not yet arrogant but definitely self-assured. The world doesn't yet belong to the jays and crows, but it will before long. No sign of the flickers this early in the day, but by midmorning they will be around, restless and in loose flocks of a dozen or more, almost ready to go south. Not a swallow in sight either, though ten days ago they were lined up, practically queued up, on the telephone wires, ready to leave but lingering another hour, another day.

A whistling of wings and four mourning doves fly past, looking for a cornfield and the day's first meal. No sign of migrant ducks or geese yet, but one looks up, sees only the mist, listens, and hears nothing.

A faint anise smell is on the air, goldenrod scent, and the plumes close by glint with dew. High-bush cranberries, really viburnums, shine translucent red. Doll's eyes seem to stare at one from white baneberry. River grapes in miniature bunches begin to purple in the festooned riverbank trees. Sumac leaves, autumn's first scarlet, make the sumac fruit clusters an even deeper maroon. Asters are frosty white.

The mist swirls and begins to open. A breeze widens the opening overhead and September shines through, the deep blue sky of September.

Burs

September 25

Burs are ripening. Walk along a roadside or across the fields and you will know it all too well. Half an hour's walk can provide half an hour's work getting them off your clothes, to which they cling with hooks and spurs and barbs and spines. But they are worth looking at as you pluck them off, simply as examples of nature's ingenuity.

Undoubtedly there will be tick trefoils, flat little three-cornered green pods covered with barbed bristles. They come from a lesser legume which a month ago had sprays of miniature lilac sweet-pea flowers. Some call them beggar-ticks, but the real beggar-tick is like a small brown sunflower seed with a pair of barbed horns at the top and comes from a relative of the marigold.

There will probably be the tiny brown burs of enchanter's nightshade, too, little balls of hooked bristles that fairly burrow their way into tweeds. They come from an unworthy member of the evening primrose family which is not even remotely related to the nightshade that bears the lovely bittersweet berries.

You may have met burdock, but there will be no mistaking its big, hook-covered burs. Perhaps you will have found a patch of cockleburs, big as a fat thumb and barbarously armed. Or you may have crossed a patch of sandburs, which come in assorted sizes, all high on the list of nuisances, all pointed in their approach.

None of these bur plants, excepting the tick trefoil, is worth a second look when in flower. Their burs should all go into the fire or you will have them for neighbors next year. But they do demonstrate that nature has various ways of getting her seeds around. She has certainly endowed some plants with a lot of stick-to-itiveness.

The Jack Frost Legend

September 26

Old tales die hard. Every year the legendary figure of Jack Frost and his magic paint pot is revived when the color begins to come to the woodland. But early, hard frost is an enemy, not a friend, of the color. Sunlight, not frost, is the vital agent.

The coloring process begins when September's shortening daylight prompts the trees to begin withdrawing vital sap into trunk and root and cut off circulation to the leaves. With no new chlorophyll, that magic green pigment that enables the leaves to make sugar from air, moisture, and sunlight, the leaves begin to fade. As the old chlorophyll disintegrates, yellow pigments that were there all the time become visible. They produce the brilliant yellows of sugar maples, birches, and all their kindred. Meanwhile, sugars left in the leaves of other trees when they were sealed off begin to oxidize in the sunlight. They become pigments called xanthophyll and anthocyanin, reds, blues, and purples. They produce the fiery leaves of swamp maples and dogwoods, the deep reds and purples of oaks.

Early frost interrupts both these processes and turns the leaves sere and drab. Cool nights and bright, sunny days hasten the processes and enhance the colors. That is why our Northeast, with its sunny autumn days, is one of the most vivid color areas in the world. The only way Jack Frost helps is by staying away until the sunlight has created the color. Or, if he must come, by tripping lightly.

Migrating Monarchs

September 27

Frost has come to rural fields and gardens and the fires of life burn low in the insect world. The bugs and beetles are nearing the end of their time. Crickets and katydids seem to sense it; when you hear them on a warm evening now there is a new sense of urgency in their calls. Bumblebees sleep late, sometimes in the shelter of a tousled zinnia blossom, and wait for the sun to warm their blood enough so they can fly. Most butterflies have had their day and slumber as hostages to tomorrow in the egg, the cocoon, or as caterpillars.

But not all of them. Not the monarchs, those remarkable big black-and-orange butterflies. They migrate, even as the birds. Some of them travel 2,000 miles southward. Their migrant flight is under way now, past its peak in New England.

Like migrant birds, the monarchs follow regular migration routes, down major river valleys, along coastlines, across the high, dry plains. They travel the length of Cape Cod, cross to Long Island, follow its length, then cross to lower Jersey and go on down the coast. They go down the Pacific Coast in record numbers.

No one is sure why these butterflies migrate, or how they navigate. All we know is that they migrate, by the millions, and that monarchs come back every spring. Some probably are survivors of the host that went south; many—perhaps most—are a new generation hatched on the way north. But they won't be back until frost-free June.

Rare September Days

September 28

Lowell wrote about the rarity of June days, and Holmes the elder wrote of chill September. Neither of them seems to have noticed that some of the rarest days of the year come in September, days when it is comfortably cool but pulsing with life.

If we appreciate such days it is not wholly because they follow August. The contrast helps, but they would be welcome at any time. Days when the sky is clear and clean, when the air is crisp, when the wind is free of dust and not yet full of leaves. Late cicadas buzz in early afternoon. Field crickets fiddle in the tall grass at the country roadside. At dusk the katydids set up their clamor. Crows caw with less than usual raucousness. Bees still hum over fading heads of goldenrod. Asters, the persistent fall windlings, spangle the roadsides.

In a properly ordered world we should all be able to go out onto the hills on such days and know that life is fundamentally good. Good enough, at least, that we should take time to see and feel and sense the strength and elemental hospitality of the natural world around us. This is man's environment, and ours should be a way of life that cherishes it. We find meaning in it when we look, when we stand in the open and see bold horizons of faith, stubborn hills of strength, horizon-wide span of enduring purposes.

First the Maples *September 29*

It is the maples that make the spectacular flame of color that comes swooping down through the Northeastern woodland. Other trees add to it, of course, but take away that first dazzling blaze of the red maples and the gold and orange gleam and glow and glitter of the sugar maples that soon follow, and the whole spectacle would lack its dominant theme.

The sumacs are early color, embers that ignite the big blaze. The scarlet flame of woodbine climbs the slower trees soon after. By then the elms have turned rusty and have begun to shed, and the white ash groves become all amethystine, even a smoky blue. Basswood and hickory turn russet and the birches show clean, clear yellows. Then the red maples spread their scarlet and cerise and crimson up the valleys, first one branch, then one tree, then a whole valleyful of trees. And the color laps up the hillsides to the sugar maples and they turn scarlet and orange and gold, so golden that they seem to radiate their own sunlight.

That's the way the color comes, with here and there the splendor of a sassafras or a sweet gum all afire with reds and oranges and gold. And the lesser flame of dogwood and black cherry, smoldering crimson. And when the first flame of color has reached its peak, just as it is about to subside, the oaks come along with antique gold and rich tans and deep reds and purples, strong, enduring colors that prolong the spectacle. But first comes that burst of breathtaking maple color, that sea of scarlet and gleaming gold.

Autumn's Treasure Chest *September 30*

By the end of September the treasure chest of autumn begins to spill over with such wealth as no royal miser ever knew. You see it everywhere, glistening in the sunrise, flashing in the dew-wet morning, glowing in the quiet afternoon, aflame in the sunset. Woodland, roadside, and dooryard will soon be gemmed and jeweled beyond a rajah's richest dreams.

Would you have rubies and garnets and carnelians? Know the woodbine, the dogwood, the swamp maple, the black cherry. Do you yearn for fire opals, sardonyx, topaz, or chalcedony? Seek out the black gum, the sassafras, the beech, and the basswood. Does your taste run to sapphires and amethysts? Then go to the white ash and the black oak, and the lesser viburnums that grow beneath them. And if you still cherish jade and jasper and Brazilian tourmaline, look to the hillsides where the white pine grows and the spruce and the hemlock, with the partridgeberry and the Christmas fern.

Richness and wealth? This is less than the half of it, for

soon will come the gold in the sugar maples and the birches, the sycamores and the aspens. Gold that will be billowed against the sky—a sky of lapis lazuli and turquoise and aquamarine. Gold that will be heaped and drifted beneath the trees, new-minted gold and Roman gold and antique gold, more gold than the Incas and the Aztecs ever mined or the galleons ever bore away.

For a few weeks now we are richer than Croesus, our world overflowing with autumn's incredible wealth of priceless color.

October

HUNTER'S MOON
Like the Harvest Moon, the Hunter's Full Moon is brilliant several nights in a row, ideal for 'coon hunters.

October

October 1

October has so many virtues one hardly knows where to begin. The woodland color is spectacular, but it really is only the backdrop, the setting which enhances blue skies, widening horizons, crisp nights, mild days, and the whole satisfaction of ripeness and achievement. Even Indian summer, a specialty of October's weather, is a kind of seasonal exultation.

The cidery tang of windfall apples is in the country air. Wild grapes hang purpling from the climbing vines, slowly sweetening. Bittersweet's bright orange and the lacquered red of barberries are brilliant accents at the roadside; the partridges come down to feed on them and whir away with a startling roar. The clean, wild, acrid odor of walnut hulls, and butternut and hickory, scents the open woodland; and squirrels are busy as beavers.

The vast bowl of sky grows wider day by day, its blue depths blue as October's own gentians. You begin to see the hilltops again, the shape of the expanding world. Distance has its haze, but now it is a mist-haze, no longer the dust-haze of hot summer afternoons. At night the stars have a frosty twinkle, the Big Dipper hangs low, and Cassiopeia sits high on her throne.

The owl hoots, the fox barks, and the hunter's hound

is restless. October makes a man want to get up and go and see and hear and feel. October is the glory and the magnificence of the year's late afternoon.

The Color

October 2

It comes quietly as mist in the night, but it doesn't vanish as the sun rises. It remains, stronger day after day. It spreads, leaf to leaf, branch to branch, tree to tree. It climbs from the valley to the hilltop. Soon it will possess the countryside.

It begins as a few scarlet leaves in the sumac while the goldenrod is still at its prime, before the asters claim the roadside. It spreads through the bushes and up the gray trunk of the dead popple where Virginia creeper climbs, a fiery beacon in the woodland. It stains the viburnums crimson and purple in the underbrush. It smolders beside the stone wall where Jack-in-the-pulpit's ember-red berries are clustered in the grass.

The elms turn lemony yellow, then rust away. White ash has a spectrum all its own, from bronze and yellowish-brown to blue and eggplant-purple. Swamp maples turn as scarlet as a tanager, fill the lowland with a tree-deep pond of stormy sunset color. Streamside basswood has a ruddy, blushing bronze on its leaves. Up the hillside, just below the pines and hemlocks, the birches flash and flutter, yellow as lemon pie—not golden but yellow. The gold comes in the sugar maples, sunlight gold and blush pink, when the swamp maples begin to darken past their prime.

And finally come the oaks, the deliberate oaks, scarlet and ruby and crimson and maroon and Burgundy and purple, and all the warm, leathery browns. We sum it all up in two words: The Color.

The Vivid Maples

October 3

As the color begins to appear in the woodlands it becomes obvious how much October's brilliance owes to the maples. Especially, here in the Northeast, to the red or swamp maples and to the sugar maples. Without them, the autumn color spectacle would lack an essential dimension.

The red maple is marked by its scarlet insistence, an unmistakable red that colors its tufted blossoms in the spring, its winged seeds in early summer, and its leaves in October. Even its twigs have a reddish twinge, and its buds are red-russet. A brook lined with red maples becomes a winding thread of scarlet in a green and gold valley. A low-lying meadow that has gone back to maple brush, on its way to becoming a maple thicket, is a scarlet pond lapping at the surrounding hillsides. Red maples color early.

The sugar maples are golden trees, for the most part. Their blossoms are yellow and later than those of the red maple. Their seeds, which ripen in the fall, have yellow vanes. And often the sugar maple's leaves turn golden yellow, sun-yellow, so that even on a clouded day in October one seems to walk in sunshine in a sugar maple grove. Some sugar maples turn red, but seldom as vivid as the scarlet of the red maples. Others mix reds and yellows, still others turn an airy peach pink. At the height of the color on the New England hills, it is the sugar maples and their close cousins, the black maples, that dominate.

There are also the birches and the ashes and the oaks, but without maples "the color" would be commonplace.

The Travelers *October 4*

Plants have a thousand different ways of scattering their seeds and, as Kipling said about the ways of telling tribal lays, every single one of them is right. They work. They insure survival of the species, which is the purpose and the destiny of the seed.

Some use the wind. Milkweed pods ripen and free their seeds to sail away on fluffy parachutes. Basswood trees launch their bangles of tiny nuts on leaflike sails to ride the autumn breeze. Maple seeds go whirling away on single-bladed helicopters. Thistles fray their fluff, each tuft bearing a seed to a distant seedbed.

Some use birds and animals. Oaks and hickories and beeches shake down their harvest of nuts, some to roll away, some to be stowed or hidden by squirrels and jays. Autumn berries, dogwood and puccoon and viburnum, barberry and baneberry and all the hollies, invite birds to feast and fly away. Wild grapes ripen with dark, juicy temptation for raccoon, opossum, and fox as well as robin and flicker and thrasher and jay.

Some use people. Walk the roadside now, or the open fields, and you soon carry a cargo of stick-tights and small burs on socks and trousers, skirt and jacket. Walk a mile and you spend half an hour ridding your clothes of them. They are seeds with hooks and spurs and spines and barbs, tiny as the tick trefoil's stick-tights, big as cockleburs, and all sizes in between. Beggar-ticks, grass burs, tack-sharp nuts, needle grass awns, chaffy bergamot seeds—they hitch rides, go places, find new seedbeds, to keep the earth green.

On the Hearth

October 5

Of all the nostalgic things man does in this age of automation, building a hearth fire is one of the least utilitarian and one of the most satisfying.

We learned long ago than an open fire is probably the least effective way to heat a house, or even one room. Out of that knowledge came the stove, the furnace, and central heating. And the thermostat, which made kindling and the match as obsolete as the stone arrowhead. Or as the fireplace itself.

The satisfaction of a fireplace fire is a combination of sentiment, emotion, and vague race memories as intangible as smoke. Man is a natural fire tender, has been since ancient times. He is the master of this flame, at least, if not of the vastly larger flame now possible. His hearth stands for his home. Here, in the glow of flames, friendship has flourished and survived winters of doubt as well as winters of ice and snow.

And back of that open flame are intangibles of a past as old as the caves. Fire enabled man to drive back not only fang and claw but darkness. In the faint tang of wood smoke is the smell of campfires that marked man's incredible journey from cave to city, from flint to atom. In the glowing coals at evening's end is the hope, the dream, that has persisted through night after long, dark, discouraging night.

Hunter's Moon

October 6

Now comes the Hunter's Moon, the full moon of October, which for night after night is a beacon to man and dog and big buck coon. Cornfields rustle, rabbits lie close, the owl courses the crisp meadow on silent wings. And even a country house is a prison, friendly, but a prison just the same. A man has to get up and go, once the moon has risen. He has to know the night smell of October, the night feel, the night wonder.

The hunt is only an excuse. There's also the country road with its long shadows and its gleam of late goldenrod and aster. There's the tang of black walnuts underfoot, the crispness of russet leaves, the bold silver of white birch boles, moonlit mottle of sycamore, dark whisper of a hemlock grove. And the soft rush and quick flash of doe and fawns startled from the orchard's windfalls.

Soon or late, the dog gives tongue, sharp, sudden, echoing all across the hills, the trail song of a dog born for such an October night. Through the cornfield, down through the woods, across the brook, up the hill, back to the stand of maples. Then the sharp yips, the dog cry: "Coon treed!" And if there's to be coon as well as hunt, the tree must be found, the quarry caught.

It doesn't too much matter whether there's a coon caught or only the chase. There's always the night, the companionship, the remembered tales beside a fire. There's man talk, and dog talk, and there's the silence of close friendship with October all around. And if a man gets home late and full of muscle-weariness, that doesn't much matter either, because a man has also filled himself with soul ease and a measure of contentment.

Put Away That Hoe *October 7*

This is the time of year when a vegetable garden needs a frost. The gardener himself secretly wishes for a frost, though it isn't quite cricket to come right out and say so. Openly he is expected to brag about the tomatoes he still has ripening. Actually, he has ripened just about enough tomatoes for this year. He is willing to call it quits and wait for May and radishes and tomato plants. By then he will be fed up with canned tomatoes, and he knows it; by then he would pay a dollar apiece for those greenish-orange tomatoes now on his vines. But right now he'll settle for a clean-up job in the garden and a weekend without a hoe, a spray gun, or a duster in his hands.

That's one of the best things about nature in a land of four seasons—frost comes and puts an end to the succulent growing things. No garden should endure, with all its dividends and demands, more than about six months a year. The other six months one should be allowed to rest and dream and yearn and get rid of the calluses. And think how wonderful is modern transportation, which brings fresh garden produce from California and Texas and Florida. And think loftily how much better home-grown lettuce and beans and corn and tomatoes are than those thus miraculously transported. Six months, as it were, to appreciate.

Hail the frost! Hail the blackened vine! Let those who make green-tomato pickles have those green tomatoes! The corn stands sere and stripped, the beans are rustling in the wind, the death rattle in their dried pods. The squash have given up. The lettuce has all bolted. Put away the hoe, close the garden gate, and let it frost.

The Summons

October 8

We might call it fall fever, but we don't, perhaps because it is restlessness rather than lassitude. It is more like wanderlust, though the wanderer merely wants to go, to see new places, and the urgency now is to see old, familiar places again. Autumn burnishes the memories as well as the hills.

It isn't only the coloring of the leaves, though that certainly is a part of it. It is a deeper sky, a broader horizon, new dimensions to the familiar world. It is the stubborn contours of the hills coming into sight again, fundamentals still at hand. It is old vistas re-opening as the birches strew their golden leaves, like thistledown, to the gusting wind.

It is there, and we know it is there; but the summons says to go and see and experience the certainty. Hills wait for the climbers and valleys invite those who prefer the stream's winding way. Paths that knew our footsteps need to know them again, and our feet remember the paths. Squirrels scold and jays spread the word of our coming. If it is morning, the mists rise. Noon, and the haze makes the far hilltops shimmer. Evening, and the long light of dusk becomes the glow of the Hunter's Moon.

It is not only the going, but the remembering, the very being. It is the knowing that there are certainties.

The Superfluous Color

October 9

If technology, with its practical laws of efficiency, were in charge of everything we would have to dispense with the autumn color in our woodlands. Not with the trees, which are models of efficiency in most of their processes, but with color itself, which apparently has no purpose whatever. People may think it is beautiful, but it isn't needed for the trees' health, growth, or fruitfulness.

In technical terms, the color is waste, sheer excess and leftover. It is created by substances revealed only when the tiring tree seals off the sap circulation and no longer replenishes the chlorophyll in the leaves. The old chlorophyll disintegrates and yellow pigments called carotene and xanthophyll, related to our daily vitamins, become visible. The reds and purples appear when the sun has oxidized sugars and acids the tree has abandoned in the leaves. When the leaves have passed their peak of brilliance and fallen from the trees, they molder into humus that eventually will feed parent tree as well as lesser plants. But the color adds nothing to the humus. Leaves that wither and turn brown make the same kind of humus as those most dazzling red or brilliant yellow. There is no difference between the leaf mold under a ruby-red swamp maple and that under an upland rock maple that was sun-gold.

Fortunately, there is no technology among trees. Especially in October, when those useless pigments and that left-over sugar and acid flare into all this superfluous color. Whether the trees need it or not, it is magnificent.

The Walk

October 10

A man can muster a variety of reasons when he goes for a walk. It's a nice day. He needs the exercise. He hasn't been out in the park, or the fields, or the woods, for quite a while. He wants a breath of fresh air, needs to stretch his legs.

Excuses, all of them, and good enough. But they aren't reasons. The reasons are both personal and complicated. How can you explain that you need to know that the trees are still there, and the hills and the sky? Anyone knows they are. How can you say it is time your pulse responded to another rhythm, the rhythm of the day and the season instead of the hour and the minute? No, you cannot explain. So you walk.

There are the trees, bigger than a man, smaller than a mountain. There are the hills, the enduring hills. There is the sky, where birds fly and white cloud-galleons sail, the vast blue bowl of sky with the certainty of day and night, the infinity of stars.

There is the earth, the sun, the wind—the turning earth, the blazing sun, the restless wind that knows the farthest ocean, the highest hill. You walk, stretch your legs, refresh your lungs. You see and feel and know some of the things a man must know about this deliberately spinning earth where man came to being, where man still lives.

The Signs *October 11*

The woodchucks are so fat they waddle, though they still can outrun the farm dog. The squirrels are hoarding nuts, and the chipmunks are garnering grass seed and lining nests with thistledown. Field mice are discovering chinks in the farmer's granary and exploring the possibilities of the cellar under the house. Muskrats are cleaning out their burrows, making new entryways for cold-weather approach. The chickadees have come down from the pine groves to see whether the feeders have yet been put up and stocked with seed, particularly sunflower seed.

It's the season for chinking the cracks, banking the foundations, putting up storm sash, seeing that the woodpile is ample and the oil tank full. Humans are forehanded too, since they don't hibernate, as the woodchuck, or depend on handouts, as a large proportion of the chickadee population seems to. It's the time when the farmer looks with satisfaction to his full silos and hay barns, to the apples and potatoes in his cellar, and the reserves, not to mention the preserves, on the shelves and in the freezer. He also looks to the state of last year's boots and galoshes and wool shirts and socks. And his wife gets out the mufflers and the heavy blankets and thinks of stews and hearty soups.

There's Indian summer still to come, we hope. And there's Thanksgiving, too, before winter. But there's no mistaking the season. The birds know it, and the beasts know it, and so does the man who can read the signs. After fall comes winter.

The Messages

October 12

Autumn's messages are written in many ways. There is the gleaming symmetry of a frosted spiderweb at dawn. There is the glistening rune of milkweed floss spilling from the pod. There are the smoke signals of morning mist. Soon there will be the penciled flight of departing geese scrawled against the sky. But now, on mild afternoons, the woolly bear caterpillars are tracing one of the most cryptic messages of all in their looping script across the lawn or along the roadside.

The woolly bear is the caterpillar of a small pinkish-yellow moth called Isabella. Unlike many other caterpillars, the woolly bear hibernates, but it does so by degrees. When the first frosty nights come it seeks shelter in an outbuilding or a pile of brush or stones, curls up, and goes to sleep. During a warm spell it emerges to bask in the sun, then goes back to its chosen shelter. And when the cold clamps down it becomes a fuzzy little knot of ice, apparently frozen to the core. But next spring it will thaw and waken, search for a plantain leaf, feed, pupate, and become an Isabella moth.

Because its furry coat is striped brown and black, and perhaps because it hibernates, the woolly bear has a reputation as a weather forecaster. Those who would read its prophecy compare the width of its stripes. A narrow brown stripe, the saying goes, means a mild winter. But, like so many prophets, the woolly bears are equivocal. One says yes, another says no. All they really agree on is that autumn brings chilly nights when a woolly bear should find shelter.

Wild Geese

October 13

Of all the migrant birds, the wild goose seems most to typify the restless spirit of autumn. A part of this comes from the fact that geese are big, spectacular birds and travel in flocks, often huge flocks. But another part is the garrulousness of geese. Most birds travel in silence, but not the goose. In the air or on the water, it chatters and gabbles, gossips and confers. Geese are not reticent birds.

You begin to hear and see them now, moving down by stages from the north. In a city street, a suburban dooryard, or a rural roadside, you hear the distant clamor. It seems to echo from the whole sky. You look up, searching, and at last you see the penciled V, high against the blue, arrowing southward.

Or you stand beside a quiet pond or lake in late afternoon and hear the chatter, like the distant yapping of small dogs. Then you see them coming in over a hilltop, a dark cloud of them, to circle once and then drop, long necks outstretched, wings cupped, feet outthrust, to land in a rush of spray.

Wherever you see them, they are something special. The sky is theirs, and far places. They come from over the horizon, like autumn itself, and tomorrow or next week they will be following summer southward again. And earthbound you will have the haunting memory, the faint echo of wild goose chatter high overhead, to remind you of autumn's footloose travelers, the proud, talkative, far-ranging geese.

Mast Season

October 14

This is mast season, or it used to be, when hogs ran loose and fattened naturally, before they were penned and stuffed with corn. Mast consisted of wild nuts, chiefly acorns, beechnuts, and chestnuts, and in the old days the hogs harvested even more of them than the squirrels. Hogs were mast-fattened in the fall and provided mast-sweet hams and bacon. The word "mast" seems to have come from the same root as "meat."

The mast still ripens, though few hogs fatten on it now. Walk through any oak grove and you will hear the acorns dropping, see the empty acorn cups beneath the trees where the squirrels have harvested. Look at the silver-bolled beech trees and you will see the bristly burs that hold brown, three-sided beechnuts. The native chestnuts have vanished, though persistent sprouts keep coming up from old roots, living a few years, then dying of the blight. You won't find chestnuts in the woods, those big, bright brown nuts, three to a pod, inside the big, spiny burs. But along fence-rows and brushy margins you will find hazel brush and hazelnuts, another—though minor—element in mast.

The really tough nuts, more shell than meat, also ripen. But hickory nuts, butternuts, and walnuts never were classed as mast. Squirrels ate them, and still do, and so do country folk who appreciate special things. Such as the look and smell and sound of the autumn woodland. Such as the remembered taste of mast-fattened ham. Such as mast season itself.

Dogwood Berries

October 15

Dogwood berries gleam in the woodland in lacquer-red clusters, bright as holly at Christmas. There's a big crop of them this fall, for the dogwoods bloomed magnificently last May, and everywhere there was a blossom there is now a bunch of berries.

Gray squirrels sometimes show a particular fondness

for dogwood berries, littering the ground beneath the trees with the bright red outer hulls. What they are after is the kernel. To reach that kernel one has to strip off the fleshy hull, which looks like the flesh of a rose haw but tastes bitter as quinine. Beneath that is a nut, bone-hard in shell and only about a quarter of an inch in diameter. Inside this shell is a kernel, a bit of white, oily meat no larger than a radish seed. To the human tongue it has a taste something like the taste of a Brazil nut. Presumably it is a delicacy in the squirrel's diet; certainly it is hard to get at and there's little of it when brought to light.

The quinine taste of the fleshy hull comes from the same tannic principle that is present in the bark of the flowering dogwood. A brew made of the bark has certain quinine properties and has been used as a fairly effective home remedy for fevers. But it is powerfully bitter on the tongue. And the oily quality of the kernel of the nut is no illusion, either. At one time the fruit of a related dogwood, *Cornus sanguinea,* was pressed in France to obtain an oil for soap making.

But to the passerby or the walker on country roads the dogwood berries are only another item of autumn beauty which, if left to themselves, will still gleam on the branch well into the winter.

The Wind's Cargo *October 16*

The autumn winds blow, and silvery milkweed pods open, and silken floss rides every gust, tufted floss bearing germs of next summer's green and urgent life. No doubt some patient botanist once counted the seeds in a single milkweed pod, but the figure is not readily at hand. It must run into the thousands, and anyone making such a count would be all but overwhelmed with floss. How nature packs so much silken fiber into one small pod is almost as much of a mystery as how she condenses such an urgent bit of life into one small seed.

But milkweed is not the only airborne seed riding the autumn air. Thistledown, loosened in the head by busy goldfinches, is wafting away, each tuft of down carrying a seed. Late dandelions are trusting their seeds to the wind. Such goldenrod as had already ripened offers minute bits of floss to the wind, each bit with its one seed attached. Dozens of plants send their seeds journeying on the wind, borne by airy fiber, nature's balloons and drifting parachutes.

Sometimes the air glistens with its cargo of floss-borne seeds, looking almost frosty even on mild afternoons. The time of leaf fall brings a crisp scuffling as the wind courses the land, but that same wind is pregnant with next summer's blossoms. The leaves come down to mulch the earth, and the winged seeds scatter among the leaves to take root in another year. And the wind shepherds them both.

October's frosts close out a season's growth, but the winds of these frosty days are rich with life, persisting life. Now is the time that nature does much of her seeding for another cycle, another green and urgent season.

Indian Summer *October 17*

There are two schools of thought about Indian summer.

One school is deeply concerned with the origin of the name and the time when the season occurs. The name, they say, is of uncertain origin, though it appears to have originated in New England. There is no reason to believe the Indians used the term. It did not occur in print in reference to the American season until 1794, by which time it was in general use throughout New England. England has a similar season, equally variable in date. If it comes early, in

September, it is known there as St. Austin's or St. Augustine's summer. If it comes in October it is St. Luke's summer, and if it is as late as November it is St. Martin's summer. None of these saints, obviously, was an American Indian.

Some members of the school say Indian summer must come no earlier than late October. Some say it cannot recur, though there is a difference of opinion here. There is agreement, however, that the season is characterized by clear, calm, mild days, a hazy horizon, and clear, chill nights. And the barometer, for those members of this school who go by such data, stands high.

The second school takes the stand that the name and the date are of minor consequence. They say that whenever it comes, Indian summer is too fine a season to spend in discussion or argument. When it comes, they say, a man should get outdoors and bask, or go tramping, or have a last fling with a fishing rod, or just gloat and be content.

We belong to the second school of thought.

The Quiet Comes *October 18*

Hard frost has come, back in the hills, and the quiet of autumn deepens. It is quiet, not silence, for the crows are loud in proclaiming their possession, and the jays are shouting at each other and the world at large. In the stillness of the night the red fox barks at the starlight and the barred owl hoots at its own echo.

But the frogs that were croaking loudly a month ago have gone into hibernation. The harvest flies that shrilled in hot summer afternoons have mated, laid their eggs, and ended their brief lives. The field crickets and their monotonous drone that marked August and September have gone and also left next year's crickets in the egg. And the katydids, save for an occasional one that found a haven from the frost, have had their say and fiddled their own swan song. The evening concerts have ended.

Now come the quiet days of Indian summer and the quiet nights of starlight and leaf scuffle. October's magnificence comes without a whisper. Listen as you may, you never hear a maple leaf turning to translucent gold or an oak leaf turning from green to tan to purplish bronze. An October wind can bring them sailing from the trees and down the road, across the meadow, with a swishing crispness and a rustle. But no frog croaks, no green cricket drones, no harvest fly shrills. The quiet deepens toward the winter silence, when snowflakes will whisper as they fall in the long night.

Autumn Sunlight *October 19*

Autumn sunlight may be no different from spring sunlight, except that days now are getting shorter instead of longer. But when a sunny day follows a day or two of autumn murk and rain with a touch of autumn chill, it is like a blessing and a promise fulfilled. The dire threats to the earth's atmosphere are no less real, but they have been postponed a little longer. The sun mankind has known all his generations still is there, and we survive in its radiance. This we know again when sunlight clarifies the day.

Spring sunshine is the awakener, rousing buds, opening leaves and flowers to clothe the earth again and bring life to the winter-dormant world. Summer sunlight is the ripener, the hot accompaniment of growth and maturity, of fertile egg and seed, the insurance of life in summers to come. Winter sunlight is a token of rest, of the long sleep, the short day; it is proof that blizzards blow themselves out, that ice eventually melts, that no winter lasts forever.

But autumn sunlight is simply perfection of the day, glory of the season, the year's high achievement, somehow. It summons one to the outdoors, where even the autumn leaves partake of it. The maples shimmer, the birches glow, and when they drop their leaves their splendor is sunlight at their feet. Roadside grasses ripen with sunlit heads of seed. The sky is clean, clear, and the sun itself is benevolent, the autumn sun making an autumn day a special moment in time.

The Gentians *October 20*

October's frosty nights and blue-sky days seem specially designed to show off the gentians, that hardy clan which waits for a minimum of competition before it comes to bloom. Only the roadside asters still make much of a show, and even they are forgotten when the country wanderer is fortunate enough to find a meadow or a woodland edge where the gentians blow.

The fringed gentian is the special beauty of the clan, certainly the most famous. It isn't a large flower, but its vase-shaped throat and four deeply fringed petals give it a particular grace, and its color is unforgettable. It is a kind of misty pale blue, practically aquamarine, and a patch of fringed gentians is like a swatch of October's blue sky on the grass. Its cousin, the closed or bottle gentian, which often grows nearby, is a deeper blue and never spreads its petals. Alone, it would catch the eye and call for exclamations; but it is usually overshadowed by the subtler beauty of its fringed companions.

One reason the fringed gentians are so admired is that they are unpredictable. One year they may deck a chosen meadow, and the next year they may be gone. This will-o'-the-wisp habit is tantalizing. It seems to be a consequence of the wind, for the gentian's seed is almost dust-fine and if it ripens on a windy day can be blown some distance from the original stand. But wherever the gentians grow they are October's special glory, as beautiful as they are hard to find.

Leaf Smoke

October 21

There are sound reasons for not burning leaves. Their smoke adds to the urban smog, their smoldering flames create a fire hazard, and unburned leaves make good mulch and compost. Burning them is both wasteful and hazardous, so nowadays enlightened folk either compost autumn leaves or let the trash men haul them away.

But now and then some suburbanite or villager forgets all these good reasons, or ignores them, and rakes a pile of leaves into some safe place and burns them, for his own good reasons. When he does, other nostalgic people sniff the evening air and remember forgotten autumns when leaf smoke was the incense of October evenings. Leisurely, uncrowded evenings, uninterrupted by television, unhurried by the delusion of protracted daylight saving time.

It isn't only the leaf smoke, pungent as it is. It is all the other remembered fragrances of the season, the spiced aroma from the pickling kettle in the rural kitchen, the acrid scent of walnut hulls, the smell of roasting chestnuts, the beady tang of apple cider, the savory simmer of mincemeat in the making, the tantalizing smell of pumpkin pie in the oven. It is frosty mornings, and Indian summer days, and the hearthside smell of wood smoke curling from an evening chimney.

It is wasteful, unwise, in some places illegal leaf smoke. And yet it is October and autumn evenings and remembered years. If you are middle-aged, don't allow yourself to smell it or you will wonder what happened to those years.

The River Grapes *October 22*

This has been a good year for wild grapes, particularly the late-ripening little river grapes. They still festoon the bushes and trees along the watercourses where the vines are vigorous climbers, the clusters of miniature grapes revealed in all their plenty as the leaves sere and fall. The birds are feasting, and the opossums; and canny country folk who know the special tang of river-grape jelly are gathering them by the pailful.

As fruit, the river grapes are inconsequential, for they are seldom as much as half an inch in diameter and their seeds are so big there is little room for flesh. But they are full of juice, deep purple juice, and that juice is the very essence of untamed flavor, tart enough to pucker the mouth. In the old days, farm folk sometimes fermented a wine from them that made a strong man sit up and take notice, but now such wine is only a memory. Those who gather these potent little grapes simmer their juice into a deep amethystine jelly that has the flavor of deep woodlands and wild, white water and makes oldsters remember roast venison.

The fox grape gave us the Concord and the Catawba, but the river grape was never really tamed. It remains as wild as the bobcat and the wily red fox. It may twine the farmer's garden fence and creep along his pasture's stone walls, but it never really belongs to him. Even when he gathers its fruit and jells its juice, the river grape is insistently, wonderfully, nostalgically wild.

The Goose-Bone Prophets *October 23*

This is the season when goose-bone weather prophets once were so articulate. They consulted the birds and beasts, weighed acorns, counted corn husks, measured the stripes on woolly caterpillars, and made their pronouncements about the coming winter. Those who were right more often than wrong achieved deserved reputations as seers.

Much of the fur-and-feathers detail, of course, was hocus-pocus. It survived because the birds and beasts couldn't talk, and the prophet would. Actually, most of the "portents" were a consequence of the summer just past, not arcane signs of the future. A good growing season, with plenty of food and only normal competition for it, always produces strong, healthy birds and animals that achieve thick coats of fur and feathers for the winter ahead. When oaks thrive they produce fat acorns. When there is a big acorn crop the squirrels are busier than usual hoarding. And the stripes of the woolly bear caterpillar vary from one individual to another, year by year.

The best of the goose-bone prophets were shrewd guessers with long memories and an uncanny sense of weather. They knew that mysterious messages from nature had an age-old appeal, and they were temporarily akin to the ancient oracles. The Weather Bureau may commune with highs and lows and jet streams and even with solar cycles, and it may run up its cautious forecasts on complex computers; but it doesn't seem to care what the owls are saying, or the geese, or the squirrels. The back-country prophets did, or said they did, and we miss them.

Autumn Evening *October 24*

Dusk comes early and the evening breeze whispers in the newly fallen leaves. The Dipper hangs low on the northern horizon and Vega is almost overhead, still dimmed by the lingering glow of sunset an hour ago. No bird sings. No katydid rasps. Sere corn blades rustle in the roadside field. The drought-low brook creeps, almost silent, across the meadow, livened only by the glint of strengthening starlight in its lingering pools.

One walks, seemingly alone with the night and the universe. But as the dusk deepens the eight-hoot call of the barred owl is heard from the far hillside. Then silence again, and one's own footsteps in the leaf-strewn road. A farm dog barks in the distance and on the highway down the valley a truck growls into a lower gear for the long grade over the hilltop. And now the silent stars gleam beyond the thinning treetops.

The owl eight-hoots again and one knows he is not alone, even in the starlit immensity of the autumn night.

The Autumn Oaks *October 25*

The sequence was established long ages ago, before man was here to see it. Soft maples turn red. Then birches and poplars turn yellow. Then the hard maples bring the color to its peak as they become shimmering clouds of blushing gold that give a sunny glow even to a dour and lowering day. And finally, but not until the other trees have passed their brilliant climax, the deliberate oaks make their concession to the season.

There's something about the oaks that won't be hurried. They are slow of growth, even as seedlings. In the spring they are late to open bud and spread their leaves. White oaks ripen all their acorns every year, but the other side of the family, the black oaks, take two years to mature their meaty nuts. All of them come late to color in the autumn, as though waiting for their impulsive neighbors to end their pomp and pageant. Then they put on their deep crimsons, their luminous purples, and their bronze and russet tans, the warm colors of late autumn, the strong, deep colors that make one think of the earth and its fundamental rocks.

Fall is for the earlier trees, the exuberant ones. Their

leaf-fall gave the season its name. But the oaks, late to color and tenacious of leaf, are autumn trees, stubbornly resisting fall frost and rain. And their colors persist, almost defiant in the woodland, as fall passes and autumn deepens. Their leaves will slowly sere and leach, but they will still be there to rattle and rustle in the winter's gales.

Half-Past Autumn

October 26

You hear, you feel, you see what time it is on the big clock of the year. It isn't quite half-past autumn, but it will be soon. Back on standard time today, the sun sets before five on the clock for the first time since January. Now the shortening days will seem even shorter and the lengthening nights will start early.

But the time was signaled by the gabbling geese, which have been coming down from the north the past ten days or more. Their flights, like penciled V's high in the October sky, go past with distant chatter, arrowing toward the southern horizon. And down here, oblivious of such far travelers, the jays and crows shout triumph and proclaim possession of the autumn woodland. Walk the country road now and you feel the mildness of midafternoon, the deepening chill of evening. Cut through a pasture and you feel ripeness all around you. Look up and you see the clarity of autumn sky through the naked branches, vistas and horizons visible again, height and breadth once more. Even the flutter of leaves on the oaks and beeches is a token of the time. And when you face the northern sky at dusk the Great Bear is down on the horizon, Cassiopeia sits high overhead, and off to the east Orion, the Hunter, is now in sight. The clock of the stars leaves no doubt about what time it is.

Star Nights

October 27

The Big Dipper now lies close to the northern horizon in the early evening. Those who call that constellation the Great Bear say he has come down to wash his paws in the northern lakes before they are sealed in by winter's ice. Cygnus, the Swan, flies high, just to the west of the zenith. Off to the east the tantalizing Pleiades are in sight again. In the southwest Aquila, the Eagle, is still on the wing but sinking, night by night, toward the earth.

These are star nights, with a late moon, and as the trees bare their branches our eyes are invited upward. The summer's dust has begun to ease away, the air clears, and the stars surpass their summer glow. Another month and they will glitter as though polished by the frost. By then Orion will be visible in the east at evening and Pegasus, the Great Square of stars will be almost overhead. The Great Bear, having washed his paws, will be climbing the skies once more in his untiring circle of the Pole Star.

There is eternity in those star patterns. They have been substantially the same in each October, and in each April and June as well, since man devised the first calendar. Caesar saw those same stars in the same places as we see them, and so did the earliest Pharaoh. The Stone Age caveman saw and was awed by them. And they will still be there 10,000 years from now. Look at the sky, these October evenings, and see the certainty of forever.

The Fall

October 28

The color comes, creeping down from the north in slow waves of gold and crimson in birch and maple, and for a little while we marvel at the sweep of beauty, cherish the spectacle of a single tree. The totality of change, of a green world gone and a dazzled, emblazoned world taking its place, is almost beyond belief. Then comes rain and wind, and the ultimate meaning of fall is at hand.

Autumn is a calendar season, but fall is the time when the color comes swirling down from the treetops. Day before yesterday the rising sun lit a vast bonfire in the maples, and at noon the light beneath them was so golden it shimmered. Yesterday it rained. Today the maples stand half naked against the clearing sky and the incredible wealth of beaten gold is on the ground beneath them. Fall has come, the fall of the leaves.

Color persists, but except in the oaks it is in tatters and remnants. And the oaks, with their deep reds and purples and leathery browns, only emphasize the fall. Birches stand slim against the hillsides. Elms are a row of witches' brooms.

On the ground the fallen leaves are restless, skittering at the roadsides, drifting into the fence corners, free as the wind itself. But their colors already begin to fade. Their brief glory is gone. Winter will quiet them, mat them, leach them, make the fall a meaningful part of the year, the whole.

Constable Jay *October 29*

Now the jays take over, the jays and the crows. The robins, the flickers, the thrashers, and all those summer songsters have gone south and it is up to the jays and crows to keep things in order here. The crows attend to the big, important matters such as crow conventions and long, loud discussions of the weather. The jays are more like local constables and truant officers. They take care of petty crime and local gossip.

Watch a jay on a frosty morning and see how he resembles a pompous officer of the old school. His feathers are fluffed against the cold and he sits and scowls. His vest is snug across an ample chest. He even seems to have a series of chins. His crest is a kind of avian hat that lends a degree of dignity. Till he opens his mouth. A jay always rasps and seems to resent the climate, the landscape, the meals, or the company.

But this must be said: The jay has an immaculate air. The white cravat at his throat, the white bars on his wings, the white edging on his tail, are crisply white. The blue of his wings is a clean, rich blue, particularly against a gray autumn sky. He has an air. He can strut sitting still.

There he is now, ignoring the clamor of crows down the valley, sitting in the leafless apple tree watching the chickadees. Not scowling, but seeing to it that the chickadees aren't too carefree. After all—harumph—Mr. Jay is a constable, isn't he?

Pumpkin Pie *October 30*

It is idle to speculate on who made the first pumpkin pie, but it wasn't the Indians. They gave us the roasting-ear and hominy and succotash, but when it came to the pumpkin they hadn't much imagination. They dried it and made a kind of mushy winter fare of it, perhaps sweetened with maple sugar eventually, but otherwise drab. It took a kitchen genius to make a pumpkin pie, and such geniuses are rare even today.

There are pumpkins aplenty, heaped at roadside stands, glowing in orange beauty on rural doorsteps, even lying like full moons in the fields. But Pumpkin Pie—and we capitalize, to distinguish the worthy achievement—is hard to find. How do you know one when you find it? By its look, first of all, golden brown, rich as an old gold coin. By its smell, savory as secret spice, autumn made manifest. Ultimately by its flavor, its texture, its very inner being. It is rich with eggs and cream, it is smooth to the tongue, it makes the taste buds rejoice with ginger, nutmeg, cinnamon, and some secret ingredient that only the artist knows. And it is tenderly enclosed, cupped like the precious thing it is, in a crust that melts in the mouth.

That is Pumpkin Pie, one of the great glories of autumn in our land. When you find it, you celebrate. You know then that the pumpkin was put into this world not to become a jack-o'-lantern or a dooryard decoration. You know that it was put here to become a very special pie, and that you were put here to discover it.

The Larches

October 31

They are like giant candle flames in the cool, damp woodlands now, preparing to shed their golden tan needles. Of all American trees of the pine family, only the larches and the bald cypresses are deciduous, and we have no cypress this far north. The larches—some call them tamaracks—are among our oldest trees; they and their kind felt the earth writhe and convulse; they knew the long, deep cold of the Ice Ages. And here they still are, brightening the woodland just when the maples, the aspens, and the ash are becoming gray and brown spectres of their summer selves.

Man knew the larches early. Long ago he learned to use their wood for hot fire at the cave's mouth. Then he learned to use larch sills for his early dwellings, since it is slow to rot. And when he learned to travel by water he found that larch keel and ribs made the best boats, since the tough wood holds its shape. Men who lived in cold countries used the larch every day of their lives.

Some think of the larch as a cautious tree, but perhaps it were better called insistently individual. Although it belongs to an evergreen family, it sheds its needles every autumn, renews them every spring. A conifer, its cones are so small that squirrels are not even tempted by them. In the spring it has tiny pink and green blossoms that make the whole tree look as though it were blushing. And in autumn, right now, it is a flame of a tree, a tall, slim candle flame in a woodland where the colors of October are underfoot.

November

BEAVER MOON
Now the beavers snug their
houses, stow food for winter,
and so do provident countrymen.

Bright November Day

November 1

We seldom think of November in terms of beauty or any other specially satisfying attribute. November is simply that interval between colorful October and dark December. Then, nearly every year, come a few November days of clear, crisp weather that make one wonder why November seldom gets its due.

There is the November sky, clean of summer dust, blown clear this day of the urban smog that so often hazes autumn. A sky so deep, so blue that April and June, in memory at least, were almost murky by contrast. When a November day is clear and blue it is the color of deep ocean water, of chickory blossoms in September.

There is the touch of November air, chill enough to have a slight tang, like properly aged cider. Not air that caresses, nor yet air that nips. Air that makes one breathe deeply and think of spring water and walk briskly. The clarity of November air, on such a day, is crystalline; it has a kind of magic, bringing the hilltops closer by day, the stars closer by night.

There is the simplified, clarified outdoor world, on a bright November day. The leafless trees are stripped to fundamentals. The horizon is in plain sight and far away. Valleys are broader, their outlines obvious. Hills are somehow higher. It is a bigger world, a world that invites wandering and exploration.

And that is November making late autumn special, making Indian summer rather pallid, making a man glad to be alive and out where he can see the clean line of that far horizon.

November's Voices *November 2*

You could throw away the calendar and still know it is November if you listened. The wind has its November voice, and so do the fallen leaves; but the unmistakable voices are those of the owls and the geese.

The wild goose is one of the few birds that chatters and calls in migratory flight. In city or country, you hear them, like the distant yapping of small dogs, a faint gabble that seems to echo from the whole sky. You look up, searching, listening, and there they are, flying high, perhaps only a thin penciling, a giant V up where the clouds belong, or a wavery line that seems to ripple in uncertain formation. Geese, Canadas if they are flying in a V, snow geese if merely lined against the sky. But calling, gabbling, chattering as they speed southward, November's haunting sound of the restless urge, the lure of the far horizon.

The owls are the voices of November nights. Dusk falls early, first stars appear, and the air quivers with that eerie hoot from the wooded hillside. It is a chilly sound, a dark and frosty sound that hints of ice and snow. And it is a fireside sound, one that goes with wood smoke and sheltered evenings. No birdsong, this, and no summons to get out and go. The owl's call is the companion of long, deep nights and the winds that rattle the latch.

The geese say, "Get up and go!" but the owls say, "Stay, and tend the fire." And both say, unmistakably, "November."

November Dusk

November 3

November brings long, chill nights of glittering stars and restless, whispery leaves. In another month the leaves will settle down for the winter and so will the rest of us. Meanwhile, the restlessness is on us too, and we walk with evening along a country road.

In the half-light this world of dusk is a world of vast simplicities. The familiar hill is almost any hill, with substance and outlines but few details. The valley has depth but few contours. The river beside the road is a winding path of luminous sky gently rippled by the evening breeze. The horizon itself is simplified, drawn with one clean charcoal stroke. Daylight horizons are a challenge to go and do, but in the vast quiet of evening this horizon makes here and now important and it urges acceptance of self and being.

Acceptance is not always easy, but here is a world reduced to elemental patterns. What is more fundamental than a tall maple, its leaves all shed, silhouetted against the sky? Or a clump of cedars on the hillside, rooted among the rocks but pointing slim, dark fingers toward the remote fires of infinity? What is simpler than the earth beneath one's feet, and the dusk itself?

One walks with the dusk, becomes a sentient of it; and one knows that the enduring mysteries are the great mysteries of all time—the stars, the eternal wind tides, the spinning earth, and man. Man, the newcomer, the wonderer. But daylight and suntime are the time to explore these matters. Dusk and night are the time to accept them and perhaps to build dreams and poems upon them.

November

November 4

The color ebbs, the leaves fall, and now November comes rustling down the valley, last summer's shade reduced to a brittle crispness underfoot. There will be a full and frosty moon tomorrow night, and only one more full moon before year's end. But there are no finalists, even now. Change and partial summary, but not finality.

On the twigs where the skittering leaves were live and green in June and July, buds are already set and visible, promise of next April and May and green again. Beneath the bark of those trees are growth rings, fiber and substance denoting another circuit of the sun, another summer's strength to help resist another winter's storms. In the grass, awaiting the warmth and urgency of spring, are the maple's samara, the oak's acorns, the hickory's nuts, tomorrow's woodland, another generation's shade.

At the roadside the September goldenrod, now here and grizzled as a granther, and the leafless milkweed, with its goosehead pods, strew fluff and floss to every breeze, seeding field and pasture with frail fertility. Cattails hold high their brown candles of bogland possibilities even while the muskrat robs them of their roots for its winter fare. The pregnant queen bumblebee, next summer's colony patterned in her unlaid eggs, sleeps dormant in an abandoned fieldmouse den. The woolly bear caterpillar, curled in hibernation, is next June's pink and yellow Isia moth.

Summaries and promises, but no finalities. November, chill, short-dayed November, but implicit with a future, with tomorrow.

Beaver Moon

November 5

In the days of woodsmen and Indians, when there was a harvest moon and a hunter's moon in September and October, November brought the beaver moon. One reason was that by November the beaver pelts were prime. Another was that by November's time of full moon the beavers, wise in the way of the seasons, were ready for winter. Their dams were sound, their ponds were full, their houses snug and well supplied with food; and any countryman with half the sense of a beaver had his own establishment similarly prepared. November, in those days of early winters and long ones, was the last chance a man had to get ready for what December and January, and often February as well, would bring in the way of snow and cold. The farmer who hadn't worked like a beaver was in for some unhappy times.

Weather has changed somewhat, and conditions otherwise have changed even more, but by the time Thanksgiving is past the provident countryman still is ready for what may come. That's why you see the leaves snugged around the foundations of old country houses by now. That's why the pump house, with its electric motor and throbbing pump, is banked and insulated. That's why the silo is full, and the mow, and the granary. That's why the freezer lid will barely close on its store of garden harvest and butchering product. That's why the blade is all ready to attach to the tractor, to keep the lane and the barnyard clear when the snow piles deep.

It's still the beaver moon, that full moon which comes tonight, though it is seldom so called. It means snugness for the winter, and it means that November has been a beaver-busy time for the family which still lives within whispering distance of the weather.

The Deliberate Oaks *November 6*

Now the oaks come into their own. They have been there right along, of course, and they turned maroon and purple and bronze and even old-gold yellow about the time the maple leaves began to fade. But the oaks weren't really visible until the earlier celebrants had lost the greater part of their finery. Now they dominate the hillsides, making maple and ash look twice as naked and pine and hemlock twice as green.

The oaks are deliberate trees, slow to leaf out in the spring, slow of growth, slow to color in the fall, and even reluctant to shed their outworn leaves which sometimes cling to the branches until new leaves burst from the buds in the spring. And the color in their autumn leaves is in good part a consequence of the tannin characteristic of the oaks, the same tannin that makes oak bark so useful in tanning leather. This tannin not only gives a brown undertone to the oak leaf colors; it makes them so durable that they rot slowly and form a mat under the trees instead of a yearly bed of humus.

So now the oaks stand tough and leathery and full of rustling defiance of autumn rain and winds. And earthy, rock-like even in their colors which reflect the colors of the fundamental soil and sand. In a sense, they prolong the season, for those leaves will still be red and brown and rustling on the branch when snow begins to whiten the woodland. All through November they will be colorful sentinels on the hillsides, challenging the rush of time.

The Fallen Leaves

November 7

The leaves come down and the glory of the autumn woodland is briefly a restless golden drift, a wine-red flurry in the wind. The gutters and roadsides are, for a little while, almost as brilliant as were the trees themselves. The countryside is festive in motley for a little while, rustling, restless, and raggedly beautiful.

But it is the last act of autumn's colorful pageant. The color fades as the leaves go back whence they came, to the earth itself. It is the old, old cycle, forever repeated, earth to earth. The leaves have had their season in the sun, and this colorful phase is but a moment in the life of a tree. First a bud, then a spreading sheet of plant fiber ingeniously packed with chlorophyll and other complex chemicals, and finally a discard.

Now comes leaf-fall, and the color rustles in the wind, skitters at the roadside, drifts in sheltered corners. The expandable leaves, the reds and yellows and russets and purples that have no meaning to the trees themselves. Color that will fade and vanish in the moldering humus. Sheer waste, some say. And yet each autumn we know again that the colorful leaf is as priceless as sunset and moonglow, priceless as butterflies and birdsong in the summer dawn.

Wild Goose Call

November 8

If it weren't for the geese, a man could get all those fall chores done and settle down, content. There really isn't much to do, now that the garden is well frosted. You put away the garden tools, hang and fill the bird feeders, stow the patio furniture, make sure the storm sash have survived the summer's sonic booms. By then most of the leaves have fallen. That's the final job, those leaves.

You can wait only so long for the wind to blow them away. Eventually you have to get out the rake and go to work. You pick a calm, bright morning and for a time it's no work at all. Then, before you are more than half through, you hear the geese, the faint, far-off gabble. You pause and search the blue November sky. There they are, a mile high and barely visible, a vast V of them arrowing southward. You watch them all the way to the horizon, listen till the last call has vanished.

Meanwhile, a gust of wind has come out of the north. The leaves are scattering across the lawn. They rattle and rustle and it is like an answer to the gabbling geese. Or is it geese, more geese? You search the sky again. Or is it an echo in your own self? You go back to raking, start all over again. But the wind is restless and the leaves are goose-wild, and you know it's useless to go on raking now. But you try, you try. And give up, put the rake away, tell yourself there'll be another day. A dark and sullen day, perhaps, when the air is calm, the leaves are damp and docile; a day when wild geese aren't flying and a man can settle down.

Frosty Morning *November 9*

Frosty November mornings reveal the beauty of simple things, for this is the season when the most fragile of all common crystals makes a dazzling wonderland of the countryside. But to see it one must be abroad at sunrise, before the night's chill has begun to relax. The white magic cannot endure the day.

For the first hour, before the sun has warmed its fingers, every blade of grass and every weed stem is transformed. Frost-edged, they shimmer in an incredible variety of patterns freshly seen. Empty milkweed pods are gleaming shells, jeweled and crusted with diamonds. Brown goldenrod stems are crowned with crystal where the tiny tufted seeds have flown. A drift of maple leaves is a miser's hoard of gold enhanced with priceless spangles. Beneath the oaks, empty acorn cups are tiny chalices carved from the rarest crystal.

The old barn, weathered by the years, reveals the tough grain of its old boards in the frost patterns. Its shingled roof is a geometric diagram of its forgotten builder's skill, inscribed in dazzling white. The pasture gate could vanish by noon, for it is fashioned of frozen mist. And the pines just beyond the house are, for this brief hour, hoary with age.

You walk with the sunrise and the frost, frost even in the gleam of your own breath. But as you walk the sun warms the air a few degrees. Here and there a thin curl of mist appears and the night's white magic begins to disappear as the day takes charge.

Plenty, and to Spare

November 10

Mingled with the leaf litter beneath the maples is a generous sprinkling of maple keys, nature's original helicopters. Ripe and loosened like the leaves, they came spiraling down, each key's own broad vane like a wing that flips and sails it away from the parent trunk. At the base of that broad vane is a fat kernel, the seed itself, from which, if all conditions are favorable, a seedling will sprout next spring. Every maple in the woodland has matured enough seeds to plant a small forest. But only a few of them will survive the hunger that prowls the woods and searches the litter.

Those maple keys are typical of nature's generosity, which man sometimes has difficulty understanding. It is so uneconomical! Virtually every plant that produces seed produces a hundredfold as much as will grow or can grow in the soil available to it. Nature has no truck with the theory of an economy of scarcity. Nature produces to the utmost of her capacity, whether it is wild berries, cattail fluff, maple seed, or domesticated wheat. Man is the only living thing that ever says, "Too much!" Man with his self-made complexities, his own systems of economy.

Periodically man apologizes for his own plenty, or he tries to limit production, trapped in his own devices. And year after year, as certain as autumn comes, nature goes her own way, oblivious. The whole natural system is based on abundance, plenty, more than enough. And the paradox becomes evident on every hillside to anyone who will look. There it is now, even on suburban streets where the maples cast their summer shade. The winged seeds come spiraling down, writing, "Plenty, plenty," on the autumn air.

The Answers *November 11*

Those who would look for simple answers to the big questions should go for a country walk on a November afternoon, out where leaves scuffle, squirrels scurry, jays cry havoc, and the fundamental shape of the hills is now revealed.

Choose a crisp leaf, no matter whether maple or oak or ash, and try to match it. And know that leaves are almost as varied as snowflakes. Watch the wind as it turns silvery in a clump of milkweed stalks, a shimmer of floss-borne seeds streaming from each open pod. Watch the glistening streamer from a pasture thistle's heads as the wind passes, airy down full of minute flecks of fertility. See how goldenrod and asters add to the aerial cargo, and know a few of the meanings of infinity, numbers that make counting a meaningless mumble.

Hold in your hand the empty shell of a beetle or the

shed husk of a locust. See the intricate parts, the ingenuity of life, now gone elsewhere, to the egg, to the pupa. Chitin, the horny substance much like your own fingernail, but only a few weeks ago a living thing, an entity. Watch a rabbit scurry, a crow fly overhead. Look at your own hand. Know that life is more than protoplasm, more than a fertile egg or ovum, that it is ultimate order in complexity.

Feel the earth underfoot. See the sky overhead. Listen to your own pulse, rhythmic as the tides. There are the answers, for those who will feel, and see, and listen.

Autumn's Leftovers

November 12

Rural and suburban householders are busy now with rake and fork and harrow, cleaning and neatening the dooryard, the lawn, and the garden. Everything must be in order for the winter. But down the road and across the valley, where autumn itself is in charge, nobody is bothering about the unkempt look. Nature isn't very neat about such matters.

Fallen leaves, restless as sparrows, rustle and scurry at the roadsides. Gray heads of goldenrod fluff spill seeds on every passing wind. Milkweed pods send streams of silken shimmer in all directions. Wild grape vines and woodbine have been left dangling from trees and bushes, nooses for unwary feet. Ripe grass is sadly in need of comb and brush.

But nature doesn't seem to care. The floor of the woodland is littered with dead twigs and branches pruned by wind and rain. Fern fronds lie sere and brown. Box elders emphasize their nakedness with tufts of keys that will dangle there all winter. The abandoned oriole's nest has begun to fray at a high, limber tip of the wineglass elm. Windrows of tan needles prove that pines, too, shed foliage in the autumn.

Man must rake and cart away, to soothe his conscience

and proclaim his tenancy. Nature doesn't bother. The tree thrives on its own trash and the seed sprouts in its parent's midden heap. Each new spring grows on autumn's leftovers.

... and Country of Quiet *November 13*

We think of it as the silence, the winter silence; but it really isn't silent at all. It merely is quiet. The distinction between silence and quiet makes all the difference, and it seldom is more evident than now.

There is no chorus of birdsong. The songbirds have gone south. There is no scratch, rattle, or buzz of insects. Most of the insects have lived out their lives and committed their future to the silent egg or pupa or fertile queen. The chittery chipmunk has finished his hoarding and settled down to quiet sleep. The chattery squirrels go about their treetop business without challenge or palaver. Even the winter jays are subdued, and the winter crows hold no conventions, are content to announce their presence and identity as they fly up and down the valley.

This doesn't add up to silence, but after the sounds of summer and early autumn it certainly is quiet. You can now hear yourself think, even in the daytime. You can hear the crisp leaves rustling in the wind. You can hear the earth sounds, the last, faint stir among the rocks and back in the woodland, as elemental things settle for the winter. You waken and hear them in the night, and then you hear the great horned owl hooting in the starlight and know it was the owl, not the wind, that wakened you. Then you know that this is the quiet of the year, not the silence.

The Witches' Flowers

November 14

The maple leaves are down, the oak leaves are leathery in texture and color, and the tamaracks stand like golden flames in the damp hollows. And now, deep into autumn, the witch hazels come to bloom.

Strange, these witch hazels are, even in form. Usually shrubs, sometimes they outgrow that stage and become dwarfish, misshapen trees. The botanical name, *Hamamelis*, comes from the Greek for the medlar or some similar tree with edible fruit, though the witch hazel's "fruit" consists of a capsule with four tough, brown seeds. When ripe this capsule pops open with explosive force and hurls the seeds up to forty feet from the parent tree.

The witch hazel blossoms appear in clusters, tousled heads of yellow petals, all long and narrow, curled and twisted. By the time the blossoms appear, last year's seed pods ripen and begin to pop out their seeds. Sometimes the flowers don't appear and the seed pods don't pop open till after the first snow is on the ground.

Where the name came from is anybody's guess. The shrub is not related to the hazelnuts, which belong to the birch family. Among the Onondaga Indians it was called *Oe-en-nah-kwe-ha-he*, which meant "spotted stick" and had no relation to witches. Its branches have long been used for dowsing, or "witching," for water, but that didn't give the plant its name. In any case, its most common use is as a demulcent, the extract from leaves and twigs being rubbed on sore and strained muscles. Witch hazel, which blooms in November.

The Signs

November 15

By mid-November, according to country lore, it should be clear what kind of weather can be expected in the winter ahead.

There are signs. The problem is how to interpret them. There are far more wild berries than usual. Black alder's vivid red berries sparkle in the lowland. Baneberry, both red and white, gleams at the roadside. There is more checkerberry, with its wintergreen tang, than there has been in years. On the floor of the woodland is an unusual scattering of partridgeberries, those little cherry-red beads that make their creeping vines look like June even in January. There was a big crop of wild grapes, which birds, possums, and raccoons have already eaten. Virginia creeper has more berries than usual.

All of which, according to one school of prophecy, means a cold, hard winter ahead. Nature, according to this reasoning, takes care of her own. Birds and beasts won't starve in the rugged weather ahead. But a little hard-headed reasoning raises questions. Wasn't this big crop a result of last spring's favorable weather? Didn't the wealth of blossoms and the cooperation of the bees produce the fruit? Did the bees foresee a rugged winter? That kind of reasoning would say a farmer who raised a big corn crop will face three feet of snow and twenty below zero on New Year's Day. All we really know is that winter will bring cold and snow, and that it will lead to April and spring.

Winter Crows

November 16

Now the crows own the rural countryside, and don't think they don't know it. Big and black, they strut the frosty pastures, haunt the harvested cornfields, fly up and down the valleys, hold loud and lengthy conferences in the leafless hill-top maples. Their voices echo, raucous and self-important, as they proclaim their sovereignty.

A good many crows migrate south for the winter, but by no means all of them. Those that remain move down from the wooded hills to the rural valleys, to the croplands, the barnyards, and the nearby meadows. They gather in noisy flocks and fly from field to field, from refuse dump to feed-lot, from orchard to pine grove. They eat almost anything they can swallow, hunting, pilfering, scavenging. Only the bitterest of winter weather limits their excursions. Despite man's enmity, they persist and thrive. There probably are more crows today than there were a hundred years ago.

One reason is that the crow is a very bright bird, full of cunning and wisdom. He can spot an enemy as far as he can see, and his eyesight is keen. He gets up early. He can outfly most of his natural enemies and out-thieve all his competitors. He lives by his wits, and they are first-class wits. That is why the crows now talk like tyrants. They are in command of the winter countryside, and they know it.

Early Snow

November 17

Snow in mid-November isn't really any colder or more slippery than it is in January. It merely seems that way because we haven't yet put on our emotional mittens and overshoes. We aren't yet ready for winter, most of us. We still have summer tans. Our hands are still shaped to the tennis racket and the canoe paddle, the hoe and the leaf rake, not to the snow shovel. Even the ski people aren't quite ready for snow in mid-November, not in our area at least.

But it snows, and there are problems. Buses and taxis

and all surface transportation begins to snarl itself in the city. Even those who travel on foot have their difficulties, with snow underfoot and slush splashing at them from all directions. And in the suburbs the buses don't run, the commuter's car stalls. Snowplows and sand trucks haven't yet got into the swing of winter. Power lines develop trouble and repair crews can't get through for hours. Nobody likes a winter snowstorm in mid-November. Nobody likes the weatherman for permitting it.

Only the countrymen, the farmers, are really reasonable about it. The farmer doesn't have to catch a commuter train or a taxi or a bus. He goes out to the barn and the feedlot, does the morning chores, looks thankfully at his ample supply of hay and his full silos, and spends most of the day doing indoor jobs that have been waiting for just such weather. Early snow is a bit of a nuisance, but nothing to fret about. It probably won't stay on the ground long, and the fields need the moisture.

Bittersweet *November 18*

Along the winding country roads and up in the edge of the woods the bittersweet dangles its clustered berries, their pale husks now open and the bright orange berries revealed. They are like mid-November flowers in the leaf-crisp evening of the year, brighter than the haws of the wild roses, far more generous than the lacquer-red berries of their creeper neighbors, the partridge berries. Bittersweet berries and sumac heads are the bright bangles of the brushland.

Bittersweet is a shrubby vine that twines its way up any handy support, but particularly up seedling birches and wild cherries. In a few years it strangles its supporter but it lifts its own head high. Its flowers are of no particular importance, small, greenish-white, and lost among the neighbors in busy, colorful June. Its color is saved for now, for this time of ripeness, when its neighbors have bowed to the frost.

The common name seems to have been borrowed from the nightshade, which came from Europe, really is not a climbing vine, and has poisonous berries about the same size but redder than those of our native bittersweet. Those who have tasted them say that nightshade berries are first sweet to the tongue, then acutely bitter. Hence the name. Our climbing bittersweet is botanically *Celastrus scandens*, a Greek-Latin combination meaning an evergreen that climbs. Our native species is no evergreen, but it has an Asiatic relative that is. Nightshade is distantly related to the potato, whose leaves are also poisonous.

The Fundamental Wind *November 19*

It isn't that the wind now has a bite; that bite isn't so sharp at midday with a bright sun and a clear sky. Nor is it that the wind has a gruff, cold voice as it howls in the night and rattles sash and storm door. It is that the wind now is unmistakably a fundamental force as surely as the river's current or the ocean's tide. It is turning the great mill wheel of the year which shapes the days to the grit of the earth, not to the shadow of the stars.

It is no longer a summer wind that can whip up a thunderstorm and be gone on an hour's notice. It is no autumn wind of whimsical gusts that whip the leaves from the birches in clouds of gold and send banners of October mist and milkweed floss scudding across the morning. This is a massive movement down from the tundra and the Arctic Sea, the wake of the whole frigid north behind it. It can be checked here and there by some feature of the earth itself and it can be diverted. But it keeps coming on, this November wind, spilling over the hilltops and surging down the valleys, a presence, an element, an agent of change. It is, at times, change itself.

At its gentlest, it moves the drifted leaves up and down the road, settles them in the brushy margins. At full strength, it prunes the woodland, adding dead branches to the mouldering litter. It shapes the autumn world for its winter coating of ice. But day after day it is the wind of change, a more potent force than the solstice itself, which is but a marker on the great mill wheel.

November Twilight

November 20

It is not yet four-thirty and the sun is setting behind the low ridge to the west. The last, long light climbs from the valley's frosted pasture grass up the gray trunks of the naked maples and seems to pause on the hilltops to the east. Then it is gone. Twilight, the glow of November evening, possesses the day.

At first there is the bright, shadowless light, a sunless daylight in which the growing moon, halfway up the eastern sky, is only a ghost. Then the glow comes, a rosy suffusion so subtle it could be a reflection of the maple leaves at the roadside or the bronze-red grass in the neglected meadow. The air seems to thin and brighten, and the chill diminishes distances. The world comes close, the familiar world of this place called home.

The glow fades. Dusk creeps in, unhurried but insistent, and the clarity of vision dims. In its place is a deceptive clarity of hearing. The farm dog barking just down the road sounds no closer than a truck shifting gears on a hill a mile away. The rustle of leathery leaves in an oak not ten feet away seems as far off as the hooting of the barred owl across the valley. And time somehow has lost its dimensions. It is evening and it is autumn, and the moon has begun to glow. The scuffle of leaves at the roadside just ahead could be a noontime cat or a midnight fox. Or the evening breeze.

Sunset, twilight, dusk, darkness, all by six on a mid-November evening, late autumn's summary of serenity.

The Golden Hackmatack *November 21*

The Algonquins called it *akemantak*, meaning snowshoe wood, and made snowshoe frames from its branches, stripped tough fibers from its roots with which to sew the birch bark of their canoes. Because it dropped its needles in late autumn, the only conifer they knew that was not green all winter, they said it slept like the hibernating *wejac*.

Then the white man came, unable to shape his tongue to the Indian words, and called the *wejac* a woodchuck, the *akemantak* a hackmatack or tamarack. The botanists later called its European cousins *Larix*, and from that came the name larch.

Hackmatack, tamarack, or larch, it is a beautiful tree that asserts its identity every spring and fall. In spring it is a tall, slim spire of lacy apple-green needles glowing with the gold and pink of its tiny blossoms. In summer it is just another green conifer in the woodland. But by the time the broadleafed trees are bare it is a startling candle flame of golden needles, glinting in the sunlight. By December it is bare as the birches.

Botanically, it is one of the ancients, one of the earliest conifers. Perhaps it learned to hibernate by enduring the ice ages. Its cones are primitive and economically small. Its wood is tough and resinous. It can live on the rocky uplands, and it can thrive in the damp lowlands. It keeled the Norsemen's longboats, it silled the settler's cabin. And, as the Algonquins said in naming it, it can give a hungry man webbed feet for the winter's chase. It is a noble tree, and a beautiful golden tree every November.

The Traditions

November 22

This is the traditional day to give thanks. Traditions, of course, are based on customs and beliefs transmitted from generation to generation. Those we observe at Thanksgiving are mostly rural—the bountiful harvest, the gathered family, the roasted turkey, the feast, the thankful prayer. And all with the generous land close about, a world of fields made fruitful by calloused hands. The thanks were for health and strength and independence.

Looking back now, in a land whose people are largely urban, the day may seem to have only token meaning. And yet, in its origins the work "thank" meant "think," and surely one day out of the year is not too much to think back and remember. The day of thanks goes back to a little band of immigrants fighting a strange wilderness, painfully getting a foothold there. They had little enough to be thankful for, yet they were grateful for survival and hoped for better days beyond the winter that was closing in. They had faith and belief and even dreams, though those dreams could not encompass what has come after them.

So the traditions are as important as the thanks themselves. The symbols are not without meaning, for they rest on the land's own bounty, on work and achievement, on obligations as well as rights. Nobody has yet outmoded harvest, or plenty, or gratitude.

Thanksgiving is more than a feast. It always was. It is recognition of the providence, the work, the hope and dreams that are in our very blood and being. It is thanks for the traditions themselves.

Owl Nights

November 23

Chilly November nights are owl nights. Not even the early-nesting great horned owl will be courting till January, so he and the barred owl and the little screech owl are merely announcing their presence. This is their time to hoot, or screech, or yammer.

There is no such thing as a hoot owl, of course, but both the great horned owl, he with a five-foot wingspread, and the slightly smaller barred owl do hoot. The barred owl has an ordinary call consisting of six or eight repeated notes, usually with a rising, questioning inflection at the end. He also barks like a dog, screams like a cat, and makes noises like two temperamental raccoons. The great horned owl has a deep, gruff voice and his call has four, often five, notes.

The screech owl is something else again. He's no bigger than a robin, and he doesn't hoot. He doesn't really screech, either. He ululates, to use the long, strange word, starting with a high-pitched note that slides down the scale, making a tremolo along the way. Traditionally it is an eerie sound, the scream of a maiden in peril, or some such awesome noise. But some who have heard it think it sounds more like laughter, or at least loud, uncontrolled chuckling. Still others call it winter's equivalent of summer's whippoorwill call.

But whether they hoot or screech, or what they do with their voices, the November owls make memorable nights. They aren't frightening, but they do make one appreciate having a roof and a door.

Bright November Days

November 24

When cold rains bring the dark, raw days of November, we think of Bryant's "melancholy days" of "wailing winds and naked woods and meadows brown and sere." Then the day wakens with a bright sun that swiftly climbs a clean, blue sky. Overnight the chill wind has been tempered to a breeze that whispers in the sere oak leaves, almost balmy, and the autumn world is bright as sunlight, crisp as dawn, broad as the far horizons. And we know that the poet's bleak November is not ours complete.

The woods are naked where ash and birch and maple grow but not where the pines make their stand, or the hemlocks. The brown of the meadow is the brown of maturity. This is an open world that invites the foot to roam and the eye to see. A season's work is done and now there is a sense of leisure on the land. The haste is ended. Now comes the long rest, the next in the endless cycles of the year.

Now one can see how life is patterned, its infinite variety. The nut nestled in this hull, the seed in this empty pod. The leaf grew on this naked twig, but where it fell is the dormant bud for another season's leaf, the succession. The beetle has left its legacy in the egg and now is an empty husk. The fledgling is flown from the empty nest.

Late autumn has its lowery, melancholy days, but they are by no means the whole of it. Autumn is also bright days of triumph and completion, days to go, to see, to understand.

Country Road

November 25

One of the forgotten benefits of the superhighways is the fact that they take the hurry-hurry traffic off the lesser roads and leave the back roads that wander through the woods and over the hills to those who would dawdle and enjoy the countryside. There one can stop to look at a tree or a vista, even to get out and walk and know the feel of autumn underfoot. There one can pause to watch a busy squirrel, or a skein of wild geese honking southward, or a brook meandering across a meadow.

The highways too often seem to lead from traffic jam to traffic jam. But the byways lead to the nearest thing to peace and leisure one can reach on wheels, to the uncomplicated serenity of woods and hills and streams. They lead back to the land itself where time is measured by seasons and years, not by hours and minutes. Back to hills that were old when man built his first cities, hills that change only on their own terms.

They lead to quiet places where one can see a hollow glowing with the golden candles of autumn larches, to hilltops where the sky is a huge blue bowl, to lowland beaver meadows, to cattail bogs, to old brown farmhouses with blue curls of fragrant wood smoke at their chimneys. In a sense, these back roads lead to a simpler yesterday, perhaps; but those who seek them out are not searching for the past. They are looking, rather, for the enduring now, the persistent reality of a native tree, uncluttered hill, a sunset.

The Paper Makers

November 26

In this age of the printed word we tend to think that man invented paper. That isn't so. The hornets did, and a walk in the leafless woods will prove it. Somewhere along the way one probably will find a gray paper ball at least a foot in diameter hanging from a low limb. It will be a hornet's nest, to be avoided all summer but now deserted and safe to examine, since all the hornets except the queen are dead and the queen is hibernating elsewhere.

Ever since there were hornets and trees, hornets have been making wood pulp, softening it with their own saliva, and building such nests of it. The nest usually has double walls for insulation—another hornet invention—and inside is a complex of cells, hundreds of them, the original of the apartment house. And every square inch of material in that nest is paper, hornet paper, the first paper ever invented.

The nests are never used more than one season. Next spring the queen will come out of hibernation, build a small new nest, lay eggs, and hatch a brood of workers. They will gather wood pulp and enlarge the nest, which by midsummer will be a fearsome hive of hornets. It may even be a colorful hive, since hornets keep up-to-date—now they use painted wood, sometimes, to make their paper, and even chew up bits of discarded paper and cardboard which litter the roadside. But it will be paper, the primitive kind of paper hornets were making long before man tamed fire, let alone learned to write or print or bind a book.

The Wind Tides *November 27*

Autumn ebbs away into winter, but there is flow rather than ebb in the unseen wind tides that now lap at the hills and send invisible breakers to hiss softly in the upper woodlands. They are the tides that curl about this earth, forever restless and eternally moving, tides that obey some subtler master than the moon.

Night is the time to hear these tides, a night when the stars are dimmed by scud that could easily be the spray of wind waves crowding swiftly one upon the next. You sit beside the open fire and hear the tides sucking at the chimney, hear the swish of their unseen waves breaking against the corner of the house, feel the quiver of panes shaken by the breakers.

You listen and you hear the rise and fall of the wind waves, the rush of one after another in crescendo until the peak has struck its battering blow. Then there is a pause, a gathering of new force, and again that succession of waves building once more to climactic height and falling away into darkness.

Occasionally you can see, or seem to see, the wind tides, breaker-white, at dawn and at dusk. They go rippling through a pasture lot and across an open knoll with its tall, golden-ripe grass. They swish through the underbrush at the edge of the woodland with the sibilant sound of cove water being crowded up an inlet. They bow the naked maple tips with the murmuring hiss of moon tides on rocky reefs.

The Lantern

November 28

This used to be the season when the farmer did his chores by lantern light, morning and evening. Nowadays electricity lights the barn and the barnyard in all but the most remote rural areas, but almost any farmer with gray in his hair can recall the days of the kerosene lantern. And so can his wife.

The lantern smelled of kerosene, it gave only a feeble light by modern standards, and it was a constant fire hazard among the livestock. But it was as much of a necessity on the farm as the milk pail or the farmer's winter boots. It was a portable lamp, a fuel can with a wick and a glass globe to enclose the flame, and a bail to carry it by. Farm work couldn't be done without it.

The farm wife knew it well. She saw that its tank was kept filled with kerosene, that its wick was trimmed or renewed, that its globe was clean. She hated it, but respected it, because it smelled of kerosene and sometimes leaked; and kerosene was not only a fire hazard, it polluted every scrap of food it reached. But it had to be kept in working order. Without the lantern, farm work could not be done.

The lantern lighted the way to the barn, the corncrib, the hen house, the woodshed. It hung on its peg in the barn while the milking was done. When a trip had to be made after dark the lantern sometimes hung from the end of the wagon tongue to light the way feebly. More often it sat at the driver's feet, under the robe, to help fend off chilblains. It was better than an open torch or a candle. But nobody regretted its passing. And nobody who ever did the chores by lantern light has forgotten. Particularly in short-dayed November.

The Perspective *November 29*

Once the autumn leaves have fallen you can see the world in its true dimensions. It happens every year, but we seem to forget. It is almost as though we are seeing things clearly for the first time, though it is merely the annual renewal of perspective.

Spring brings a burgeoning world, a world of opening buds and spreading leaves and early blossoms. Summer brings a world so busy with growth, so verdured with chlorophyll and so bright with bloom, that the rootstock of life is not only hidden but almost denied. All that summer exuberance seems so spontaneous it needs no roots. Late summer and early autumn bring the ripening, the incredible natural harvest. And by October this overwhelming generosity has become the glory of the woodlands, a spectacle to make anyone forget that the hills have rocky cores, the trees are slow-grown fiber, the seeds and nuts are next spring's grass and tomorrow's woodlands.

Then the leaves come down and the contours stand revealed, hill and valley, ledge and chasm. You can see the shape of things around you. It's something like the thoughtful pause after the loud voices have had their way. There's time to look beyond the mask of summer, to see down to the root of things and know where stand the real importances, the fundamentals with which you have to live.

And that is one of the rewards of living with four clear-cut seasons. You have this annual season of simplicity, of rocks and rootbeds plainly visible. You can, if you really look, see things whole again.

The Enduring Voices

November 30

Now that autumn's silence is upon the land, one can hear the big, enduring voices which seldom shout the things they have to say. One can hear the earth declare that ice, the counterpart of fire, must be reckoned with. One can hear the hills assert their stony structure which forever underlies the soothing green of leaf and shade. One can hear the wind and water discussing polar regions and the fundamental wedge of frost that can level mountains. Listen closely, and one can hear the patient throb of almost suspended life in the root, the bulb, the seed, the egg, waiting for another spring.

It is pleasant to walk with May and hear the song of mating birds and see the glint of fresh violets in the new grass. It is satisfying to sit in summer's shade and know the fragrance of roses and the hum of bees through the long afternoon. It is exhilarating to watch the color come to the woodlands and feel the lure of wanderlust in blue sky and opening horizon. But when the blossom has become the seed, when daylight has been abbreviated by the southward swing of the sun, when the trees stand naked in the frosty woodland, such transient pleasures give way to the big assurances.

Now we approach the nadir of the year, the neap tide of daylight. But the earth still turns, the stars are still there, the seas maintain their vast expanse, and the hills still stand. Another spring is already patterned, as inevitable as sunrise. Time flows, and with it life and change. That is what the enduring voices are saying, if we only listen.

December

COLD MOON

In the natural year, winter begins with the calendar year's December. Now come long nights, cold days.

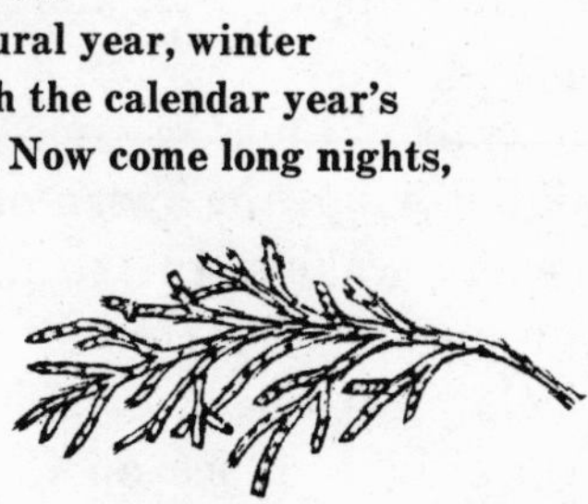

December

December 1

The arrival of December means the definite end to autumn. Even the leaf-rustle of the November wind whisking October's brilliance along the country road is muted as the leaves settle down. The early clamor of crows no longer starts the day, and the jays go about their business for the most part in blue silence. The chickadee is the most vocal bird in the dooryard, and his brief song is interrupted by the tap-tap-tap of his beak as he cracks a sunflower seed. In the country house, the fly-buzz and wasp-flutter in the attic have quieted down, the insects dead or dormant.

The barred owl hoots in the night, and from time to time the fine-spun yapping of a red fox is heard. But their voices only punctuate the silence, which lies deep in the rural valley where frogs, only a few weeks ago, thumped the darkness. Brooks are quiet, their shallow waters beginning to clog with ice. The woodchuck sleeps. Chipmunks drowse in their fluff-lined nests, and squirrels go chatterless in the treetops.

December comes, a time of earth sounds, the moan of the chilling wind, the swish of driven snow. Sometimes the countryman wakens in the night and thinks he hears the faint groan of rocks restless in their age-old beds, nudged by the slow expansion of silent frost. Sometimes he hears the slow crunch of ice on the pond. December comes, and winter.

Winter Color

December 2

The color, we say, is gone, remembering vivid October and verdant May. What we really mean is that the spectacular color has passed and we now have the quiet tones of winter around us, the browns, the tans, a narrower range of greens, with only an occasional accent in the lingering winter berries. But the color isn't really gone.

The meadow is sere tan, but that is a tan of a dozen different shades from gold to russet. The fallen leaves have been leached of their reds and yellows, but theirs is no monotone by any means. The bronze curve of the goldenrod stem emphasized the ruddy exclamation point of the cattail. The rough brown bark of the oak makes the trunk of the sugar maple appear armored in rusty iron. The thorny stalk of the thistle stands beside the cinnamon seed head of the pungent bee balm. Dark eyes stare from the white parentheses of the stark birches, bronze tufts of one-winged seeds tassel the box elder, miniature "cones" adorn the brown-black alders at the swamp's edge.

In the woods, the insistent green of Christmas fern and partridgeberry leaf compete with the creeping ancients, ground cedar and running pine. Hemlock, spruce, and pine trees cling to their own shades of green, individual as the trees themselves. And on their trunks are paint patches of the ancient lichens, tan and red and blue and green, like faint reflections of vanished floral color.

The color is still there, though its spectrum has somewhat narrowed. Perhaps it takes a winter eye to see it, an eye that can forget October and not yearn for May too soon.

December

December 3

This first week in December brings the earliest sunsets of the year, though not the shortest days because sunrise will continue to lag for another month. We are approaching the winter solstice and, in terms of daylight span, the very depth of the year. Now we begin to pay that promissory note we signed last summer for those endless sun-tanned days with early dawns and long, lingering twilight. Nights now are as long as the days were in June.

We pay the debt with coin that has an icy clink, and the coin itself is important as a corrective. These December days are in themselves a challenge to our environment. Man boasts of his power and his control over the world around him. True, he can cut the trees, bulldoze the hills, drive out the animals, discourage the birds, even kill a few billion insects. But he still can't divert the course of a blizzard, temper the winter wind, or put a legal limit on the depth of a snowfall. All he can do is armor himself against them or hide from them, which is something less than domination.

December is going to be itself, no matter what we say or do. Sometimes it has all the trappings of late autumn, and sometimes it is a full-fledged partner of January. It will bring a full moon this week, with moonlight that makes one wonder why we can't leave the moon alone. It will be green with pine and bright with berry, and it probably will be spangled with frost and snow as well as tinsel. And before it ends the days will be lengthening toward spring again.

On Its Own Terms *December 4*

It wasn't an outdoor poet who coined the phrase "bleak December." It was someone who probably slept late, had sluggish circulation, and was afraid of catching cold. December was bleak because it wasn't June, loud with bees and bright with blossoms.

True, December can be raw and cold and its days sometimes are dark, but it is neither bleak nor colorless. Go outdoors soon after sunup, which now comes late, and even on a lowering day you probably will find a frosty scene of dazzling beauty. If the day is clear it can be a world transformed by frost or snow, newly created, fragile as spun glass, ephemeral as the passing hour.

Go to the woodland and see how the green of pine and hemlock is twice as bright against leafless elm and ash and maple. Underfoot are those humble ancients, running pine and ground cedar, greener than summer grass; and the creeping partridgeberry is gay not only with evergreen leaves but with dewdrop-size rubies. Sumac has fat clusters of bloodstone-fruit. Black alder stems are decked with garnets. Bittersweet is festive with bangles of coral and carnelian. The barberry bushes are loaded with topaz and rubies.

The meadow grass is bronze and antique gold. Empty milkweed pods are lined with mother-of-pearl. Fraying thistle heads are spun silver. The gray beech tree's crisp leaves are beaten gold.

Taken on its own terms, no December day is really bleak. December wasn't meant to be June.

December Moon

December 5

The full moon of December, which occurred last night, is no summer serenader's moon, no sentimental moon of silvery softness to match the rhyming of the ballad singer. It is a winter's moon with more than fourteen hours of darkness to rule in cold splendor.

It is not a silvery moon at all. This is a moon of ice, cold and distant. But it shimmers the hills where there is a frosting of snow and it makes the frozen valleys gleam. It dances on the dark surface of an up-country pond. It glitters in the frost-spangled air over the ice-defying brook. It weaves fantastic patterns on the snow in the woodland. It is the sharp edge of the night wind, the silent feather on the great horned owl's wing, the death-scream of an unwary rabbit when the red fox has made its pounce.

This winter's moon is a silent companion for the night-walker, a deceptive light that challenges the eye. It dims the huddled hemlocks on the hillside, and it sharpens the hilltop horizon. It wreathes the walker's head in the shimmer of his own breath, and it seems to whistle in his footsteps. It makes wreaths of chimney smoke and sweetens the smell of the hearth-fire.

It is the long winter night in cold splendor, night wrapped in frost, spangled and sequined and remote as Arcturus.

Living Thermometers

December 6

An outdoor thermometer is a handy thing to have, these December mornings, especially one hung at the coldest corner of the house. Note the temperature there as early as possible and you are armed to compete in the daily "coldest spot in town" contest.

But if you merely want to know relative temperatures, whether you need heavy gloves and a muffler, you needn't even glance at a thermometer. Suburbanites and rural folk can simply look out the window on their way to breakfast and see what the birds and the broadleaf evergreens are doing. If the chickadees coming to the feeder are fluffed fat as tennis balls the temperature is in the low thirties, plenty cold enough for a muffler. If the leaves on the rhododendron are closed like folded hands, get out the heavy gloves and the storm boots.

The fluffed feathers on a bird trap warm air, the bird's own body heat, and provide insulation. They create a special overcoat. A ruffed grouse fluffed against the cold can look big as a barnyard hen. The closing of leaves on a broadleaf evergreen does somewhat the same thing. It reduces the area of evaporation. Heat and moisture are lost through the pores of the leaves, so when the leaves are folded that loss is reduced. The plant rests, its leaves closed to business, until the weather moderates. They have built-in thermometers.

Fundamental *December 7*

There is a deceptive simplicity now in the natural world that makes winter a season of fundamentals. The meadow's grass is frosted, its seed heads empty. Queen Anne's lace, a gleaming saucer of white petals in August, has become a dark fist of brittle stems. Milkweed pods are empty and their silky iridescent linings have lost their sheen. And leafless trees, maples, birches, elms, and willows are naked as skeletons, their bare limbs rattling in the wind.

The green of summer that makes this a softer, gentler

place to live seems to celebrate complexity. Who can count the leaves on a single willow tree? Who can number the blades on one grassy acre? Who can measure the growth of one swamp's cattails? The blossoming, the set and ripening of seed is an incredible achievement, magic created of a raindrop, a sunny day, a breath of pollen, an ovum.

Then they are gone, leaf and blossom, seed and fragile stem. The world is reduced to its visible, elemental parts. Or is it? Behind the vanished complexity of leaf and blossom is the greater complexity of their source. Beneath the frosted, stem-tangled meadow lie the roots of next summer's grass. The empty pod and windblown tuft signify seeds waiting to sprout and flower and seed again. And the trees, those stark winter trees, are already budded with next April's leaves. The source of leaf and flower and seed stands rooted in all the yesterdays, fundamental, itself the ultimate riddle of complexity, for it is the root of life itself.

December

December 8

December emphasizes the basic realities, even in a world of machines and complex organization. There is little subtlety about December's wind and weather, which are winter in the making. The winter landscape is already reduced to fundamentals. Ice, in one form or another, is now obvious, whether it is morning hoarfrost or a glaze on the pond or snowflakes in the air—ice, a primal element. And life itself faces the reality of two basic necessities, food and shelter.

In a simpler past, before the individual was so largely lost in norms, averages, and common denominators, we accepted a vast and awesome world and knew that our problems demanded human solutions. Winter was one of those problems, and we had to live with it. If we were cold, we built shelter and a fire. If we hungered, we went to the cold cellar and the smokehouse for food produced from the soil with our own sweat and blisters. In need of tools, we made them with our own hands. The necessities demanded simple, direct, human answers, and got them.

That past is gone, with its essentially intimate, personal relationships to society and to the world itself. It was not ideal. Few of us would welcome its return. But some of its solutions had a human warmth that glows in memory. Particularly in December, which is little changed. It still reduces this world in which we live to essentials, to cold, unarguable fundamentals, and we wish that life could be simplified again.

Fence Posts *December 9*

The sound of the ax in the back-country woodland these days doesn't necessarily mean that somebody is cutting firewood. Now is the time when the farmer "gets out" his fence posts. He is harvesting his pasture cedars, those slim, straight, blue-green trees that fill the open spaces and creep out onto the grassland. For the brushland just below the rocky ledges is not wasteland; it grows a crop that every farmer needs, fence posts.

They are red cedars, those trees, technically junipers, and their wood rots slowly. They have small blue berries, dark blue with a whitish bloom, and birds eat the berries and plant new cedars with their droppings. So now, when the farmer cuts his cedar posts, he thinks well of the birds which relieve him of one job of planting.

There he is on the ridge, cutting cedars, and the bite of his ax is good to feel. The echo is loud and lingering in the crisp air, and after a while the jays come to see what is going on and the chickadees come closer. A man cutting posts can create a good deal of excitement in the woods, and yet he is somehow at home there, and the birds know it. He's a little like a tree himself, rooted in the soil and living with the seasons, shaped by the weather and patient with the years.

So he cuts his posts, and he thinks that maybe no man should quarrel too much with the world around him. Good things grow in odd places, and what's poor land for one crop is good land for another. It depends on what a man wants and what he needs. Cropland needs fences, and fences need posts, and posts grow where crops for market won't grow. Maybe it all evens out. It seems to, in a minor way, when a man is up there on a December day getting out his posts.

Energetic Idlers

December 10

One reason so many people feed the winter birds may be that they represent a degree of freedom and an attitude toward life that man likes to dream about. They have their problems and they face their hazards; but, as someone once said, birds are energetic idlers. They live uncluttered lives with no possessions to protect, no homes to maintain, no family responsibilities once the nesting season is ended. Even their social obligations, ties to their own kind, are minor and loose.

True, they have special problems in winter, but most of them involve food. All birds have a high metabolism and run what we would call a high fever, which simply means their inner fires are intense and require constant stoking. But those that stay north all winter stay by choice and inheritance. They are free to fly south if instinct prompted. Instead, equipped to face the weather, they stay here and brighten the dooryard and help those who would remember that dream of the good life.

Their songs help. On bright, sunny days even the least of them twitters fragments of song, and not merely tribal calls. They are voicing some sense of well-being if not actual happiness. And why not? The chickadee that comes to hand for a sunflower seed has no regrets for yesterday and no worry about tomorrow. The cardinal that whistles so brightly on a frosty morning is not hiding from a hawk. The downy woodpecker at the suet pauses between bites to chitter his satisfaction. Who would put out food for a regimented ant? Or for katydids, or crickets? But birds—well, birds are independence itself.

A Song for a Supper *December 11*

Among the daily customers at the winter bird feeder, the tree sparrows are almost as common as the chickadees, and usually as welcome. One reason is that the tree sparrow, that fellow with a single dark button on his light gray vest, will volunteer a song for his supper even in the midst of a snowstorm. He doesn't go into ecstasies over the weather in December, perhaps, but he is more than a mere twitter even now. By January he will be as much of a songster as a chickadee, and by February he will sing about spring, regardless of the weather.

The name is deceptive, for this fellow is essentially a bird of the bushes and the underbrush. Even at nesting time—and the tree sparrow nests up around Hudson Bay—these sparrows stay close to the ground. And the summer habits are carried south in the winter. For the tree sparrow is a migrant, sometimes going as far south as the Carolinas. Those that winter here will be on their way back north no later than April.

Every farmer and every gardener who knows his birds welcomes the tree sparrow, who probably consumes as many weed seeds, ounce for ounce, as any bird alive. In a state the size of Connecticut the tree sparrows alone will eat as much as eleven tons of weed seed in a single season. What they eat at the feeding stations is small pay for such a service. And even the handouts are paid for in song as well as in service. Who could ask more than that?

December Sunrise

December 12

Sunup is late, past seven of the clock, and dawn is brittle. The night's cold seems to intensify as daylight comes. The grass is crunchy underfoot, each blade crystalled. Fallen leaves, their color leached, lie in frosty heaps where the vanished wind left them in its gusty haste down the valley. Rooftops gleam as with lingering starlight. A man can see his own breath.

A new day comes, a dazzle of sun in a sky as cold as clear blue ice. The pines stand green on the hillside, the hemlocks dark on the ridge, making maples and birches look twice as naked in their elemental shapes. The brook, not yet prisoned by the ice, chatters in its rocky bed as though alive and sentient. But the owl and the fox are back at roost and den and the day belongs to the crow and the jay. And to man.

In a den on the far side of the meadow the woodchuck sleeps, the deep sleep of hibernation. On a ledge in the barn the woolly bear caterpillar lies curled in cold insensitivity. The acorn and the hickory nut, vaguely patterned with another summer's trees, neither throb nor stir, and the egg and the seed wait.

Sleep and hibernation are upon the land. But man is abroad, knowing the year complete. Knowing dawn, knowing the wonder of a new day even in December, seeing the wonder of his own breath, knowing the wonder of wondering itself.

December Snow *December 13*

December snow is no whiter when it falls than the snows of February or March, and its flakes are no more magnificently intricate in their symmetrical crystalline beauty. But snow still is wonderful and mysterious in December. It hasn't become commonplace and worn out its welcome.

Now we can exclaim over the beauty of a snowflake. We can even admit that we know very little about snow except that it is a crystalline form of water. We can't create a snowflake. The best we can do is set up laboratory conditions of temperature and humidity under which snowflakes will form themselves. The chemical formula of water is no help. Mathematical formulas for hexagonal shapes are little more than statements of fact. The whys and hows persist, the wonder of the evanescent flakes, so frail they vanish in one warm breath, so substantial they form ice sheets and glaciers.

Each summer we have proof that there are other, less exquisite means of emptying a cloud than by turning it to snow. Each winter we see that ice can be glass-clear, iron-hard, that it can cut and gouge and rend apart even the granite mountains. Or that it can be snowflakes, feather-soft, incredibly varied, perfectly beautiful. Snow that can transform a woodland overnight, make a wonderland of a weedy meadow, sculpture the invisible wind, robe a woeful world in innocence. For a little while now we can sense and see the wonder of snow. Its cold, factual identity will assert itself later.

The Pines

December 14

By December the woodlands have become simplified into winter's pattern, most of the hardwoods leafless and stark, the pines sighing in the wind, green and reassuring even on a raw, dark day. Here and there an oak or a beech rustles, with its tatter of withered leaves still clinging; but it is a dead sound, as dead as the rustle of fallen leaves at the roadside. But the pines whisper, live and almost sentient. The pines are alive.

They are the oldsters of the woodland, the pines—and the family includes spruces, hemlocks, and firs as well as those we specifically call pines. Their kind was here before there was one broad leaf to wither and fall in any autumn. They saw the mountains rise and the rivers carve the valleys. They slowed the thrust of the great ice sheets, and they crept back northward when the ice began to melt.

Green, eternally green, the color of the living plant. They make no big concessions to either cold or long, dark nights. There they stand, the hemlock thicket on the mountainside, the tall, pointed firs in the northland, the soft-needled spruces, the tall, graceful, ubiquitous pines. They are a part of winter's simplicity, of the green statement that outlives all winters. There they stand, whispering in the breeze, a certainty in a time of questions.

The Throb of Time

December 15

Now we are on the last steep slope of autumn, with the winter solstice ahead. The span of daylight is almost six hours less than it was six months ago. The tides of light and darkness, day and night, approach the year's neap and

December, the counterpart of June, reminds us that elemental ice is the twin of fire.

The lesser voices are stilled, but the throb of time and change beats beneath the sighing of the wind in the hemlocks and the rush of the wind in the naked maples, the cold and wintery wind. Restless, surging life has retreated to the root, the bulb, the seed, and the bud. Life sleeps in the egg, awaiting another spring. And the elemental strength of the hills, the substance of growth itself, communes with the wedging frost and the gouging ice. The wind may howl and roar, but the earth and its insistencies of life whisper of time and eternities.

Another spring is already patterned, but the inevitability has its own rhythms and patterns. The sign of the Archer rules among the stars, with the Goat to follow, and the Water Boy and the Fishes before the Zodiac brings the Lamb and spring. The mysterious perfection of the snowflake has its season, to be followed by the miracle of melt. But time flows, and change, and the great tides wash over the enduring hills. And man, privileged to know the year whole and complete, can hear the whisper of certainty in the deep throb of the earth and the answering beat of his own pulse.

The Snowbirds *December 16*

Of all our winter birds, only two are known as snowbirds, and both are as true to the weather as the barometer. Just now our only snowbird is the junco, the genial slate-gray dooryard bird that comes south ahead of the snow. But when winter really arrives, with a biting wind and swirling snow, our midwinter snowbirds, the snow buntings, will seem to come on the very wings of the storm.

Small wonder these little buntings are sometimes called

snow larks or snowflakes, for they are the whitest of our land birds. Like the snow-clad weed patches they haunt, they are marked sparingly with black and brown above. On a blustery day they ride the wind like real snowflakes, and a flock rising from the ground seems to roll right over itself, like drifting snow. Find a windblown, winter-bound weed patch, especially of ragweed or pigweed, and you almost certainly will find a flock of snow buntings making a meal. Listen between gusts and you will hear them, twittering as though they actually revel in rough weather.

It is still junco weather, and nobody is begging for a change. The juncos are pleasant company in any dooryard. But snow-bunting weather is sure to come eventually, and when it does it almost certainly will bring the midwinter snowbirds. They won't improve the weather one whit, but they will make it official, in a way, and they will add a cheery note even to a stormy day. Meanwhile, the juncos are quite satisfactory snowbirds to have around.

White Birch

December 17

Of all the leafless trees in the winter landscape, the most eye-catching and spectacular is the white birch, particularly when seen against the grays and browns of a snowless hillside. It has a grace of line, a slimness of bole, a clean, sleek look that is sheer beauty.

From the earliest days the white birch has been storehouse and source of elemental materials for both the settler and the woodland wanderer. Its bark provides a usable paper, tinder for fires in the wet woods, enough nourishment to save man or beast from starvation; and from it came the canoe, shaped and sheathed by the tough, enduring bark itself before man adapted cedar and canvas and, eventually, aluminum, to the same purpose. Wigwams were roofed with that bark, and buckets and boxes were made from it. And in the springtime the rising sap of the white birch was boiled down, like maple sap, for a syrup and a sugar that sweetened the woodsman's diet and disposition. The white inner wood, easily worked, provided an infinite variety of woodenware for the pioneer cabin and still provides everything from spools to bowls for the contemporary household.

One can scarcely imagine our Northeastern hills without the white grace of the birch against the gaunt winter hillsides of naked oak and maple or the deep greens of pine and hemlock. Other birches have their own qualities and virtues, but the white birch is the noblest of them all, beautiful to look upon and full of simple utility. In spring it rouges the gray hillside with its buds. In summer it is a whispering canopy of shade. But in winter it is simply beautiful, white beauty in a drab gray world.

Snow *December 18*

Snow really belongs to the open country. It has no reason for being, in the city, where it is a wet and slushy nuisance with little beauty, once it has fallen. And in the city it has almost none of the white mystery that it brings to the meadow and the woodland. A snowfall itself, the shifting curtain of flakes drifting down, has its brief loveliness even in the city's canyons; but once on the streets it is just so much cold, wet inconvenience.

In the country, where it can lie as it falls, snow is full of magic. It softens the stark outlines of the leafless season. If it comes wet and clinging, it accents the clean, simple structure of every tree. It powders and decks the roadside weed patches. It smooths the meadow and frosts the field. It fringes the brooks and makes their dark waters look almost black. It makes the pinewoods festive.

Snow creates a brand-new world out in the open country. It smooths and softens the contours as even the grass can't do in summer. It covers the autumn litter, heals the scars that mark the land. Even the open sky seems broader and deeper over the snow-clad hills. It adds a new dimension to the old, familiar world.

There is such magic in any snow, but the first few snowfalls of the season, the tentative ones, so to speak, are special occasions. Later the freshness will be gone and snow will no longer be new or particularly welcome, even in the country. But the first few snowy mornings of any winter are filled with wonder and crisply beautiful. Especially out where a snowdrift is not a nuisance to begin with.

The Clown *December 19*

Of all the winter birds the clown of the lot is the nuthatch. Not that he shows any signs of conscious clowning; far from it! The nuthatch is as serious a bird as you will meet at any feeding station. That is a part of his absurdity. He is short and fat. His bill is ridiculously long, and slightly tip-tilted. His tail is too short. So is his neck. And his beady black eyes are set so close together that he looks either cross-eyed or ridiculously near-sighted. And, to cap it all, he doesn't know that a bird can't go down a tree trunk headfirst. Not knowing it, he turns his stubby tail to the sky and blithely walks down, headfirst, searching the bark for bugs as he goes. Maybe other birds can't do it, but the nuthatch can.

And his voice! Technically, and by ornithological classification, the nuthatch is a songbird. He has vocal organs. And how does he use them? To utter a nasal, "Yark, yark, yark," a little petulant, a little questioning. No variation. Nothing approaching a melody. Just "Yark, yark, yark," always in the same key, always the same note, whether he is gloating over a fresh piece of suet or warning a chickadee to stand off. In the spring the nuthatch has what passes for a song, a mating song. It is sometimes like "Too-too-too," as tuneless as the "yark" call, but in a different key.

None of this is to belittle or berate the nuthatch, an exemplary bird if there ever was one. He is not quarrelsome, or noisy, or pilfering. He is a good neighbor, and a welcome winter guest, and he eats his full share of noxious bugs the year around. But he is a funny bird, for all that. He would look right at home with a slapstick tucked under one wing and a jester's cap with bells on his head.

The Ancients *December 20*

One need not go into history to find the reasons for veneration of the evergreen tree or bough as a part of the Christmas season. They are of the enduring things of this earth, and man has known them as long as man has been here. The pine, the spruce, the hemlock, the fir—all those conifers that know no leafless season—have been held in special favor when man would have symbols of life that outlast all winters. And even more enduring, in geologic time, are the ground pine, the ground cedar, and the club mosses, most venerable of all the evergreens.

We gather them now, even as the ancients gathered them reaching for the reassurance of enduring green life at the time of the winter solstice. For the pines and their whole family were old when the first man saw them. Millions of years old, even then, even at a time when millions of years had no meaning. When we gather them we are reaching back, back into the deep recesses of time. But, even as the ancients, we are reaching for reassurance, for the beauty of the living green but also for that green itself, the green of life that outlasts the gray winds, the white frosts, and the glittering snow of winter.

So we go forth and bring in the pine, the spruce, the

hemlock—and now, because of the cultivation of Christmas trees on a wide scale, we can do so without desecrating the natural forest. We bring the festoons of ground pine and partridgeberry, feeling a kinship with enduring things. They help us to catch, if only briefly, that needed sense of hope and understandable eternity.

The Winter Nights

December 21

Now the year balances its accounts. The short days and long nights are upon us. The winter solstice, the technical beginning of winter, does not occur until tomorrow, but the daylight sunrise to sunset, will shorten only another minute or so. We are already at the year's nadir. We have passed the year's earliest sunset. Sunrise will continue to lag through the year's end.

In our latitude we know that every year brings this time when not only the candle but the fire on the hearth, figurative if not literal, must burn at each end of the day. The sun cuts its smallest arc off there to the south and shadows lie cold and deep. It is for this time that the countryman lays up a store of firewood and fodder. Now we pay for the long days of summer in the simple currency of daylight.

And yet the short days provide their own bonus. The snows come, and dawn and dusk are like no other time of the year. We know again the long winter nights when the moon rides over a white world and the darkness thins away. The full-moon night on a snow-clad world is as long as the longest summer day, and the winter world glows with an ethereal shimmer.

Year to year we remember the short days and we tend to forget the long nights of moonlight and starlight, when it seems one might stand on a high hill and touch the Big Dipper. Who would not cut wood and burn a candle for a few such nights each year?

Winter Solstice

December 22

The year achieves another solstice as the great wheel of time turns with the earth and the seasons. Winter, by the calendar, begins in midmorning today, though the year's shortest days have been upon us for almost a week. The solstice is a marker on the charts, but winter abides by its own schedule of wind and weather.

Since man was first aware of the changing seasons, the winter solstice has been occasion for awe and wonder and a challenge to faith. Hope and belief are easy in a warm, green world, but when the cold days come and the sun edges farther and farther south, cutting a constantly smaller arc across the sky, the imminence of utter darkness and oblivion seems at hand. Then the sun stands still. The turn comes. The crisis passes and the sun slowly climbs the sky once more, reaching toward another spring, another summer.

It was, and it still is, an annual miracle. Hope and belief were, and still are, once more justified. There is order in the universe. The seasons still march in their eternal sequence, and winter is neither pause nor punishment, but a part of the year's whole. Ice and stormy wind are inevitabilities, but they pass even as the leaf and the blossom, equally inevitable in their own season, ripen and are gone.

The year has its own fourfold truth, indelibly marked on the turning earth. Now we know it whole for another turn of the great wheel. The cold verity of winter completes the cycle.

Winter

December 23

Whether winter is a corrective or not, a means of balancing the year, is debatable. But it certainly clears the air in more ways than one. It strips the natural world to its fundamentals, hill and valley, tree and bush. It gives the great wind tides both strength and substance as they surge and sweep across the land. It reasserts the elemental power of cold and ice; and it makes of fire a comforting and rehabilitating primal force. It makes life, the very persistence of life, important.

Even such a simple thing as a snowflake or an ice crystal is, in a way, a fragment of universal truth. The form and beauty, the infinite variety within a sixfold pattern, of a snowflake is beyond human achievement. But there it is. The power in an ice crystal manifested in winter dwarfs the energy in a man-fractured atom.

Even so rudimentary a thing as a root, a seed, or an insect egg is an expression of insistent vitality, of life itself. Somehow the germ of growth is hoarded and protected through the cold, dark weeks and months, awaiting another spring. Life, which will persist whether man is here to see it or not. Winter, which is as simple as a snowdrift and as complex as protoplasm itself. We live with it, and wonder at it, and occasionally we catch a glimpse of its elemental meaning.

The Celebration *December 24*

No matter where you are today, you are surrounded by a sense of wonder and the excitement of celebration. There isn't a town or a village in America without the gaiety of lights and tinsel, gifts and carols, not one. This is a festival of lights. They mark every street. Wherever you look there is a lighted tree twinkling in a window. And tonight will occur the mythical visit of the most generous folk hero of all time. Tomorrow will bring the solemnity of the rituals and the celebration of the festivities.

The wonder is there, and the miraculous, in the Biblical

story of the Nativity. The Christ child was born in a stable in Bethlehem. But almost equally miraculous is this holiday itself, for it is both a very holy day and a unique secular celebration. It is not only a festival of faith, but one of generosity and goodwill.

There is no other occasion quite like this, no other holiday, no other holy day, that unites so many of us in a common spirit. It is the solemn festival of the Nativity, of the birth of Jesus; it is also Christmas, not a mass or a sermon but a secular festival to the innocence of children and the goodness of mankind.

The Hope, the Dream *December 25*

There is the tree, there are the evergreen boughs and wreaths, there are the lights and the tinsel and the gifts and the old, old songs. But beyond these things, all with their half-forgotten meaning, is the simplicity of the event itself. What we celebrate is the birth of a Child into a time of dissension and oppression and a world of cruelty and suspicion, one who grew up to teach peace and justice and love of fellow man. It was as simple as that.

The story of the birth itself is brief and eloquent, rich with awe and wonder, and yet marked by simplicity. It was in a simple hill town of no particular importance. The priesthood had no hand in it. The birth was in a stable because there was no room at the inn. The first visitors were shepherds from the nearby hills, men of no consequence in church or government.

Yet it changed the whole history of mankind. Out of it grew the Judeo-Christian ethic to which our whole concept of truth and justice owes an enduring debt. The consequences of that night of wonder in Bethlehem still shape the thought and aspiration of much of the world.

And so we celebrate, with the trappings of long tradition now become more habit and custom than belief. But what we are really celebrating is the obscure birth of One who lived, and died, for a simple creed, so simple that we still find it difficult to accept complete. We celebrate the hope, the dream.

The Tiniest Ham

December 26

Go almost anywhere in the suburbs or the country now, even to the edge of a city park if there is a bird feeder nearby, and you will see chickadees.

A full-grown chick seldom weighs more than half an ounce, about the weight of an ordinary letter. Inside that tiny body is a heart that beats close to 700 times a minute, so fast that through a stethoscope its sound is practically a buzz. Its body temperature ranges around 105 degrees, which accounts for that high-tension activity.

On a cold day a chickadee needs its own weight in food to keep the inner fires burning. Its small fraction of an ounce of feathers, which can fluff it to the size of a sparrow, helps hold warmth while the dark back and head gather additional heat from the winter sun.

But these are details; this bird is more than the sum of its anatomical parts. It is a lively spark of personality. It can be a ham actor, a bully, a wheedler, an acrobat. It loves a human audience and comes to the dooryard feeder as much for companionship as for a snack. As an entertainer, it is all pro, the feathered song-and-dance performer who gets, and deserves, top billing on the winter circuit of the dooryard feeders.

The Winter Stars

December 27

The Great Bear is now down on the horizon at evening, come down, the legends say, to wash his paws in the deep December lakes before they are all iced in. And the Little Bear hangs by his tail from the North Star. Cassiopeia, the Queen, sits high in the sky, and off toward the west Cygnus, the Swan, is in flight toward another hemisphere, the eternal migrant. The Big Dog and the Little Dog, off to the east, watch Orion, the Hunter, as he faces Taurus and the zenith. Almost overhead are the Pleiades, those seven shy sisters who are best seen from the corner of the eye.

These are star nights, with the moon late rising, in its last quarter today, and with winter-brilliant skies. Walk the countryside these evenings and the whole universe accompanies you, for the earth is all open now to the starlight, leaf-fall complete. The stars lean so close that if one stood tiptoe on the highest hill he might grasp at least one star in his tingling fingers.

It is illusion, of course, but the December stars seem twice as brilliant as those of June, for the sky is doubly clear, the mist chilled out of it and the dust of summer settled at last. An illusion, but a pleasant one on a brittle night; the sun seems so far away that the stars should come closer. We should be able to glimpse eternity through those spark-holes in the blanket of the long night. And perhaps we do. Where else is such order, such an eternal pattern, as in those stars that light the winter sky?

Daylight

December 28

Almost any way you look at it, December is the year's shortest month. Anyone who insists that February is shorter is simply niggling. True, December has thirty-one days, but can you honestly call those frantic little spans of daylight that come zipping past between Thanksgiving and Christmas days? Pause long enough to check them off on the calendar and you have no time to keep track. The turkey vanishes and right in front of you is the tree, waiting to be decorated. Then someone shouts, "Happy New Year!" and that is the end of December.

In round figures, there are 288 hours of daylight in December, even counting those dreary hours when the sun sulks behind a mass of clouds all day. Even March, month of evil reputation, can muster that many hours of daylight in twenty-four days. And June, magnificent June, does as well by us in only nineteen days.

What is a December day, after all? Nine hours of daylight, with a few minutes left over at each end to turn the lights on and off. And fifteen hours of darkness. With a moon part of the time, and with a great many brilliant stars. But darkness, even so. You eat breakfast by lamplight, hurry off to work in demi-dawn, and get home in darkness. You have four weekends to watch the sun scurry across the sky off there toward the south.

December? By sundown tonight we will have had only a little more daylight than we will get in next July's first week. Enough said?

The Owls Know

December 29

The owls know it. The owls are wise in ways that man may only guess at, and they give us few clues in their midnight conversations. They probably feel change in their bones. Birds do that, since their hollow bones are built-in barometers. They know when storms are coming, when change is due.

So the owls know we have passed the winter solstice, that we now are on that long, cold slope that leads so slowly upward toward spring. That may be one reason the ancient shamans venerated the owls—because they, too, were aware that there are arcane answers to simple questions. Those ancients checked the shadows at midday, they performed their incantations, they watched the apparent movement of the sun. And they listened to the owls.

We are wise. We are sophisticated. Believing that because there was a yesterday there will be a tomorrow, we take it on faith. Last year and last summer are sufficient proof that another year, another summer, lie ahead. In taking it on faith we have lost a measure of the wonder that once marked this time, this turning of the year. We have forgotten a miracle of time.

But the owls remember. The great horned owl hoots with that deep, gruff, announcement voice, and the barred owl hoots his questions in a whole range of voices. They know. And soon they will be mating and nesting, ignoring winter, defying cold and snow. They will have owlets in the nest, feathered and almost ready to fly, by April.

A Summary *December 30*

December thins away, the old year wanes, and we automatically reach for the marker. Any tally-line we draw will be as evanescent as the shadows on the snow, which shift hour by hour, but habit is strong. We need to count and sum up totals, to imagine we are summarizing.

What we really do in such tallying up is prove again that the year is round as the day and that the whole is an endless continuity. Try to summarize the yesterdays and you come to now, and beyond the now is an endless procession of tomorrows. When all other details are stripped away, it is the summary of spring rain and green leaves, summer and blossoms, autumn and ripeness, and another winter. As always, as far back as the race memory runs. But even that is heartening, both in its repetition and in its enduring truth—as long as the sun shines, rain falls, water flows, and green leaves work their miracle there is life, there is hope.

A good deal of it must be taken on faith, also, as always. The dormant bud on the dogwood twig, the latent root in the hidden acorn, the fetal fawn in the hungry doe, the hibernating frog and turtle, snake and woodchuck all await the summons of time and the April sun.

We have passed the solstice. Shadows now point toward the vernal equinox. Daylight slowly lengthens. The great pulse beats on and on, and we need no tally-line to feel its echo in our own heart, the ultimate summary for all of us.

Year's End

December 31

Year's end, we call this final week of December, hoping thus to tie a knot in the endless cord of time, bid it cease running while we draw up summaries and conclusions. But we might as well try to summarize the tides or halter the wind.

Time has no divisions, save as we make them. The continuity persists and, willing or not, we partake of it. Winter begins, and the dormant bud upon the twig is yesterday's preparation for tomorrow. The hidden egg contains the germ of another summer's gnawing, buzzing, bright-winged insect. The wasp queen sleeps, pregnant with another season's brood. The doe, sheltering in the hemlock thicket, carries the fetal fawns that will perpetuate her kind. Earth and sun and time proceed in their cyclic rounds, and only man presumes to summarize.

No year is complete in itself. Even the seasons overlap the arbitrary divisions we make, and year's end is neither an end nor a beginning but a part of the infinite whole. The most we can do is say, "Up till now," knowing that now itself has no meaning without a yesterday and a tomorrow. Any year is a vast procession of nows, which add up to the continuity of foreverness. The totals are eternally incomplete, eternally changing. What is past is past, a part of experience. That is the only summary, and it leads on and on, beyond endings or beginnings to the hope that is tomorrow, all the tomorrows mankind will ever know.

Index of First Publication Dates in *The New York Times*

January

1. January *1/5/69*
2. More Sun *1/14/62*
3. The Killer-Wind *1/6/63*
4. The Winter Voices *1/7/78*
5. The Unseen Tides *1/12/64*
6. Winter's Moon *1/21/62*
7. Winter Green *1/21/73*
8. The Handsome Jay *1/28/68*
9. Ice *1/7/62* 11
10. Dogwood *11/18/45*
11. The Truth of Trees *1/22/67*
12. The Long Night *1/14/73*
13. Color and Contrast *1/22/64*
14. The Primitive Sleep *1/8/64*
15. The Waiting Trees *1/19/64*
16. The Dooryard Birds *1/2/66*
17. The Day's Commitment *1/9/66*
18. The Open Fire *1/16/66*
19. The Ice Booms *1/23/66*
20. The Remembering *1/30/66*
21. The Long, Slow Climb *1/3/65*
22. Winter Dusk *1/5/64*
23. Owls in the Night *1/17/65*
24. The Unremitting Change *1/21/68*
25. Wolf Moon *1/10/71*
26. That January Thaw *1/21/64*
27. Squirrels in the Treetops *1/27/63*
28. January Wind *1/15/50*
29. Simplicity *1/14/51*
30. Midpoint *1/26/64*
31. January Evening *1/7/68*

February

1. Groundhog Day ("This week brings . . .") *1/30/77*
2. Groundhog Day ("If one wanted to be . . .") *1/31/65*

Index of First Publication Dates

3. Half Past Winter *2/3/74*
4. Whimsical February *2/1/78*
5. The Flutterers *2/15/76*
6. The Maples *2/4/68*
7. The Promise *2/17/63*
8. The Secret *2/9/75*
9. Reynard *2/1/76*
10. The Green Wishes *2/9/69*
11. Snowstorm *2/12/67*
12. The Difference *2/16/69*
13. Mr. Redbird *2/14/60*
14. Valentine *2/13/66*
15. Subtle Signs of Spring *2/7/65*
16. The Courting Owls *2/14/71*
17. Those Attic Wasps *2/16/74*
18. Purification *2/9/64*
19. Jaunty Mr. Chick *2/16/64*
20. Sunrise *2/14/65*
21. Sap-Rise *2/20/66*
22. The Signs *2/22/76*
23. Twilight *2/18/62*
24. In the Sun *2/18/68*
25. The Deliberate Buds *2/24/63*
26. Hunger Moon *2/10/63*
27. Winter Is Still Winter *2/2/64*
28. Prophets of Tomorrow *2/7/60*

March

1. March ("March comes, a kind of interregnum . . .") *3/1/64*
2. Weather and Prophets *3/3/63*
3. March ("March has a dubious . . .") *3/3/68*
4. Song Again *3/12/67*
5. The Signs *3/14/65*
6. Winter Robins *3/3/64*
7. Partridge in the Apple Tree *3/4/62*
8. March Winds *3/7/65*
9. Promises *3/10/74*
10. Shade-Tail *3/10/57*
11. The Home-Coming *3/13/66*
12. The Big Melt *3/24/68* 70
13. Washing Winter Away *3/17/64*
14. The Response *3/8/64*
15. Beyond the Promise *3/10/68*
16. Sap *3/15/64*
17. The March Buds *3/16/74*
18. Coltsfoot *3/9/75*
19. The Quickening Willows *3/16/69*

20. Still in Order *3/19/67*
21. Ready for Spring *3/10/66*
22. The Primitive Peepers *3/21/77*
23. March Doth Make Liars *3/17/74*
24. Waiting *3/28/65*
25. Red-Wings *3/14/76*
26. Dawn *3/31/63*
27. Three Gardens *3/25/62*
28. The Spring Furrow *3/29/53*
29. March Dusk *3/6/66*
30. Hepaticas *4/3/66*
31. The Wings of Spring *3/27/66*

April

1. First Smell of Spring *4/5/64*
2. Easter *4/10/66*
3. The Buds *4/1/62*
4. Wild Goose *4/7/63*
5. The Pressures *4/4/65*
6. When the Robins Arrive *3/10/63*
7. The Silence Ends *4/6/58*
8. The Newness *4/20/60*
9. The Green *4/13/69*
10. The Songs *4/1/65*
11. Spring-Hungry *4/12/64*
12. The Bee and the Crocus *4/20/75*
13. The Songless Songster *4/4/54*
14. Crimson Maples *4/17/66*
15. April Rain *4/19/64*
16. The Migrants Return *4/21/65*
17. Morning Fog *4/15/62*
18. Spring Plowing *4/8/62*
19. Breathing Space *4/17/77*
20. Green Again *4/21/74*
21. The Ferns *5/6/51*
22. The Dipper *4/25/76*
23. The Beautiful Dandelion *4/27/75*
24. Partner of the Elements *4/18/74*
25. The Belief *4/23/67*
26. Obvious as Sunlight *4/16/67*
27. The Digger *4/27/47*
28. Catching Up *4/25/77*
29. The Miracle of the Bud *4/25/77*
30. April Summary *4/26/64*

Index of First Publication Dates

May

1. May ("April is promises . . .") *4/29/62*
2. The New Leaves *5/3/76*
3. The Truth of May *5/5/68*
4. Orioles and Apple Blossoms *5/21/67*
5. The Baltimore Bird *5/28/61*
6. Inevitable May *5/5/63*
7. Shadbush Shimmer *5/8/66*
8. Bluet Time *5/10/64*
9. The Shy Thrasher *5/2/65*
10. Apple Blossoms *5/6/62*
11. May ("May is a consequence . . .") *5/3/64*
12. Change *5/7/67*
13. Scarlet Tanager *5/19/63*
14. A Day Begins *5/15/66*
15. Halfway to June *5/17/64*
16. A Boy and a Brook *5/2/64*
17. May and Violets *5/1/66*
18. Jack, the Preacher *5/12/63*
19. The Sunrise Hour *5/27/62*
20. The Green Canopy *5/20/62*
21. Salamander Weather *5/19/46*
22. The Busy Birds *5/11/75*
23. The Ancients *5/9/65*
24. Mister Mimic *5/14/50*
25. The Rush Toward June *5/23/65*
26. The Persistent Mustards *5/22/60*
27. June-Bugs *5/27/75*
28. Laughter on Wings *5/13/62*
29. The Golden Dust of Life *(5/26/63; republished on 5/31/77)*
30. Wild Strawberries *5/24/64*
31. The Abounding Earth *5/30/65*

June

1. June Dawn *6/7/64*
2. Generous June *6/4/67*
3. Chokecherries *6/11/67*
4. June *6/1/69*
5. Wild Roses *6/14/64*
6. The Hayfields *5/31/64*
7. Not Forever *6/8/69*
8. June Days Begin Early *6/2/63*
9. The Flags of June *6/3/56*
10. The Green Leaves *6/9/63*
11. Five Crimson Doves *6/6/76*
12. The Wheelbarrow *6/9/43*

13. The Thrush Still Sings *6/16/74*
14. The Chattering Popples *6/13/65*
15. The Bumblebee *6/10/62*
16. The Nestlings *6/13/76*
17. Wild Strawberries *6/12/66*
18. Knee-Deep in June *6/14/59*
19. No Time to Sing *6/26/66*
20. Summer Solstice *6/20/65*
21. Summer and Time *6/23/63*
22. Whippoorwill *6/15/58*
23. Fishing *5/22/55*
24. Firefly Nights *6/17/62*
25. Wings in the Dusk *6/25/67*
26. The Exodus *6/29/69*
27. Rubythroat *6/26/60*
28. The Moths and the Birds *6/30/74*
29. Corn *6/27/54*
30. June-Becoming-July *6/28/64*

July

1. July *7/2/67*
2. Honey-Sweet July *7/3/66*
3. Bee Balm *7/15/62*
4. Independence *6/30/68*
5. Summer in Blossom *7/6/69*
6. The Hordes *7/26/70*
7. Ox's Eye and Farmer's Curse *7/3/77*
8. The Succulent Bean *7/6/58*
9. Hot-Season Color *7/21/63*
10. Jewelweed *7/8/45*
11. The Beetles *7/7/63*
12. Rain *7/12/64*
13. Bouncing Bet *7/26/64*
14. The Pause *7/19/64*
15. The Dragonflies *7/17/66*
16. Summer's Song *7/14/63*
17. Milkweed *7/9/67*
18. Midsummer ("Dusk comes a few . . .") *7/20/75*
19. The Wings of Summer *7/18/65*
20. Elderberries *7/10/55*
21. Summer Songster *7/16/67*
22. Chicory *7/5/64*
23. Midsummer ("Midsummer is the power . . .") *7/23/67*
24. The Fiddlers *7/28/63*
25. Beyond the Fact *7/8/62*
26. The Untamed *7/25/65*
27. The Byway *7/10/66*

28. Queen of the Night *7/20/69*
29. The Everlasting Hills *7/24/66*
30. Dog Days *7/21/68*
31. The Chromatic Harvest *7/29/62*

August

1. August *8/2/64*
2. Feast of the Green Corn *7/31/66*
3. Serenity *8/1/76*
4. Goldenrod Surf *8/1/65*
5. Summer's Maturity *8/6/61*
6. Catfish *8/13/44*
7. Queen Anne's Year *8/30/64*
8. The Katydid's Clock *8/8/65*
9. The Worts *8/8/54*
10. August Moon *8/11/46*
11. Tam-o'-shantered Acorns *8/21/66*
12. Askutasquash *8/18/46*
13. The Meteors *8/12/74*
14. Tomatoes *8/22/54*
15. The Pause *8/15/65*
16. The Little Lakes *8/18/66*
17. Poisonous Pokeberry *8/28/63*
18. Milkweed *8/25/76*
19. Fiddlers in the Night *8/27/67*
20. The Overlap *8/25/68*
21. Sumac Flame *8/14/66*
22. Festival *8/18/63*
23. Crab Apples *8/25/46*
24. Mist at Sunrise *8/25/74*
25. Zinnias *8/27/44*
26. Still August *8/22/76*
27. "A" is for Apple *8/27/61*
28. Time to Go *8/24/75*
29. Berries for the Birds *8/31/58*
30. The Monarchs *8/16/64*
31. Purple Majesty *8/31/76*

September

1. September *9/3/67*
2. September's Spectacle *9/13/64*
3. Deliberate September *9/4/66*
4. The Trees *9/2/62*
5. The Ripeness *9/10/67*
6. The Aster Season *9/9/62*
7. Autumn Miracle *9/20/64*
8. The Pulse of Autumn *9/5/65*

October

Index of First Publication Dates

5. December Moon *12/13/70*
6. Living Thermometers *12/7/75*
7. Fundamental *12/10/67*
8. December ("December emphasizes . . .") *12/4/66*
9. Fence Posts *12/5/54*
10. Energetic Idlers *12/15/68*
11. A Song for a Supper *12/6/59*
12. December Sunrise *12/12/65*
13. December Snow *12/3/67*
14. The Pines *12/7/70*
15. The Throb of Time *11/28/65*
16. The Snowbirds *12/3/61*
17. White Birch *12/13/53*
18. Snow *12/15/63*
19. The Clown *11/17/51*
20. The Ancients *12/15/74*
21. The Winter Nights *12/20/76*
22. Winter Solstice *12/22/63*
23. Winter *12/5/64*
24. The Celebration *12/24/67*
25. The Hope, the Dream *1/25/63*
26. The Tiniest Ham *12/5/77*
27. The Winter Stars *12/11/60*
28. Daylight *12/12/76*
29. The Owls Know *12/28/75*
30. A Summary *12/29/68*
31. Year's End *12/26/65*

A Note About the Author

Hal Borland was born in Nebraska, grew up in Colorado, and lived in New England from 1945 until his death in 1978. He is the author of more than thirty books—including the classic *When the Legends Die*, his memoirs, *High, Wide and Lonesome*, and a recent favorite, *Hal Borland's Book of Days*—and he was for many years a contributing editor of *Audubon* magazine. In 1942 he wrote the first of the "outdoor editorials" that became an institution in the Sunday edition of *The New York Times*. Mr. Borland received many honors and awards, among them the John Burroughs Nature Award in 1968 for *Hill Country Harvest*. With his wife, author Barbara Dodge Borland, he lived on their 100-acre farm in Connecticut beside the Housatonic River in the lower Berkshires.

A Note on the Type

This book was set on the linotype in Century Expanded, a type designed in 1894 by Linn Boyd Benton (1844–1932). Benton cut Century Expanded in response to Theodore De Vinne's request for an attractive, easy-to-read type face to fit the narrow columns of his *Century Magazine*. Early in the nineteen hundreds Morris Fuller Benton updated and improved Century in several versions for his father's American Type Founders Company. Century remains the only American type face cut before 1910 still widely in use today.

Composed by The Maryland Linotype Company,
Baltimore, Maryland

Woodcuts by James Grashaw
Typography design by Karolina Harris